DORSET AT WAR

Rodney Legg

HALSGROVE

Dedication

To Winston's grandson,
Nicholas Soames, *who asked me to write more.*

British Library Cataloguing-in-Publication Data
A CIP record for this title is available from the British Library

ISBN 978 1 84114 981 3

HALSGROVE
Halsgrove House,
Ryelands Industrial Estate,
Bagley Road, Wellington, Somerset TA21 9PZ
Tel: 01823 653777   Fax: 01823 216796
email: sales@halsgrove.com

Part of the Halsgrove group of companies
Information on all Halsgrove titles is available at: www.halsgrove.com

Printed and bound by CPI Antony Rowe, Wiltshire

Contents

Foreword

THIS IS the story of Dorset in World War Two – from 1939 to 1945 – condensed from files of more than a thousand events and incidents which I have been compiling and expanding since 1986. I claimed then and repeat it now that it is no exaggeration to say that there is no other single county in the British Isles that contributed to victory in so many decisive ways and on such a variety of levels and fronts.

Dorset not only withstood the defensive phase but proved to be pivotal in waging the offensive war that followed – by developing the ideas of secret science into operational apparatus, by deploying assault battalions of the county regiment, and by providing the major American springboard for the D-Day landings.

Putting the book together has at times been its own detective story. That some of the 1940 anti-invasion photographs have been identified was thanks to Peter Spinney of Parkstone pointing out that the Sandbanks Hotel had been wrongly called a 'Bournemouth clifftop hotel'. Holdenhurst Farm also eluded identification in the earlier research.

Not only were names removed at the time in accordance with Defence Regulations but censorship ensured that Poole, for instance, was described as 'an East Coast resort'. Misinformation was an official way of life and 'facts' were deliberately distorted to avoid compromising security.

I spotted two glaring examples of this, in print from contemporary captions, in Imperial War Museum archives. Firstly, an iconic photograph showed an infantryman pacing anti-invasion wire between Thorncombe Beacon and Golden Cap which was described as 'the Scottish coast'. That was because a single soldier and a strand of wire were fair enough as a defensive measure in the wilds of Scotland but pathetic on the real front-line in the English Channel. Secondly, from a very different period of the war, there was 'Torquay' showing Lieutenant-Colonel James Rudder and his elite United States Rangers marching along the Esplanade at Weymouth.

Many of those taking part had no idea where they were, as proved by the veteran who drew me a map of Portland Harbour, insisting it was called Plymouth. The other cautionary tale is that memories telescope into single events through the passage of time. One fire-fighter recalled a midnight bomb at Woolworth's, in the Square at Bournemouth in 1941, but merged it into the Sunday lunchtime raid that destroyed Beales in 1943. It takes an anorak like me to know that the twin-engine aircraft towing Horsa gliders from Tarrant Rushton on D-Day were Albemarles (not Dakotas, as I have just read).

Reminiscing and nostalgia have a wonderful authenticity but need to be handled with care as events go through their 70th anniversaries. The checking process, against contemporary and declassified information, often throws up details and facts utterly unknown to the participants at the time. This is particularly the case in 'need to know' situations and spoof activities such as Operation Fortitude which worked so well in tricking Hitler into thinking the main thrust of D-Day would be around the mouth of the Seine rather than across to Normandy. Those unwittingly acting out deceptions had to believe in what they were doing. Churchill had a neat little phrase about the truth requiring protection from a bodyguard of lies.

This is my bullet-point selection of the highlights of the war – seen from a Dorset perspective – that has endured as the cathartic event in the national psyche for three generations of Britons and shaped the modern world.

* shipping losses off Dorset were enormous – the Channel was one big minefield and battle-ground for both Allied and German convoys.
* the Royal Naval Cordite Factory at Holton Heath was one of just two establishments in the country making propellant for the Navy's shells.
* Winston Churchill, on becoming Premier, flew across the Channel three times from RAF Warmwell in desperate bids to stop the Fall of France.

* flyers from Warmwell, in their Spitfires, were in the thick of the Battle of Britain.
* Telecommunications Research Establishment scientists at Worth Matravers won the secret war and gave the RAF its victory by perfecting radar equipment and devising anti-bomber counter-measures.
* old Shirburnian Alan Turing, creator of the world's first programmed electronic digital computer, honed the technology that cracked the German top-secret 'Enigma' machine-coded radio traffic, to give the Allies advance notice of enemy actions throughout the war.
* civilian homes in Bournemouth, Poole, Christchurch, Weymouth and Sherborne took a hammering from enemy bombs but few were to fall on vital military installations and factories.
* the Major Strategic night Decoy on Brownsea Island, devised by the pyrotechnics department at Elstree Studios, attracted more than 1,000 tons of Luftwaffe bombs that would otherwise have fallen on Poole and Bournemouth.
* German invasion, had it come, would have been here – with both Lyme Bay and the sandy coastline between Studland and Christchurch being prime targets.
* as the tide of war began to turn, commandos from Poole raided the French coast.
* American top-brass – including Dwight D. Eisenhower, Jimmy Doolittle and Lyman Lemnitzer – left in an air armada from Hurn to Gibraltar to oversee the Allied invasion of French North Africa.
* development in Dorset of H2S airborne mapping radar – first tested over Bournemouth – enabled Bomber Command to carry out massed raids at night against German cities.
* Barnes Wallis tested his freelance wonder weapon – the Dambusters' bouncing bomb – along The Fleet lagoon where it panicked the Abbotsbury swans.
* the county's own warship, HMS *Dorsetshire*, delivered the coup de grace to the *Bismarck* (a year before being sunk by Japanese aircraft off Ceylon).
* Poole flying-boats restored the air links across the Atlantic and the Empire routes to Africa, India and Australia, with BOAC 'land-planes' doing much the same from Hurn.
* the village of Tyneham and other parts of Purbeck were secretly requisitioned on the orders of the War Cabinet, six days before Christmas in 1943, to train Sherman tank crews for the forthcoming Battle of Normandy.
* King George VI and the military top-brass watched the major live-fire rehearsals for the D-Day landings from the massive Fort Henry observation post overlooking Studland Bay.
* invasion, when it came, saw the United States Army occupying Dorset and using Portland and Weymouth as stepping stones to Omaha Beach and the bloodiest of the D-Day landings.
* American flyers, from Warmwell and Christchurch, paid a heavy price to harry German lines and logistics.
* gliders from Tarrant Rushton took British airborne forces to victory near Caen – being the first Allied soldiers to land in France on D-Day – and a disastrous 'Bridge too Far' across the Lower Rhine.
* RAF Typhoons flew from Hurn against V1 flying-bomb sites and anything that moved in northern France, whilst the home skies were protected by Mosquito night-fighters directed by Sopley radar station.
* prefabricated steel Bailey Bridges, which speeded the war across both Europe and Asia, were developed at Christchurch.
* battalions of the Dorsetshire Regiment spearheaded Britain's infantry after recovering from retreat at Dunkirk to carry out assault landings in Sicily, Italy and Normandy.
* the Dorsets were the first infantrymen to cross the Seine and to enter the Reich.
* three battalions of the Dorsetshire Regiment found themselves holding a salient in the Netherlands and showed heroism en masse in a valiant struggle to rescue airborne forces from the Arnhem debacle.
* on the other side of globe, 2nd Dorsets fought the Japanese – often hand-to-hand through the jungle – in a long advance from Kohima in India to Rangoon in Burma and then provided the guard for the Imperial Palace in Tokyo.
* casualties of the Battle of the Bulge were flown in their hundreds on a shuttle-service of Dakota transports to Tarrant Rushton and the United States Army General Hospital at Blandford Camp.
* Dorset's worst air crash, killing 27 RAF personnel, took place in 1945 when a Liberator transport bound for India flew into the hill above Encombe House.
* Christchurch scientists test-fired captured V2 rockets and began Britain's guided weapons programme.

1939

The year it kept raining

THE POLITICIANS split into hawks and doves. Viscount Cranborne, South Dorset's MP, cautioned Wyke Regis Women's Institute in January 1939 about the threat posed by Hitler and Mussolini:

> 'These dictators have tasted blood and have applied a policy of force and had considerable effect with it. We must make England an impregnable fortress.'

Clement Attlee, the leader of the Labour opposition, was a little less specific when he addressed farm workers in the Corn Exchange, Dorchester:

> 'People may ask what I would have done at Munich. Suppose you had a man who was driving a heavy lorry. He drove it mile after mile on the wrong side of the road, and after narrowly missing other vehicles, came to a position where a collision seemed inevitable, swerved and ran over a child. You might ask me what I would have done had I been driving. I would not have driven on the wrong side of the road. The trouble is that the Government has been driving on the wrong side. I would remind you that the right side for an Englishman to drive is on the left.'

Speaking at the annual Territorial Army dinner in Christchurch Drill Hall, Lieutenant-Colonel Arthur Malim was unequivocal that it was 'the duty of every young man who is patriotic is to be in the Territorial Army'. He was scathing at a suggestion that the Auxiliary Fire Brigade had no shortage of recruits because of the attractions of the blue and scarlet uniform:

> 'We can supply the uniform, not blue with scarlet facings, but His Majesty's khaki. That is where the young men of Bournemouth ought to be – not running around with hosepipes. It will be a bad day for Bournemouth and other towns if they cannot get men to take an active part in a battalion of His Majesty's Army, as part of the field force that will defend the lives and liberties of the people when the time comes. Fit young men of the right age ought to be in the Territorial Army – not in those civilian organisations which are all very well for old men who are not fit.'

By March, Dorchester Evacuation Committee was prepared for 4,612 evacuees, with Abbotsbury and Maiden Newton being the only significant places that had failed to respond, though it warned the Ministry of Health that water supplies and sanitary facilities could prove inadequate. Billeting Officers met local government officials at a conference in Dorchester on Friday 2 June to discuss how the Reception Areas would handle the expected influx of children from London. The reception centre was Maud Road School in Dorchester, where light refreshments would be provided plus a bag of food each, sufficient for 48 hours. They would then disperse. Arrangements were approved for sending 1,600 children into the borough of Dorchester, 1,900 to the surrounding rural district, and 1,300 into the Beaminster area.

That very day there was a tragic reminder of things to come. The Portland-based 6th Destroyer Flotilla of Tribal-class vessels, led by HMS *Mohawk*, was ordered to sail immediately for Liverpool Bay where a new submarine failed to surface during sea trials. They were to render assistance to the 1,095-ton H.M.S. *Thetis* and 90 men trapped aboard.

Nothing could be done. It was to be the worst peacetime submarine tragedy, with the agony also being extended for days for those on the surface ships as well, knowing they had no means of helping their comrades who were trapped on the seabed. As for *Thetis*, she would be raised, restored, refitted and renamed. HMS *Thunderbolt* joined the British Mediterranean Fleet in the autumn of 1940 (and had an active war until reported missing in 1943).

(Left) 76th Heavy Regiment, Royal Artillery, on manoeuvres in the rain at Bere Regis

(Right) Gunners going under canvas at Bere Regis with a 25-pounder gun and limber

During June the 310th Anti-Aircraft Battery, with 130 recruits training at the Mount Street Drill Hall in Poole, was issued with the new 3.7-inch Ack-Ack guns. The 375th and 376th Queen's Own Dorset Yeomanry Batteries, recruited from Shaftesbury, Blandford, and Sherborne, were amalgamated. The new Territorial Army unit retained the historic name, as the 141st (Queen's Own Dorset Yeomanry) Field Regiment, Royal Artillery. Likewise the 218th Field Battery, based in the Drill Hall at the Lansdowne, Bournemouth, was merged with the Dorchester and Bridport 224th (Dorset) Field Battery to form the 94th (Dorset and Hants) Field Regiment, RA.

Lunch-break for the 76th Heavy Regiment training at Bere Regis

The 1st Battalion of the Dorsetshire Regiment – the county's Regular Army infantrymen – left for Grand Harbour, Valetta, aboard the troopship HMT *Neuralia* from Bombay. They had been serving in India since 1936. These Regular Army soldiers are to man the south-eastern sector of the Mediterranean island's defences. Malta had been occupied by Britain since 1800, with its naval dry dock having been opened in 1871. In Italy, Sir Percy Loraine was received as British Ambassador in Rome on 27 May, to be lambasted by Mussolini for 'the manifest British policy of encirclement' blamed for sabotaging the Anglo-Italian Agreement.

Wireless tent at the Bere Regis exercise, preparing for the first electronic war

Dorset and 14 other southern counties tested the Black-out at 04.00 hours on Sunday 9 July. Aeroplanes monitored the results. Air Raid Precautions directives stated that even a light of one candle-power could be seen from a height of two miles on a clear night. Urban kerbs, posts, and poles were being painted white to lessen the need for street lighting.

DORSET AT WAR

Colin Dowell (tallest) and boys of Weymouth Grammar School with newly-issued gas masks

A huge tented camp sprouted over Blandford's downland. More than 100 marquees and 500 smaller tents were concentrated on Race Down across the former hutted lines around Cuckoo Clump that were used in the Great War to train the Royal Naval Division which landed at Gallipoli in the Dardanelles. It was at Blandford Camp that Sub-Lieutenant Rupert Brooke wrote those immortal lines:

'If I should die, think only this of me: That there's some corner of a foreign field that is for ever England.'

The mobilisation in 1939 was for a Militia Camp to provide volunteers with basic physical and weapons training in a gentle introduction to military life. It was followed on 1 August by the reforming of the Poole-based 5th Battalion of the Dorsetshire Regiment – a Territorial unit – under the command of Colonel Sir John Lees of Post Green, Lytchett Minster, who was wounded twice in the Great War. The battalion became part of the 43rd (Wessex) Division.

Trying to counter national fears that mobilisation meant conflict, Sir Thomas Inskip, Minister for the Co-Ordination of Defence, announced on 3 August:

'War today is not only not inevitable but is unlikely. The Government have good reason for saying that.'

Thousands of visitors packed Weymouth on 9 August to see King George VI review the Reserve Fleet in Portland Harbour. A total of 120 ships have gathered. For most in the Royal Navy Volunteer Reserve, the last summer of the Thirties had already ended, but on shore the holidaymakers had their last fling. An estimated 45,000 converged on the station and the situation worsened with the delays to trains that the royal visit caused. Many fainted in the crush and the St John Ambulance Brigade commandeered the waiting room and parcels office as a field hospital for casualties.

As for the King, he failed to see the ships off Bincleaves because of mist and drizzle. The Mayor expressed regrets about the rain. Laconically, the King replied:

'Don't worry, Mr Mayor, it's raining everywhere.'

Continuous rain postponed the second major test of the effectiveness of the Black-out on 11 August – for 24 hours – but Bournemouth's 11 zones of the Auxiliary Fire Service, each with its own local emergency station, went ahead with their own mass turn-out. Fifty-four mock incidents had been devised and 500 firemen called out.

The system we know as radar was put to the test over four days from 8 August 1939. A total of 1,300 aircraft of the Royal Air Force were split between 'Westland' (defenders) and 'Eastland' (attackers) with the result that the country's 25 Radio Direction Finding stations detected almost all incoming formations. This was despite appalling weather – rain, wind and fog – causing frequent suspension of both attacking and interception flights.

(Left) Reserve Fleet gathering in Portland Harbour for royal inspection

(Right) King George VI (closest to camera) passing Royal Terrace, Weymouth, on 9 August 1939

THE YEAR IT KEPT RAINING

The taller aerials at radar stations sent out radio waves from 350-feet altitude, which were reflected back from the intruding aeroplanes and received on the station's lower set of 250-feet aerials. The fractional difference of time between transmitted and returned signals was measured on a calibrated cathode-ray tube to indicate the altitude and direction of intruding aircraft whilst they were up to 150 miles offshore. Air Chief Marshal Sir Hugh Dowding, Air Officer Commander-in-Chief at Fighter Command, made a BBC wireless broadcast on 12 August to tell the nation that the exercise had been successful, though he stopped just short of directly mentioning the art of Radio Direction Finding:

Whitehead Torpedo Works carnival float in Rodwell Avenue, Weymouth

> 'It only remains for us to see that our technical equipment keeps ahead of that of our potential enemy. What we have been doing is to work at increasing interception towards one hundred per cent which is our goal. I am satisfied with our progress, and I confidently believe that a serious attack on these islands would be brought to a standstill within a short space of time.'

Those were prophetic words. 'Our technical equipment' now included secrets of the German 'Enigma' military cipher machines, courtesy Polish cryptanalysts in July.

Air-raid sirens sounded across south Dorset at 00.15 hours on Sunday 13 August and a Black-out was enforced. The lights went out on the ships of the Reserve Fleet at anchor in Portland Harbour and there was a continuous drone of aerial activity. Destroyers were deployed as 'enemy' vessels to test defences at the entrance to the harbour.

In villages the death-bells tolled and bewildered country people staggered out of bed to find what was happening. In Weymouth the news had already got around, or at least among those who had been out on the town, dancing and drinking, or laughing with Elsie and Doris Waters. There had been a noticeable absence of sailors for a Saturday night.

Dorchester Rural District Council decided on 30 August that:

Carnival queens Anne Morgan (right) from Weymouth and Olive Browning from Swindon

> '. . . in view of the imminent outbreak of war, that the whole power of the council so far as allowed by law, be delegated to an Emergency Committee until further orders.'

Some, however, still planned for peace. Imperial Airways and British Airlines were to amalgamate as the British Overseas Airways Corporation, under the chairmanship of Lord Reith, founder of the BBC. Its fleet of Short C-class 'Empire' flying-boats moved with their support facilities from Hythe, on Southampton Water, to Poole Harbour. Salterns Pier and its club-rooms were requisitioned as a Marine Terminal from Poole Harbour Yacht Club. Water runways – called 'Trots' – were marked out by lines of tyres in the Wareham Channel off Hamworthy and along the Main Channel between Salterns and Brownsea Island.

Airways House opened in a Poole shop – 4 High Street – and the showrooms at Poole Pottery became the reception area and customs clearance point for incoming passengers. Harbour Heights Hotel was the rest centre for those due to embark from nearby Salterns Pier on early morning flights.

(Left) Ansons of Coastal Command operated from Warmwell Aerodrome

(Right) Dorset Territorials in wet summer camp at Corfe Castle pull-through their Lee-Enfield rifles

9

DORSET AT WAR

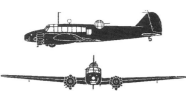

Avro Anson

Everyone in Britain had a gas mask

Door-to-door Black-out salesman

Prime Minister Neville Chamberlain

Avro Ansons of 217 Squadron (identity letters 'MW') became operational in August for coast patrols at an aerodrome near Warmwell, east of Dorchester, where the Royal Air Force set up its School of Air Firing in May 1937. Their last public display, as Warmwell Armament Training Squadron, was a bombing exercise for a 10,000-strong crowd at an open day. Five Ansons came in and a bomb dropped on a make-believe factory, a building on the other side of the grass airfield, as attacking planes were buzzed by three Hurricanes. One Anson was 'disabled' and forced to land. Forty planes took part including a squadron of Singapore reconnaissance flying-boats from Southampton Water.

More practice bombs were heard across Dorset as the Air Ministry announced that 16 square miles of Lyme Bay – lying six miles off Lyme Regis – was a bombing range for daylight use. A limit of 120-lb was been placed on live bombs that could be dropped. It was known as Lyme Bay Bombing Range. Inland, a bombing range was also established on Crichel Down in the chalky foothills of Cranborne Chase.

Sensational stories appeared in national newspapers that the Air Defence Research and Development Establishment at Somerford, Christchurch, had perfected the 'death ray'. This intensely strong electromagnetic wave, it was said, could heat up anything in its path – including living tissue – to the point at which it exploded. It was, however, no precursor of the laser or star-wars, or even the microwave oven. As long ago as 1935, Arnold Wilkins had demonstrated at the Radio Research Establishment, at Slough, that the energy needed for death rays was way beyond present technology. It was, on the other hand, a convenient cover for the development of radar systems.

Reverting to the equestrian age, there was a seemingly endless convoy of horse-drawn wagons around Blandford as contractors removed thousands of tons of earth and chalk from the site of the military encampment being built across Race Down. The lights went out across the land on Friday 1 September with enforcement of a full Black-out. Henceforth all street lighting and illuminated advertisements were turned off and curtains made light-tight to prevent seepage through windows. Regulation masks were fitted to car headlights. Sidelight lenses had to be dimmed with double sheets of paper.

Poland had been invaded and the mobilisation of British Armed Forces took place on Saturday 2 September as the rains fell once more. In Bournemouth the 750 men and 26 women of the Auxiliary Fire Service were called-up to their places of duty and found themselves answering 15 flood calls in the middle of the night. Bobby's department store in the Square had to be pumped out, with the loss of two tons of sugar, as did a flooded air-raid shelter. Electrical transformers exploded and the Pier Approach Baths had an embarrassment of water in its basement. Ironically, it was regarded as an emergency reservoir for fire-fighting, with 150,000 gallons, so this turned into a useful exercise.

In the morning, the Sun came out and the country went to church, as war hummed through military communication lines from 10.00 hours. All units were informed that unless Germany pledged to remove troops from Poland, war was to be declared by Great Britain. At 11.15 the Prime Minister, Neville Chamberlain, broadcast to the nation from the Cabinet Room in No. 10 Downing Street:

> 'This morning the British Ambassador in Berlin handed the German Government a final note stating that unless we heard from them by eleven o'clock that they were prepared at once to withdraw their troops from Poland a state of war would exist between us. I have to tell you now that no such undertaking has been received, and that consequently this country is at war with Germany. You can imagine what a bitter blow it is to me that all my long struggle to win peace has failed . . .'

Evacuees were leaving London by every train. A billeting allowance of 8 shillings 6 pence was promised to each host family. On the water, in sea trials off Portland, the newly commissioned flagship K-class destroyer HMS *Kelly* – named for Admiral of the Fleet Sir John Kelly and commanded by the King's cousin Captain Louis Mountbatten – received a signal midway through the morning lecture. Chief Petty Officer Primrose handed it to Captain Mountbatten. 'Thank you,' he said, before continuing.

'This is the stage in my lecture at which I usually point out how valuable the automatic station-keeper would be in wartime, when the captain and other officers on the bridge have so many things to do besides keeping the ship in station [position] on the other ships of the flotilla. I usually say, "Now I have given you the basic principles of operating my gear. If war should at this moment break out, you know enough about it to work it." Well, war has at this moment broken out.'

Mountbatten proceeded to read the signal:

'FROM ADMIRALTY TO ALL CONCERNED – HOME AND ABROAD. MOST IMMEDIATE. COMMENCE HOSTILITIES AT ONCE WITH GERMANY.'

Dorset-bound London evacuees

In *K Destroyer Flotilla News*, the daily newspaper of the Royal Navy's 5th Destroyer Flotilla, Bob Knight reported to the crew of HMS *Kelly* on the fishy sequel resulting from anti-submarine depth charges that had claimed a U-boat off Bridport on Monday:

'That's war – that was; but we must not lead ourselves to believe that some of the catch will always appear on the breakfast table. The presence of mind of Posty in producing a gaff to lift the whales inboard while the ship had stopped to obtain a sample of the oil on the sea is much to be admired. We all hope that *Kelly*'s and the *Acheron*'s efforts [another destroyer] did away with one of the pests that sank, without warning, the liner *Athenia* on Sunday night [3 September, off Ireland] – and, of course, we hope that the lucky messes in the *Kelly* enjoy their breakfast. There is plenty of corroborative evidence to show that there were two U-boats here yesterday – one in Weymouth Bay and one in West Bay. The periscope of the former was seen from the signal bridge of the *Resolution* [battleship] and the MASB and the tracks of two torpedoes fired at the *Kelly*. They missed us by 30 or 40 yards, so certainly we were lucky. To be missed by one submarine and bag another [later, in Lyme Bay] all in the first day [at sea] is good going.'

By 11.00 hours on 12 September, the *Kelly*'s crew had put two and two together following a report in the *Daily Mirror*:

'One of Britain's fastest and newest destroyers is being sent to France to bring home the Duke and Duchess of Windsor.'

They were ordered to put to sea from Portland 'to raise full steam and make for Le Havre'. There they met 'Officer X' who was Major Randolph Churchill, son of Winston, the First Lord of the Admiralty. With him were the Duke and Duchess of Windsor (former King Edward VIII and his wife, Wallis Simpson). They had just driven half-way across France. *Kelly* brought them back to Farewell Jetty at Portsmouth.

Volunteers at Dorchester distributed 14,000 gas-masks and 24 men came to the council's depot in Poundbury Road and offered to fill sandbags. In a day they stacked 5,000. The ladies helped as well, notably the staff and pupils of the Dorset County School for Girls, who cycled around the district delivering gas-masks. Many had been assem-

Destroyer on patrol out of Portland

(Left) Cookhouse queue at Chickerell Camp for the 4th Battalion, Dorsetshire Regiment

(Right) Tank crews raise glasses, dining at Bovington Camp

bled by the inmates of Dorchester Prison. In Poole, lifesaver Harry Davis (66), who had saved many from drowning, made himself personally responsible for delivering 7,500 gas-masks.

The first sounds of war were explosions heard in Weymouth on Saturday 16 September. The 6,000-ton Belgian passenger liner *Alex van Opstal*, empty and homeward bound from New York to Antwerp, was blown up by a German mine south of the Shambles, off Portland. All 49 crew, plus eight passengers, were rescued by a Greek steamer.

Having attended upon the tragic scene of the torpedoed aircraft-carrier HMS *Courageous* in the Western Approaches and on 17 September recovered pillows and a lavatory door from the sunken *Accrington Court*, brought up by depth charges, HMS *Kelly* returned to Portland. She joined HMS *Kingston* – newly arrived second ship of the 5th Destroyer Flotilla – for working-up trials. Torpedo discharges were the order of the day.

On 23 September, in an echo of the Great War, the 2nd Battalion of the Dorsetshire Regiment left Aldershot on their way to join the British Expeditionary Force in France. The 2nd Dorsets, the 1st Battalion of the Queen's Own Cameron Highlanders, and the 7th Battalion of the Worcestershire Regiment, comprised the 5th Infantry Brigade. It and the 4th and the 6th Infantry Brigades made up the 2nd Division, commanded by Major-General M. G. H. Barker. Commander-in-Chief of the BEF was General Lord Gort VC.

Three Sundays on from the declaration of war, mystic writer Adela Curtis told sisters of the Christian Contemplatives' Community at St Bride's Farm, Burton Bradstock, that she abhorred pacifism and regarded 'faithful prayer' as 'the most effective of all weapons in our warfare'. A Royal Artillery Anti-Aircraft Regiment, giving basic training to recruits at Blandford Camp, might well have resorted to prayers. Theirs was very basic training – without any guns.

In the first four weeks of war 1,000 tons of contraband cargo intended for Germany were confiscated, mainly from neutral vessels, and impounded at Weymouth. A total of 513,000 tons had been searched in 74 ships bound for European ports. Seizures accumulated on the quayside. The prize went to ten bags of fine coffee beans from a Danish vessel. They were labelled: 'Adolf Hitler'.

Auxiliary Leading Fireman Reg Cooper slipped from a moving Auxiliary Fire Service van and was killed by its wheels in an accident outside a disused church in Nortoft Road, Bournemouth, on 6 October. The building was a fire station for No. 7 Zone of the town's AFS. Bournemouth had 11 auxiliary fire stations. Eighty emergency fire pumps had been delivered to the town. Twenty-five pumps were required to turn-out for each major wartime incident.

On 7 October another ship was sunk by a German mine off the Shambles Lightship, south-east of Portland Bill. She was the Dutch steamship *Bynnendyk*, returning to Rotterdam from New York. The 42 crewmen abandoned the blazing wreck and watched her gradually sink, from the bows, from the rescue vessel taking them to Weymouth. More survivors arrived on 12 October from the Whitby steamer *Sneaton*. The U-boat commander had surfaced to watch the men abandoning ship and called to them in perfect English:

'So long, boys. Sorry I had to do it, but it was my duty.'

The whole country was stunned on Saturday 14 October with news of an audacious attack on the Royal Navy's main Fleet base in Home Waters. A German submarine slipped into the Royal Navy anchorage of Scapa Flow, in the Orkney Isles, between 01.30 and 01.45 hours, and torpedoed the 29,000-ton battleship HMS *Royal Oak*. She turned over and went down into the cold, grey waters with 786 men still inside her.

There was hardly a district or town in the country without a wife or mother who was suffering personal grief. In Weymouth, Petty Officer William Helmore left a widow in Hillcrest Road with three children, the youngest of whom he had never seen. Billy Savage (17) came from Holton Heath. Petty Officer Charles Beeling's parents lived at Plush. John Hocking (20) had been living with his grandfather at Martinstown. Poole's losses included Dennis Brown of Broadstone and Vernon Fay of Branksome Park.

(Left) Trailer-pump fire tenders at the Central Fire Station, Bournemouth

(Right) Lord Gort VC (second from right) leading the British Expeditionary Force in France

For others, however, the eventual knock on the door brought relief after a day of despair. Able Seaman Victor Ayles and Stoker Cecil Lucking from Weymouth survived. So too did Ronald Kenny of Ackerman Road, Dorchester, though the news was not brought to his mother until 02.00 hours on Sunday. Another call in the early hours was made to St Helen's Road, Broadwey, where Weymouth police were able to tell Mrs Barrett that she still had a husband, Petty Officer W. Barrett.

Lieutenant-Commander Gunther Prien and his crew in *U47* were feted as heroes on their return to Berlin. Prien would write his memoirs before losing his life in the North Atlantic, on 7 March 1941.

Armistice Day took on a new meaning on 11 November. Previous services often included expressions of pacifism and reflected communal revulsion at the memory of the carnage in the trenches of the Western Front and Gallipoli. In 1939, however, they reverted to militarism as the country stepped back into uniform. 'Once war seems inevitable again, a million martyrs will have died again,' Labour Prime Minister Ramsay MacDonald said at the Cenotaph in 1934. Joining the armed forces had gone out of fashion. Even with high unemployment the level of Army recruitment remained inadequate. All that was changing, with the only partially acceptable pacifists being 'Chocolate Soldiers' of the Friends Ambulance Unit, re-formed by the Quaker Cadbury, Fry, and Rowntree families.

A celebration in Dorset saw Hamworthy Engineering's 300 employees marking their firm's silver jubilee with a weekend dance at the Woodlands Hall, Parkstone, on 18 November. The Poole-based company was formed at the start of the previous war, in 1914, so it did not seem inappropriate to be celebrating the occasion at the beginning of another one.

The German mines floating off the Shambles claimed yet another vessel, the Greek steamship *Elena R*, and the Royal Navy nearly lost a corvette. Five ratings were killed, and though she was listing, HMS *Kittiwake* was able to limp back into Portland Harbour on 22 November.

Wedding of the year with Major Randolph Churchill marrying the Honourable Pamela Digby from Minterne Magna

On Saturday 30 December the First Lord of the Admiralty – Mr Winston Churchill – visited the Contraband Control Centre at Weymouth and went on to Castletown Royal Naval Dockyard at Portland. He called it 'my first day off for nearly four months' as he departed to spend the night with Lord and Lady Digby at Minterne House, Minterne Magna. One of their daughters, Pamela, had married Mr Churchill's son, Randolph, in the social wedding of the year.

Sunday was New Year's Eve but Mr Churchill was unable to enjoy it relaxing in the Dorset countryside. He spent the morning working on despatches that followed him from the Admiralty and had to leave for London after lunch.

The song of the year, on both sides of the Atlantic, was *There'll Always Be An England* by Ross Parker and Hughie Charles:

'There'll always be an England
While there's a country lane
Wherever there's a cottage small
Beside a field of grain.'

1940

The Battle of Britain

DORSET'S KEY role in the secret scientific war began on Friday 5 January with the arrival of a 45-year-old boffin. John Darwin – a cousin of the Victorian naturalist – from Section VIII of MI6, the Secret Intelligence Service, at Whaddon Hall, Buckinghamshire brought a Mark III high-frequency transmitter and HRO receiver with aerials to install in the chartroom of the 750-ton Royal Navy trawler HMT *Hartlepool*, in Portland Harbour for experimental wireless tests. Captain William Powlett and his crew were briefed to assess its anti-submarine potential.

Winter then stopped the conflict. For three weeks in January the obvious enemy was the weather. Intense cold restored a quiet dignity to the countryside. Hedges and river-banks were enlivened by the bright colours of flocks of birds driven south by severe conditions. Siskins, little yellow green seed-eaters from Scandinavia, descended on the alder cones of trees beside the River Yeo at Sherborne. There was a water-rail, for the first time anyone could remember, also showing no fear of human observers. No mention appeared in the newspapers, nor on the wireless, of the record snowfall of 27 January. There could be no public weather reports. Meteorology remain classified for the duration.

The secret war resumed on 28 February when several young radio research scientists were posted to the Isle of Purbeck. Alan Hodgkin and Bernard Lovell arrived at Worth Matravers with the advance party from the Air Ministry's Telecommunications Research Establishment (TRE) at Dundee to set up a new base between Worth village and Renscombe Farm. They were joined by Dr Robert Cockburn. The group's sole lecturer was Leonard Huxley who endeavoured to explain to RAF personnel how to use the complex equipment that was being devised. All four went on to knighthoods in their eminent post-war careers.

By 5 May 1940 the rest of TRE had been evacuated from Scotland to Dorset. Ironically, though the coast facing Norway had become dangerous, that towards France was regarded as safe. With 200 staff, and previously known as the Air Ministry Research Establishment – when it was at Bawdsey – the unit was headed by A. P. Rowe and Robert Watson-Watt. They worked on RDF, standing for Radio Direction Finding and then Range and Direction Finding, though soon both were replaced by the American description Radio Direction and Ranging thanks to its catchy palindrome mnemonic – radar

Indications that this might no longer be a secure coast came on 2 March when long-range German aircraft from Kampfgeschwader 26 attacked shipping in the English Channel east of St Alban's Head. The steamship *Domala* was set on fire. In a repeat incident on 20 March they sank the 5,439-ton freighter SS *Barnhill* off Purbeck. The crew escaped by lifeboat.

The important and worrying discovery of the month was in a Heinkel He.111 bomber (call-sign 1H+AC) of Kampfgeschwader 26 – the celebrated Lowen-

Peter Franklin of Bovington with his father's rifle and helmet

Geschwader (Lion Wing) – which had been shot down. It contained a navigation note confirming the existence of a radio directed beam-bombing system. 'Radio Beacon Knickebein from 06.00 hours on 315 degrees,' it revealed on being translated. This provided a puzzle for TRE.

On 12 April a laurel wreath was attached to the door of the Hardy Monument, the memorial tower to Nelson's flag captain on the hills above Portesham – the village known to Thomas Hardy as 'Possum' – in memory of the men of the Royal Navy killed in Narvik fjord, Norway:

> **'To the unfading memory of Captain Warburton-Lee, R.N., H.M.S.**
> ***Hardy*****, and the gallant men who died at Narvik. Nelson's Hardy and**
> **Hardy's Possum salute you.'**

Slit-trenches reminiscent of the Western Front at Hengistbury Head, Bournemouth

HMS *Hardy* was named for Vice-Admiral Thomas Masterman Hardy. His commemorative tower is owned by the National Trust. Bernard Warburton-Lee caught the enemy by surprise in on 10 April when he penetrated Ofofjord with the Royal Navy's 2nd Destroyer Flotilla. He then took *Hardy*, *Havock* and *Hunter* into Narvik harbour. *Hotspur* and *Hostile* stood guard outside but then joined the action. Two German destroyers were sunk for the loss of *Hardy* and *Hunter*. Warburton-Lee, mortally wounded, was posthumously awarded the Victoria Cross. *Havock* and *Hotspur* were damaged, but fought on as they escaped into the open sea, setting fire to the German transport *Rauenfels*. The ship was carrying ammunition and the destroyers 'were peppered with ironmongery as she went up'.

The first bombing targeted on Dorset was to a munitions factory on 24 April. An oil incendiary bomb exploded beside the wash-water settling house of the nitro-glycerine complex at the Royal Naval Cordite Factory, Holton Heath. This began burning but Walt Dominey and his fire-fighting team brought the fire under control and averted what could have been a major disaster. Paper was a key material at Holton Heath – 1,910 tons of it being used in 1939 – for guncotton pulp which was mixed with nitro-glycerine for the basis of cordite SC, the propellant for the Navy's shells.

The situation became hopeless in northern Norway as the Germans advanced. Two Short Empire flying-boats, *Cabot* and *Caribou*, which had been scheduled to operate planned peacetime Atlantic services in 1940, had been seconded by BOAC at Poole to 119 Squadron at Invergordon. They took radar kit for beleaguered British troops at Harstadt but were attacked by a Heinkel He.115 floatplane in Bodo fjord on 4 May. The equipment was destroyed though the injured crews were rescued and brought home by a British destroyer. A further raid sank the flying-boats.

The Air Ministry's Special Duty Flight arrived at Christchurch Aerodrome from St Athan, Glamorgan, on 8 May. It comprised six Ansons, four Blenheims, two Harrows,

Training for a gas attack in the exercises at Hengistbury Head carried out by the 12th Battalion, Hampshire Regiment

Bayonet practice (with dummies) in sand dunes beside the Sandbanks Hotel, Poole

two Fairey Battles, and three adapted 'Special Aircraft'. These were a Hurricane, an Anson, and a High Altitude Machine. The aeroplanes, which were augmented by further arrivals of a variety of types, carried experimental radar aerials and secret apparatus. They were for the use of the Christchurch-based Air Defence and Research Development Establishment and scientists of the Telecommunications Research Establishment at Worth Matravers.

Unarmed combat in the grounds of the Sandbanks Hotel, Banks Road, Poole (name removed in accordance with Defence Regulations)

Tommy gunner in an Allen-Williams steel turret

The debacle was having far-reaching political consequences. On Friday 10 May Clement Attlee and Arthur Greenwood were recalled to London from the Labour Party Conference in Bournemouth as the Chamberlain Government recoiled in crisis following the German invasion of the Low Countries. Neville Chamberlain had offered the Labour leaders positions in a proposed new National Government.

They accepted the posts (Attlee as Lord Privy Seal; Greenwood as Minister Without Portfolio) but rejected Chamberlain's leadership. This exemplified Parliament's mood, characterised by an intervention in full uniform by Sir Roger Keyes. The most devastating attack on Neville Chamberlain came from behind, three days before, with a verbal dagger wielded by one of his own back-benchers. The Right Honourable Leo Amery MP spoke during the debate on the failed Norway campaign:

'This is what Cromwell said to the Long Parliament when he thought it was no longer fit to conduct the affairs of the nation. "You have sat too long here for any good you have been doing. Depart, I say, and let us have done with you. In the name of God go".'

Camouflaging a pillbox 'Somewhere in England' (Wareham, actually)

Speeches of the Opposition, of Duff Cooper from Chamberlain's own benches, and a vehement attack by Lloyd George, were followed by a Pyrrhic victory. In this the Prime Minister carried the vote but lost the confidence of his party – 33 Conservative rebels had voted against and a further 60 abstained. Chamberlain went at once to Buckingham Palace to tender his resignation to the King. The Prime Minister's final public act was a broadcast to the nation:

'You and I must rally behind our new leader, and with our united strength, and with unshakeable courage, fight and work until this wild beast, that has sprung out of his lair upon us, has been finally disarmed and overthrown.'

(Left) Dragon's Teeth anti-tank trap below a railway viaduct in Bourne Valley, Poole

(Right) Pillbox and anti-tank obstacles beside the railway bridge over the River Avon, Christchurch

Gunner's slit, looking outwards, from a pillbox at Langton Herring

The King sent for Winston Churchill to form a new three-party coalition Government. It was noted with approval in Dorset that his most distinguished ancestor, John Churchill, the first Duke of Marlborough, was the son of Winston Churchill of Round Chimneys Farm, Glanvilles Wootton, 'of a good Dorset family'. Winston Spencer Churchill was the grandson of the seventh Duke of Marlborough. In 1939 his son, Randolph, married the Hon. Pamela Digby of Minterne Magna.

Following the sudden Nazi invasion into the Low Countries an armada of dozens of overloaded Dutch vessels was shepherded by the Royal Navy into Poole Harbour. Refugees camped on Brownsea Island where they were screened by doctors, police, and the Security Service before being admitted into the country.

'Ou est la route pour France?' a Dorsetman heard as Algerian troops were beaten back by the German advance. The 2nd Battalion of the Dorsetshire Regiment then withdrew through Belgium in the face of the same overwhelming odds. Pulling back to Tournai near the French border, on 19 May, they saw the bodies of civilians bombed and strafed by German aircraft. The town was on fire.

With German radio announcing that the ring around the French, Belgian, and British Armies had 'definitely closed' the 2nd Dorsets – at La Bassee, south-west of Lille – were showered from the air on 24 May. Leaflets invited them to desert:

'You are surrounded – why fight on? We treat our prisoners well.'

Back home 'too much fraternisation' was taking place between military and civilian units. Dorset's local commander of the Observer Corps, Wing Commander Stewart, told his men:

'Head observers must consult their officers before making any commitments with the Local Defence Volunteers. No instruction has been received with regard to co-operation and any tendency to mingle at posts should be discouraged.'

Major-General Harry Marriot-Smith organised these armed civilians under instructions from the War Office. Dorset was covered by six battalions. Churchill would soon have them renamed – as the Home Guard – and the 3rd Dorset Battalion was split to form another, the 7th (Wareham) Battalion, and a Motor Transport Company as part of the Hants and Dorset Transport Column.

Prime Minister Churchill flew in a twin-engine de Havilland Flamingo transport aircraft from Hendon, via Warmwell Aerodrome on the Dorset coast, to Paris for secret discussions on the deteriorating military situation on 30 May. Nine Hurricane fighters from 601 (County of London) Squadron escorted the Premier's aeroplane. They waited overnight to bring it safely home. Churchill met the French Premier and talked with Major-General Edward Spears, his personal representative with the French Government and armed forces. The clutch of young pilots, even after their night on the town, reminded the Prime Minister of 'the angels of my childhood'.

Among them was Flying Officer William Rhodes-Moorhouse, whose father was the first airman to win the Victoria Cross, in 1915, and is

Home Guard volunteers firing Lee-Enfield rifles at the Nothe, above Weymouth Harbour

(Left) Emplacing a 9.2-inch anti-ship gun on East Weares to protect Portland Harbour

(Right, upper) Bournemouth firemen's Zone Control with 'X' marking regular stations and 'O' for wartime emergency bases

(Right, lower) Bournemouth No. 2 Zone fire station at Palmerston Road, Boscombe

Firemen torch a derelict thatched cottage in a training exercise at Castle Lane, Bournemouth

Bournemouth No. 5 Zone fire station at Maxwell Road, Winton

buried on a Dorset hillside at Parnham, which was the family home near Beaminster (with Willie interred next to him after being shot down over Tonbridge, Kent, on 6 September 1940).

After five days and nights of marching and fighting northwards to the Channel coast, the main contingent of the 2nd Battalion of the Dorsetshire Regiment completed their withdrawal, under fire, to the Mole at Dunkirk. On boarding a Thames dredger they were appalled to see that she seemed to be half-full of water but heard that dredgers were always like that.

The first train carrying Free French soldiers arrived in Weymouth at 05.00 hours on 1 June. They were being taken to Christ Church, opposite the station, which was turned into a refugee Welcome Club. On being issued with rations – half a loaf and a tin of bully-beef – they dispersed to various schools, halls, and private accommodation.

The centenary of author Thomas Hardy's birth was marked by a ceremony beside his statue in Dorchester on Sunday 2 June (though the precise anniversary was on the 4th). Speakers emphasised that Hardy was a patriot. Earl Baldwin of Bewdley (Conservative Prime Minister Stanley Baldwin) laid a wreath and admitted that he felt during the week that the event should be postponed due to the dismal news from France. On further consideration, however, he decided there was nothing unseemly even at such a moment for the English people to gather together in the part of England made famous by a very great Englishman, to express their sense of what they owed to him:

'He has for many increased their knowledge and love of England – for which her sons today are laying down their lives.'

Pleasure craft from Poole and Weymouth were in the armada of Operation Dynamo that evacuated the British Expeditionary Force from the beaches at Dunkirk. Among the flotilla heading to Dover from Poole had been Harvey's *Ferry Nymph* and *Southern Queen*; Davis's *Felicity* and *Island Queen*; and Bolson's *Skylark VI*, *Skylark VIII*, and *Skylark IX*; plus *Thomas Kirk-Wright*, the harbour's inshore lifeboat. These vessels were commandeered by the Royal Navy. The lifeboat, with its shallow draught, had the distinction of going into the beaches and survived shore-fire from Germans less than 40 yards away.

The pleasure craft stood offshore and proved ideal for taking aboard soldiers by the dozen. *Island Queen* and *Southern Queen* were sunk and *Skylark VI* abandoned, though she was later salvaged and towed back to Bolson's Shipyard in Poole for conversion to an Air-Sea Rescue craft. As for Poole's fishing fleet, which also loyally responded to the Admiralty's appeal, they were summarily rejected by the Navy. The Poole fishermen, who considered themselves something of an elite – as the port's only true seamen – felt humiliated on being sent home from Kent by train when their vessels were impounded for possible reserve use.

Retreat from the jaws of defeat turned into a miracle of defiance with a successful evacuation of unprecedented proportions. A total of 338,228 soldiers were brought out to fight again another day. Of these a third were French and 6,000 of those, from Flanders, were sent to Weymouth. There, at least, the seaside had hotels and facilities, but concern was expressed in Dorchester that in the wake of the military collapse there would be a further civilian influx for which the county town was totally unprepared. A further 2,300 evacuees were earmarked for Dorchester Rural District where work had only just started on constructing air-raid shelters.

Lieutenant-Commander Charles John Thompson Stephens (35) was among those lost on 8 June in the sinking of the aircraft-carrier HMS *Glorious*, off Narvik by gunfire from the German battlecruisers *Scharnhorst* and *Gneisenau*. Commander Stephens was the son of Major John August Stephens of Evershot.

Overnight on 8-9 June the Germans mined the Swash Channel into Poole Harbour in anticipation of its use in a relief operation to bring out beleaguered British Army units struggling in Normandy. Overall, Operation Cycle failed to live up to the Admiralty's expectations of a second mini-Dunkirk, but for some of the Poole boats taking part it was a triumph. By 12 June they had played a key role in rescuing 3,321 soldiers – a third of them British – from the salient at St Valery-en-Caux. This time the Germans had been ready for a maritime exit mission, though it was fog that disrupted efforts in the early hours of the 11th, and sent 6,000 Scottish troops into prisoner-of-war camps.

Navy divers from Portland cleared the Swash Channel, but not completely, as the *Princess Juliana* found. Sailing out of Poole, she hit a mine off the Training Bank, and was lifted clear of the water. George Brown, the pilot, was saved with three Dutch crewmen. Ivor Holland, instrumental in the rescue of survivors, was awarded the Order of the Red Lion by the Netherlands Government-in-exile.

Nine Spitfires of 609 (West Riding) Squadron from RAF Middle Wallop deployed to Warmwell Aerodrome in the Frome Valley for 72 hours to act as fighter escorts for Prime Minister Churchill's Flamingo. He flew to France twice between 10-13 June, on the first occasion with Secretary of State for War Anthony Eden and Generals Dill and Ismay from the Imperial General Staff, to try and persuade Prime Minister Paul Reynaud to continue fighting the Germans. On the second occasion the London party comprised Churchill and Ismay with Lords Halifax and Beaverbrook.

The first flight was to Briare, near Orleans, and the second to Tours. Churchill saw the journeys as encapsulating the state of the nation:

> '**Eight thousand feet below us on our right was Havre, burning. Presently I noticed some consultations going on with the captain, and immediately after we dived to a hundred feet or so. They had seen two German aircraft firing at fishing boats. We were lucky that their pilots did not look upwards. Arrived over Tours, we found the airport had been heavily bombed the night before, but we and our escort landed smoothly in spite of the craters.**'

Farm memorial at South Admiston, Tolpuddle, to Adrian van de Weyer of the Rifle Brigade who was killed at Calais, 26 May 1940

Navigation across the ground was equally fraught. The Prime Minister's car could hardly move through a stream of refugees.

On 13 June, three of a flotilla of 15 craft returning from St Valery-en-Caux with remnants of the British and French Armies ran the gauntlet of the Swash Channel into Poole Harbour. The fourth and unlucky craft was the *Abel Tasman*, fortunately returning empty. She hit a mine and was blown to pieces, killing all eleven of her complement from the Royal Navy Volunteer Reserve. An order was then flashed to the remaining ships for them to turn around and sail to Southampton instead.

The steam tanker *British Inventor* struck a mine off St Alban's Head. Although she stayed afloat long enough to be put under tow the line had to be released as the stricken vessel began to go under. Channels into the ports of Weymouth and Poole were kept open through the efforts of two Portland-based minesweepers, HMS *Kindred Star* and HMS *Thrifty*.

Mines in the Swash Channel were of a new magnetic type that exploded when they come close to a steel ship. These C-type mines had not been retrieved intact for examination and on 15 June the first attempt to do so burst into spectacular failure on Studland beach. Harold Cartridge with the Poole fishing boat *Smiling Through*, operating under Navy orders, managed to tow one on a 700-feet line from the Bar Buoy to the sandy shallows off Studland – where it exploded, though without delivering more than a shock and a shake to Cartridge and his craft. The Germans proved to be slow in deploying this potentially devastating weapon. The first to be dismantled by the British would be recovered from Shoeburyness, Essex, on 22 November 1940; the Germans had been lax in not incorporating an anti-handling device.

A London coal-barge, *Alnwick* from Fulham Dock, chugged into Poole Quay at midday on 17 June 1940, having successfully dodged both the Luftwaffe and the mines. She carried a cargo of fully-armed British soldiers withdrawn from Cherbourg. They were greeted by a crowd of cheering civilians who tossed the men packets of cigarettes and bottles of beer. An infantryman of the 51st Highland Division played the bagpipes as remnants of Ark Force, the 154th Infantry Brigade who had been tasked to protect the evacuation, stepped ashore. They were then treated to a wash in municipal swimming baths and accommodation at St Walburga's Catholic School, Malvern Road, Bournemouth.

Condition Red on 20 June triggered the first air-raid warning at Christchurch, though there had been earlier alerts for Condition Yellow, the precautionary message from Fighter Command that enemy air activity was to be expected. Red, however, signified that enemy air activity was being monitored – by radar – and heading towards places given the warning. It was an instruction to take to the shelters, given as a two-minute warbling blast on the sirens. Observers at Christchurch reported enemy aircraft sighted at 8,000 feet, and a burst of gunfire heard, but no bombs were dropped. Later a continuous two-minute wail from sirens declared All Clear.

Tearful farewells on 20 June marked Weymouth's parting with the French soldiers, the last of whom left to resume the war with fighting units. They were taken to heart, in a way that Londoners and others weren't – but the town had experienced an influx unprecedented for anywhere in England. In one sad incident a Catholic priest attempted placating an unhappy Belgian woman. 'Are they all yours?' joked Father Jules Ketele when he saw she had three children with her. A good Catholic should have known better! She burst into tears and sobbed that she had seven children when she left home eight days before; they were all she had left.

The total number of arrivals for the week had been 27,400 refugees, of which the bulk – 23,743 of them – had come from the Channel Islands, which faced impending German invasion. This took place at the end of the month, on 30 June and 1 July, and they remained enemy-occupied for the duration of the war.

The daring rescue of General Wladyslaw Sikorski, the commander of Free Polish forces, from the chaos surrounding the Fall of France was carried out by a British flying-boat. Captain Donald Bennett landed on a coastal lake at Biscarrosse, 30 miles south-west of Bordeaux, to pick up his highly important passenger. Although they took off from within sight of German armoured vehicles the only fire that came in their direction was from a British cruiser in the Bay of Biscay. The flying-boat touched down in the comparative safety of Poole Harbour at 09.00 hours on 21 June. Air Vice-Marshal Donald Bennett, as he became, led Bomber Command's elite Pathfinder aircraft. He held the world record for a long-distance seaplane flight, from Dundee in Scotland to Alexandra Bay, South Africa. General Sikorski died in an aeroplane accident at Gibraltar on 4 July 1943.

As Sikorski landed at Poole, TRE organised a special mission for that evening, with three Ansons of the Special Duty Flight at Christchurch Aerodrome. They tried, in poor weather, to use American radar receivers to track the course of a German radio direction signal intended to aid the navigation of bombers. This appeared to lead inland from the North Sea in the vicinity of Spalding, Lincolnshire, after which it intersected with another similar 'beam' from the south, above the Rolls-Royce aero-engine factory at Derby..

On Sunday 23 June, a British Avro 504N biplane took off from Christchurch Aerodrome to tow a German Minimoa glider into the middle of the English Channel and released the wooden craft at 10,000 feet for it to glide back towards the Isle of Purbeck. The pilot, Philip Wills, returned below cliff level at St Alban's Head and braced himself for impact but was saved by the phenomenon of currents rising on sunny days beside south-facing vertical surfaces.

The purpose of the exercise was for TRE to establish with radio direction finding aerials whether short-wave radiation bouncing off metal bombers would also reflect from wooden gliders.

The answer was affirmative; to the relief of the scientists and the War Cabinet as the country feared a mass invasion by German gliders. As for the Avro 504, it had a remarkable pedigree dating back to the beginning of the Great War, when it took part in the first organised bombing raid – that on the Zeppelin sheds at Friedrichshafen, Lake Constance, on 21 November 1914.

69th Infantry Brigade, late of France and the Dunkirk beaches, returned to the front line at Poole and east Dorset on 25 June. It took over anti-invasion defences from the Queen's Bays. The Officer Commanding, Brigadier Barstow, was based at Bovington Camp. The Brigade comprised the 7th Battalion of the Green Howards; the 5th Battalion of the East Yorkshire Regiment; and the 6th Battalion of the Green Howards, with the latter being dispersed into the countryside. Their Adjutant found that the unit no longer possessed a duplicator and asked Poole Corporation to loan theirs.

The 554th Coast Regiment of the Royal Artillery, with its headquarters at the Conningtower, West Road, Canford Cliffs, emplaced former naval guns (taken from warships at the end of the Great War and put into store) as the teeth of anti-ship defences around Poole Bay. They were emplaced in fortifications built by the Royal Engineers:

> **'Two 6-inch guns at Battery Hill, Brownsea Island, manned by 347 Coast Battery. Two 5.5-inch guns on Hengistbury Head manned by 172 Coast Battery. Two 6-inch guns at Mudeford manned by 175 Coast Battery. Two 4-inch guns at Swanage manned by 386 Coast Battery. Each set of emplacements to have a complement of 100 men.'**

An Examination Ship was positioned in the Swash Channel at the entrance to Poole Harbour. The duty was rotated between ex-Belgian trawler *Rose Arthur*, as His Majesty's Trawler *XVI*, with her sister craft HMT *XVII* (*Roger Robert*) and HMT *XVIII* (*Marguerita Marie Louisa*). 'Blackbird' was the alert code for sighting of enemy forces, 'Gallipoli' for a landing of troops, and 'Caterpillar' for tanks. Once a warning of invasion had been radioed and received on the mainland the craft's duty was to suspend the watching brief with a final signal – 'Finish' – and head to sea to intercept and engage enemy vessels.

The harbour entrance, from Sandbanks to Shell Bay, had a steel boom with suspended torpedo heads provided by the Royal Naval Cordite Factory at Holton Heath. There was a passage that was opened at the centre during the day and closed each evening by boatman George Mitchell. Inside the harbour, six pleasure craft were requisitioned by the Royal Navy, armed with machine guns, and designated *H1* to *H6* of the Poole Harbour Patrol.

In the Main Channel an old steamship, the *Empire Sentinel*, was been packed with explosives. In the event of invasion the Harbour Patrol was to sink her, to block the approaches to the port. Their prime duty was to ensure the closure of this channel. The Naval Officer Commanding, Poole, organised the laying of a minefield between Sandbanks and Brownsea Island to prevent the intrusion of German submarines or surface vessels.

Anti-tank 'Islands' of urban coastal areas, impregnable to armoured attack, were established behind concrete obstacles, minefields, and flame traps, at the Old Town in Poole and between the railway and the rivers at Christchurch. The Garrison Headquarters was also strongly defended in the centre of Bournemouth. The whole of the conurbation, from Upton to Highcliffe, was under the control of the Garrison Commander in Bournemouth.

Seaplane training for Fleet Air Arm pilots moved to Poole in mid-June, from Calshot on Southampton Water to Sandbanks, with the arrival of 765 Naval Air Squadron and the Royal Navy Seaplane School. The school and its squadron trained pilots on the Walrus biplane, the Fleet and Air-Sea Rescue workhorse, which was one of the most distinctive maritime aeroplanes. It had a characteristic chugging sound and a high profile with a stabiliser on the tail and floats at the tips of the wings. Sailors called it the 'Shagbat'.

On Sandbanks slipway the machines were stored with their wheels down and wings folded back. The unit also flew veteran Swordfish torpedo-reconnaissance biplanes – the 'Stringbag' – and Kingfisher and Seafox floatplanes. The base was known as Royal Naval Air Station Sandbanks. To Poole people, however, it was the more prosaic HMS Tadpole – because it handled beginners with seaplanes that were dwarfed by the flying-boats operating from Poole Harbour with BOAC and RAF Coastal Command. The name HMS Tadpole was later adopted by the Royal Navy for real, in 1943, for a pre-invasion Landing Craft Training Establishment.

The unique collection of the world's first tanks at the Armoured Fighting Vehicles School, Bovington Camp, was dispersed to help the war effort. Many were taken away for scrap and others are placed in strategic positions as stationary pillboxes. The vehicles had been put in a shed after Rudyard Kipling visited Bovington in 1923 and expressed disappointment that nothing was then being done to preserve them.

As the exhausted evacuated armies are dispersed from their reception ports a detachment of 400 French soldiers were told to report to Bournemouth for a short recuperation while billets were found. Bournemouth School became a refugee reception centre. Town vicar Canon Hedley Burrows found French troops being directed to St Peter's Hall. He telephoned the Town Clerk to ask who was in charge of these men. 'You are!' he was told. Canon Burrows arranged their accommodation at hotels and with his congregation. There was growing competition for space as thousands more passed through the town. Militarily, there was just one fully-equipped operational division in the whole of the British Isles, and that was Canadian.

In Bridport a pub name moved with the times. Historically, it was the King of Prussia at 52 East Street. Then it became the King of Belgium when he was the nation's darling for standing up to the Kaiser in 1914. Sadly, King Albert the hero was killed in a climbing accident on 17 February 1934, and his successors were noticeably lacking in qualities of defiance in defeat, being quick to capitulate to the next wave of invading Germans. Palmer's Brewery solved the problem by choosing a hero who could not be deposed by deciding that Lord Nelson had stood the test of time.

On the morning of Monday 1 July, Ration Books for food came into force, with green coupons for meat, yellow for butter and margarine, and orange for cooking fat. Identity Cards were issued to everyone living in the Military Control Areas, which in Dorset included the entire coast and its towns and extended 20 miles inland.

The Commissioner responsible for the control of civilians in the South-West Region was Sir Geoffrey Kelsall Peto. The process of issuing the National Registration Identity

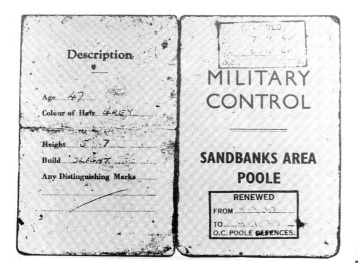

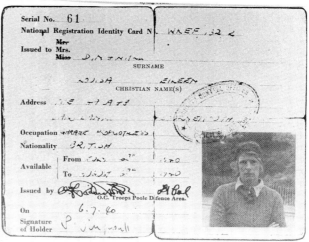

(Left) Military Control passport for Sandbanks at Poole

(Right) Identification for Sandbanks garage proprietor, horse-trainer and chauffeur Mrs Louisa Dingwall issued on 6 July 1940

Cards was delegated to local officials. Those issued at Sandbanks, for instance, were signed by the Officer Commanding Troops, Poole Defence Area:

> 'Persons without cards who have business or private reasons for entering Military Control Areas will be required to give their names and addresses, and those of the people they are visiting, at police or military vehicle check-points. Passengers and pedestrians are also asked to co-operate. Police will be carrying out spot-checks inside these zones, such as on buses, and at random in public places.'

The following day it was announced that all beach chalets and huts had to be removed from the vicinity of beaches at Poole, Bournemouth, and Christchurch, having been subjected to a blanket requisition order by the military. Their clearance was deemed necessary to ensure a field of fire from the cliffs and across the sands. The low-tide line for the ten-mile entirety of Bournemouth beach, from Sandbanks to Hengistbury Head, was given priority for wiring-up with barriers. These defences were erected by the Green Howards who also built emplacements at intervals and guarded weak-points such as the Chines. They began by sealing-off Sandbanks with strong-points at the Haven Hotel and Sandbanks Pavilion.

Newly knighted, General Sir Alan Brooke arrived in Wiltshire on 26 June, to take over Southern Command with Command Headquarters in Wilton House. He drove south on 2 July to visit 30th Division and inspect Dorset's defences. His itinerary was Blandford, Bovington, Blandford again (for lunch), Yeovil and then back to Salisbury. He confided in his diary:

> 'The more I see of the nakedness of our defences the more appalled I am. Untrained men, no arms, no transport, and no equipment. And yet there are masses of men in uniform in this country, why I cannot think after ten months of war. The ghastly part of it is that I feel certain that we can only have a few more weeks left before the Boche attacks.'

Southampton received its first enemy bombers on 19 June and at 00.12 hours on 3 July came Bournemouth's turn. A single high-explosive bomb fell at Cellars Farm Road, Southbourne. It set a house on fire and damaged 18 other properties. The explosion and blaze caused considerable consternation. Rumours as the suburbs awoke were that at 02.45, on the other side of the River Stour, Christchurch police had issued a warning that German parachutists had landed.

For Dorset the phoney war ended on Thursday 4 July. Ninety Junkers Ju.87 Stukas attacked Convoy OA 178 between Portland and Hengistbury Head, sinking the steamship *Elmcrest* and three other vessels. A further nine ships were damaged. The dive-bombers then turned to the west and attacked Portland Harbour at 08.50 hours, sinking two ships,

German bombs dropping towards the Outer Breakwater of Portland Harbour and the East Ship Channel (bottom left)

Portland Harbour with *Foyle-bank* burning after attack by Stuka dive-bombers on 4 July 1940

Capsized hulk of the *Foylebank* in which 60 seamen died, including Jack Mantle who won the Royal Navy's first Victoria Cross in British territorial waters

including anti-aircraft auxiliary HMS *Foylebank*, moored beside the Admiral's Buoy. A dozen Stukas came at her and one of the first casualties was Leading Seaman Jack Mantle (23) who went to school at Affpuddle. Despite having his legs shattered as bombs tore the ship apart, causing loss of electrical power, he stayed at his pom-pom. He continued manual firing of the starboard 20 mm barrels even as he suffered further wounds and knew he was mortally injured. Anti-aircraft fire accounted for one Stuka which was sent crashing into the harbour. It belonged to the 3rd Staffel Stukageschwader 51 and took with it Leutnant Schwarze and his crewman.

Fifty-nine of Jack Mantle's comrades were also killed and a total of 60 were injured. Somehow one in three, the further lucky 60, came out of it unscathed as the burning vessel turned over and sank. Perhaps the unluckiest people on Portland were nine contractors from McAlpine's who had been digging a tunnel. They sheltered inside it during the raid and came out of it when it was thought to be over; to be killed by the last bomb from a single German aeroplane that turned back from the sea. Four of the workers were boys.

The attack confirmed that the Luftwaffe had moved its squadrons forward to occupied airfields on the Cherbourg peninsula only 70 miles from the Dorset coast. There were repercussions. The Admiralty closed the English Channel to ocean-going merchant vessels though coastal convoys continued.

The initial death toll from *Foylebank* rose to a total loss of 72 men. Jack Mantle, would be gazetted on 3 September 1940 – the war's first anniversary – with the only Victoria Cross that the Royal Navy has won inside United Kingdom territorial waters. He is buried in Portland Naval Cemetery with the epitaph:

'Because we did not choose to shame the land from which we sprang.'

The young man's mother spoke with pride:

'Jack didn't seem to be the heroic type. He was a quiet boy. He had an intense dislike of pain and was always afraid of the dentist.'

Open-air gatherings were henceforth restricted. Only family mourners were allowed to attend funerals that resulted from the day's events. At one of the services the Methodist minister of Fortuneswell, Rev F. Jowett, said:

'We owe a tribute of gratitude and affection to the one who has departed. He has given his life for his King and country, and those things for which we Englishmen stand.'

Survivors of Convoy OA 178, which had suffered so considerably, were harassed on the night of 4 July by E-boats. The flotilla of German Schnellboote attacked off Poole Bay. One Allied ship was sunk and two more damaged. E-boat was the generic term for these craft, being the Anglicised shorthand for the German 'Eil-Boot' meaning 'Fast Boat'. Specifically they were Schnellboote (plural), or Schnellboot (singular), being the German motor torpedo-boat (or S-boat in alternative Anglicised shorthand).

SS *Hartlepool*, a British freighter, sank beside Weymouth Harbour after being crippled by the Stukas. She was put in tow with the intention of beaching her on Weymouth sands, but shipped too much water and went down in four fathoms, half-a-mile offshore.

In view of their potential use to the enemy, not only for German airborne landings, but also as supply points for any conventional invasion force, the precautionary measure was taken of 'blowing' the seaside piers at Bournemouth and Boscombe. The Royal Engineers carried out a series of explo-

sions to demolish the central sections of both structures. The seaward ends – the scene of the famous end-of-the-pier shows – were left as islands to signify the state of siege that was now 'England alone'.

It was a short war for the destroyer HMS *Brazen*, sunk in the Channel in July 1940

Fighter aircraft were to be based beside the Dorset coast in order to counter the Luftwaffe's increasing threat to Channel shipping and in direct response to the audacious attack on the Royal Navy base at Portland. The Deputy Chief of the Air Staff, Air-Vice Marshal W. Sholto Douglas, issued the redeployment order and on 6 July RAF Warmwell, near Dorchester, became a front-line defensive aerodrome with the arrival from RAF Northolt of the Spitfires of 609 (West Riding) Squadron commanded by Squadron Leader Horace Stanley 'George' Darley (26). The aircraft carried the squadron code letters 'PR' and their motto was 'Tally ho!'.

Deadly silhouette of the Junkers Ju.87 Stuka dive-bomber

Control of the grass airfield at Warmwell was transferred to 10 Group of Fighter Command with headquarters at Rudloe Manor, Box, near Bath. The airfield's pundit code

Warmwell Spitfire etched in wet cement by Bere Regis boy Fred Pitfield

was 'XW', displayed in huge white letters 10 feet high, and also flashed in Morse code at night, in red light, from a mobile beacon. Warmwell's sector base and home aerodrome was Middle Wallop, near Andover, Hampshire. The pilots returned there in the evening and came back to Dorset the following morning. Scramble time was 15 minutes and the accommodation tented.

Spitfire P9450 – the reassuring presence in Dorset's sky – fielded by RAF Warmwell

The advent of the eight-gun fighter revolutionised aerial warfare. There were 187 Spitfires in squadron service when war was declared. By the end of that month 4,000 were on order. Their production had the highest priority.

The Special Duty Flight, based at Christchurch Aerodrome and fulfilling aviation needs of TRE scientists, received a Sunday visit from top-brass on 7 July. Air Marshal Arthur William Tedder, the Director-General of Research and Development, was accompanied by Air Vice-Marshal Roderic Maxwell Hill as Director of Technical Development for the Air Ministry and Ministry of Aircraft Production.

Premier Winston Churchill inspecting a pillbox in the Sandbanks dunes on 17 July 1940

Dive-bombers attacked Channel shipping off Portland on the evening of 9 July and 609 Squadron was scrambled from RAF Warmwell. Three of its Spitfires closed in on two Stukas but then at least nine Messerschmitt Bf.110s pounced on the British fighters from above and behind them. These attacking aircraft were spotted by Pilot Officer David Moore Crook (26) in Spitfire P9322. He yelled a radio warning to his two companions.

England alone, at Seatown, with one soldier and a coil of wire between Golden Cap and the Wehrmacht

The iconic figurehead and signature cigar from the *Dorset Year Book*

'We shall never surrender' – Churchill defiant in Dorset on his 17 July visit

Pilot Officer Michael Appleby had just switched his set from transmit, in time to hear the word 'Messerschmitts', and pulled his Spitfire clear. The third Spitfire, flown by Pilot Officer Peter Drummond-Hay, must still have had its radio on transmission mode and was lost in the action, over the sea south of Portland Bill. The pilot was declared missing, presumed dead. Then, David Crook writes, in his combat report:

> 'I found myself very near to a Ju.87 so stalked it through cloud and when it emerged into clear sky I fired all the rest of my ammunition at very close range. He turned over and dived in flames into the sea.'

The dive-bomber was piloted by Hauptmann Friedrich-Karl Freiherr von Dalwigk zu Lichtenfels, the 33-year-old Staffelkapitan of I Gruppe, Stukageschwader 77 who was posthumously awarded the Iron Cross. Writing his memoirs, published as *Spitfire Pilot* in 1942, Crook recalled the interception and his thoughts on achieving his first kill:

> 'I saw dimly a machine moving in the cloud to my left and flying parallel to me. I stalked him through the cloud, and when he emerged into a patch of clear sky I saw that it was a Ju.87. I was in an ideal position to attack and opened fire and put the remainder of my ammunition – about 2,000 rounds – into him at very close range. Even in the heat of the moment I well remember my amazement at the shattering effect of my fire. Pieces flew off his fuselage and the cockpit covering, a stream of smoke appeared from the engine cowling and he dived down vertically. The flames enveloped the whole machine and he went straight down, apparently quite slowly, for about 5,000 feet, till he was just a shapeless burning mass of wreckage. Absolutely fascinated by the sight, I followed him down, and saw him hit the sea with a great burst of white foam. He disappeared immediately, and apart from a green patch in the water there was no sign that anything had happened. The crew made no attempt to get out, and they were obviously killed by my first burst of fire. I had often wondered what would be my feelings when killing somebody like this, and especially when seeing them go down in flames. I was rather surprised to reflect afterwards that my only feeling had been one of considerable elation – and a sort of bewildering surprise because it had been so easy.'

David Crook made 'a perfectly bloody landing' at Warmwell and returned to RAF Middle Wallop at dusk:

'We got back and I went to my room in the mess. Everything was just the same as Peter and I had left it only 18 hours before; his novel was still in the window where he had thrown it during our hurried dressing. But he was dead now. I simply could not get used to such sudden and unexpected death, and there flashed across my mind the arrangements we had made to go up to London the following day. It all seemed so ironical, so tragic, so futile. I felt that I could not sleep in that room again, and so I took my things and went into Gordon's bed next door and slept there.'

It was unoccupied. Gordon Mitchell had been grounded with a damaged Spitfire and was spending the night in a tent at Warmwell.

'But I could not get out of my head the thought of Peter, with whom we had been talking and laughing that day, now lying in the cockpit of his wrecked Spitfire at the bottom of the English Channel.'

There would be more grief. 'It was the last time I ever saw him,' David wrote of Gordon. Another friend, 'Pip' Barran, answered the telephone to find it was Peter's wife:

'The telegram had not yet reached her, and so Pip had to tell her the news. It all seemed so awful; I was seeing for the first time at very close quarters all the distress and unhappiness that casualties cause. I walked out of the mess and drove to the station, very thankful to be doing something that took my mind on to other subjects. And I never saw Pip again, either.'

Poole became a sealed-off town on 9 July, as part of the Defence Area, with access restricted to those who had reason to enter the town, under a regulation signed by Regional Controller Harold Butler. The Battle of Britain had begun but the British Empire's air link resumed with the arrival in Sydney of a BOAC flying-boat from Poole. Another reached Durban. They both flew horseshoe-shaped routes to Lisbon and then across the southern Sahara. From there the Australian plane turned northwards, via Khartoum and Cairo, to join the usual peacetime flight-path across Palestine, the Persian Gulf, India and Malaya. The other route, to South Africa, was via Lagos and Leopoldville.

Among various anti-landing traps laid to discourage enemy glider forces were rows of telegraph poles, cut into sections, dug into fairways of Parkstone golf links and across Branksome playing fields.

Two more Spitfires from Warmwell's 609 Squadron were shot down over the English Channel on 11 July while fighting off Stukas dive-bombing a convoy of British merchant ships. Flying Officer Philip Henry 'Pip' Barran (31) and Pilot Officer Gordon Thomas Manners Mitchell (29) were killed.

Channel watch by the 12th Battalion, Hampshire Regiment, at Hengistbury Head, Bournemouth

Sergeant-Pilot Frederick John Powell Dixon, in a Hurricane of 501 Squadron from RAF Middle Wallop, was shot down at 08.00 hours off Portland Bill. He baled out and his body was washed up on the French coast. Hurricanes of 238 Squadron from Middle Wallop claimed the double distinction that day of being the first RAF unit to bring down a German aircraft on Dorset soil, thereby delivering the first Germans to be taken prisoner in the conflict which became known as the Battle of Britain.

Infantrymen of the Hampshire Regiment scaling cliffs in an exercise at Bournemouth

Oberleutnant Gerhard Kadow, who crash-landed at Povington, was the first pilot to be taken prisoner in the Battle of Britain

The two enemy flyers were in Messerschmitt Bf.110C (2N+EP) which crash-landed at 12.05 hours on Povington Heath in the parish of Tyneham. They were Oberleutnant Gerhard Kadow, pilot, and Gefreiter Helmut Scholz, gunner, of III Gruppe, Zerstor-ergeschwader 76. They flew from Laval, refuelling at Dinard, and were among the fighters escorting Stuka dive-bombers that attacked Channel shipping. Their twin-engine aeroplane had twisted propellers and a dented underside but was otherwise undamaged. The pilot failed in an attempt to set it ablaze.

Luftwaffe losses off Portland included a Junkers Ju.87B of II/LG 1 shot down at 11.30 hours by Flight-Lieutenant Sir Archibald Hope, in a Hurricane of 601 Squadron from RAF Tangmere. His colleagues claimed a Messerschmitt Bf.110C of III Gruppe, Zerstor-ergeschwader 76, killing Oberleutnant H. D. Göring – nephew of the Commander-in-Chief of the Luftwaffe – and crewman Unterofficer Zimmerman.

They completed the hat-trick when Flight Lieutenant Hugh Joseph Riddle took a third of the credit for destroying another Bf.110C, with pilot Leutnant Schroder and his crewman. This was a multi-squadron kill for a pack of Hurricanes, with Wing Commander John Scatliff 'Johnny' Dewar, of 87 Squadron from Exeter, plus the Green Section of 238 Squadron from Middle Wallop contributing their gunfire.

An unblooded support squadron, 152 (Hyderabad) Squadron, flew into Warmwell Aerodrome on 12 July, led by Squadron Leader Peter Devitt (29) who learnt to fly as a teenager in 1930. Their markings were 'UM' and motto 'Faithful ally'. Equipped with Spitfires, they had their practice flights in Northumberland.

Veterans of Dunkirk, the 4th Battalion of the Royal Northumberland Fusiliers arrived in Bournemouth, after a short stay at Yeovil and a few days in tents at Piddlehinton.

On the seaside they took over coastal defences from the Royal Artillery as well as mine-laying and the erection of wood, steel, and concrete anti-invasion obstacles. Much ingenuity was displayed in concealing fortifications. One large pillbox built upstream from Iford Bridge was camouflaged as a refreshment kiosk. Another was disguised as a hay-rick.

Simulated fire towards a realistic depiction of the road across the heath, at the Gunnery Wing of the Armoured Fighting Vehicles School, Lulworth Camp

Learning from the chaos brought to Belgium and France by refugees blocking the roads in the hours that preceded the arrival of German troops, the three mayors of the Bournemouth conurbation emphasised that there was to be no civilian evacuation if the enemy invaded. Major roads would be sealed-off for the use of the Army. Resistance would continue from the 'Fighting Boxes' garrisoned by upwards of 50 armed men, and in some cases 200 or more. These were 'fortified, supplied, and organised to withstand siege without outside assistance'.

Spitfires from 609 Squadron, whilst flying a convoy protection patrol over the English Channel on 13 July, encountered German aircraft at 15,000 feet, off Portland. Flying

Officer John Charles Dundas (24) came out of the sun at a Messerschmitt Bf.110 which he claimed to have destroyed – it in fact limped back to France – and had a dog-fight with other German fighter-bombers. As he returned to Warmwell, Radipole-born Pilot Officer Rogers Freeman Garland 'Mick' Miller (20) took on and damaged a Bf.110, and then found a Dornier Do.17P, a photo-reconnaissance aircraft. This was almost finished off by Hurricanes of 238 Squadron from Middle Wallop on the Hampshire Downs. Leutnant Weinbauer and Oberleutnant Graf von Kesselstadt attempted to crash-land it on Chesil Beach, close to the oil-tanks on Portland, but the aircraft slid into the sea. Harry Buckley of Buckland House, Buckland Ripers, recalled that wreckage was recovered from the water at the time, and found some himself more than half a century later:

> 'Strangely enough, in the spring of 1997, I picked-up a radial engine piston and a condensing rod at the spot of the crash. They had been washed ashore.'

Australian volunteer, Flying Officer John Connelly Kennedy (23), from Sydney, was killed on 13 July at South Down, above Preston, near Weymouth. His Hurricane, of 238 Squadron from Middle Wallop, was being watched by an observer through a telescope:

> 'It was flying slowly north at about 1,500 feet and the cockpit cover was slid back. Suddenly as I watched it nosed down and crashed into the ground almost vertically. The crash was at the top of South Down Hill.'

Luftwaffe 'Enigma' machine-coded radio messages carried a directive from Hitler on 16 July. The translation of the deciphered intercept, passed to Prime Minister Churchill by the Government's Code and Cipher School, read:

> 'I have decided to prepare a landing operation against England and if necessary to carry it out.'

The cryptographic headquarters, at Bletchley Park, Buckinghamshire, was headed by Commander Alexander Dennison and formed a department of MI6, the Secret Intelligence Service. The 'Ultra Secret' of the Second World War was the extent to which cryptanalysts could read the enemy's mind by breaking codes which the Germans believed were secure.

The following day Winston Churchill visited Dorset to see the invasion precautions along one the most vulnerable beaches of the South Coast when he inspected units at Branksome Chine and Sandbanks. He showed his skill as a bricklayer at Branksome with practical contributions to the defences. While driving to Dorset from Gosport, the Prime Minister recalled to General Sir Alan Brooke, the chief of Southern Command, that it was from the rustic bridge at Alum Chine that he had fallen 20 feet in 1892, at the age of 17, and very nearly plunged to his death. He was unconscious for many days.

They dined at the Armoured Fighting Vehicles School, at Bovington Camp, and were taken to Wool Station for 20.00 hours and Churchill's train back to London. While maintaining 'a confident exterior' Brooke was unimpressed with what they saw:

> 'What has been going on in this country since the war started? The ghastly part is that I feel certain that we can only have a few more weeks before the Boche attacks.'

Churchill, however, realised he had a considerable asset in Brooke – who two days later was promoted Commander-in-Chief Home Forces. On Christmas Day in 1941 he became Chief of the Imperial General Staff.

On 18 July 1940, Brooke spent the day with the 50th Division and toured the Dorset beaches from Lulworth Cove, Swanage, Studland Bay, Sandbanks and Bournemouth, around to Christchurch Bay and Hurst Castle. He then discussed an anti-invasion exercise with Major-General Bernard Montgomery before dining with General Sir Bernard Paget.

Warmwell's Spitfire pilots returned on 18 July to celebrate their first undisputed kills. Two German aircraft were shot down, with the honours being shared by 152 Squadron and 609 Squadron, thereby restoring the latter's morale after recent losses. The engagement over Lyme Bay was the first action for newly-arrived 152 Squadron. Flight-Lieutenant Edward Sidney Hogg (21) claimed the destruction of a Dornier Do.17M bomber of the Staff Flight of Kampfgeschwader 77 which had been attacking Channel shipping. Oberleutnant Strecker and his three crewmen were killed.

On the debit side, 609 Squadron lost another Spitfire, and had a second machine awash on a beach, though both pilots were safe. Flight-Lieutenant Frank Jonathan Howell parachuted into the sea from Spitfire R6634 during a mid-afternoon dog-fight five miles from Swanage. He had been shot down by a Junkers Ju.88. A Royal Navy launch picked him up.

The Navy then found Flying Officer Alexander Rothwell Edge (32) on Studland beach. He had brought Spitfire R6636 down on the sands after return fire smashed its cooling system. As the tide came in the fighter was covered by the sea. It was salvaged to fly again.

Three RAF fighters were shot down off Swanage on 20 July. Pilot Officer Frederick Hyam Posener (23), a South African volunteer, was the fourth Warmwell Spitfire pilot to be killed. He was flying K9880 with 152 Squadron. In the same action, 15 miles south of Durlston Head, Sergeant Pilot Cecil Parkinson (25) was critically injured. He was flying Hurricane P3766 of 238 Squadron, from Middle Wallop, which was shot down in flames. Though Parkinson baled out, and was picked-up a destroyer, he suffered extensive burns and died the following day. Pilot Officer Edmund John Hilary Sylvester (26), in a Hurricane of 501 Squadron – recently returned from France – was shot down by Leutnant Zirkenbach of I Gruppe, Jagdgeschwader 27.

The Hurricanes of 238 Squadron claimed a Dornier Do.17P (5F+OM) which was shot down at 15.00 hours on 21 July over Nutford Farm, Pimperne, a mile north of Blandford. Its three crew were wounded in the crash and taken into the farmhouse before being driven to hospital. The '5F' identification markings on the fuselage indicated that it belonged to reconnaissance unit Aufklarungsgruppe 14. The normal crew for a Dornier bomber was four. In a reconnaissance role, however, it carried three – as they left out the bomb aimer.

Swanage Coastguard reported a vessel on fire, about ten miles out in the English Channel directly south of Durlston Head, at 18.15 hours that evening. The lifeboat *Thomas Markby* was launched from Peveril Point and made good speed in a light sea. She headed towards the distant smoke and found the Norwegian tanker *Kollskegg* burning towards the bow after being dive-bombed by the Luftwaffe. Her crew had already been taken off by a British destroyer. The lifeboat waited until a dockyard tug arrived to take the tanker in tow and sent a party aboard to fasten lines.

No. 4 Commando, newly formed at Weymouth, held its first parade on Sunday 22 July, followed by the commanding officer's opening address, which was given in the Pavilion on the Esplanade. Though it would spend only a few weeks training in south Dorset in the summer of 1940, the battalion returned to the Weymouth area in August 1942, to prepare for the Dieppe Raid.

The Vichy French liner *Meknes* sank after being torpedoed by German submarine *U572* off Portland on 24 July. She was carrying 1,100 neutral French sailors, of whom 400 were estimated to have perished. Inland, enemy aircraft shot down a barrage balloon over a VP [Vulnerable Point] near Dorchester, and punctured two others.

Squadron Leader Devitt led the Spitfires of 152 Squadron from Warmwell on 25 July in their second successful interception. Calling 'Tally ho!' – the hunting motto of their sister squadron – and hearing an 'Achtung, Spitfire' response, his fighters attacked a Dornier Do.17 of the Staff Flight of Kampfgeschwader 1 which was accompanied by a group of Stuka dive-bombers, passing over Portland.

The Dornier crashed at 11.23 hours at East Fleet Farm, Fleet, near Weymouth, killing one of the crew. A second man broke a leg and was taken to Weymouth Hospital. The pilot, who only suffered bruises, recovered in John Nobbs's farmhouse. He passed Players cigarettes to his captors; they had been looted in France. As that drama was being acted out on the ground one of the Stukas was seen to be streaming smoke and dropping towards the sea. Both kills were claimed by Sergeant-Pilot Ralph 'Bob' Wolton (26), with the coup de grace to the Dornier being delivered by Flying Officer Edward Christopher 'Jumbo' Deanesly. He then went after the stricken Stuka but received some return fire and ended up baling out wounded, as Spitfire K9901 crashed into the sea, five miles south of Portland Bill. Deanesly was picked-up by the SS *Empire Henchman* and dropped off at Lyme Regis. He was taken to hospital for treatment to a minor injury.

An E-boat Flotilla, comprising three German motor torpedo boats – Schnellboote *S19*, *S20*, and *S27* – sank three merchant vessels in attacks in the Channel between Portland and the Isle of Wight on 26 July.

Losses resumed for 609 Squadron on 27 July when Pilot Officer James Richebourg 'Buck' Buchanan (25), leading Green Section in Spitfire N3023 from RAF Warmwell, lost his life in combat over Weymouth Bay. His fighter, on a convoy protection sweep, was attacked by a group of Messerschmitt Bf.109s after he apparently spotted a Junkers Ju.87 and dived down through broken clouds to attack it. Two other Spitfires, guarding his tail, lost sight of him and could do nothing to help.

Reviewing the unacceptable rate of losses amongst merchant shipping in the waters between Dorset and the Cherbourg peninsula, the Admiralty suspended coastal convoys in the English Channel on 27 July. Thirty-six merchant ships had been sunk during the month so far, five of them when Convoy CW8 was mauled by Junkers Ju.87 Stuka dive-bombers. Three Royal Navy destroyers had been lost in the English Channel and the North Sea.

The sinking of HMS *Delight* revealed the existence of German radar

A fourth succumbed on 29 July. HMS *Delight*, a 1,375-ton 'Defender'-class vessel, was dive-bombed by Stukas and set on fire 20 miles south of Portland Bill. She was a floating wreck when put in tow and brought into Portland Harbour. Shortly after she was attacked an intercepted German radio message in the Enigma code was deciphered at Bletchley Park. It stated that the warship 'had been sunk with the aid of Freya reports'. This was clearly a codename for some device. Her name was plucked from Norse mythology and Dr Reginald Jones, head of scientific intelligence at the Air Ministry, had already heard of 'Freya Gerat' (Freya apparatus). Jones saw a mention of 'Freya-Meldung' (Freya reporting) on 5 July and bought a book on myths from Foyle's:

'Freya was the Nordic Venus who had not merely sacrificed but massacred her honour to gain possession of a magic necklace, Brisingamen, This necklace was guarded by Heimdall, the watchman of the Gods, who could see a hundred miles by day or night.'

Luftwaffe combat film of bombs hitting HMS *Delight* off Portland Bill on 29 July 1940

The last phrase was the crucial one – making Heimdall a wholly appropriate code for radar, though rather too obvious. Freya was chosen, by association, in its place. Either way, the German obsession with things Nordic had compromised their security. Twelve days before the loss of *Delight*, Jones used this reasoning to predict the exis-

Masts and huts of the top-secret Telecommunications Research Establishment at Renscombe Farm (left), Worth Matravers

tence 'of a coastal chain and detecting system with a range of a hundred miles'. The loss of the destroyer removed any possibility that Freya was detecting associated objects in the sky – for *Delight* had neither balloon protection nor a fighter escort.

'The apparatus must have been able to detect her directly,' Jones concluded. It appeared to be sited near the village of Auderville on the Hague peninsula north-west of Cherbourg, but it had to be very different from our own coastal chain stations, since it was completely undetectable on the best air photographs that we possessed of the area.

'This confirmed the idea that Freya was a fairly small apparatus which had already been suggested by the fact that it had been set up so quickly after the Germans had occupied the Channel coast.'

The story would resume in February 1941 with the picking up of a German radar signal on St Alban's Head by a scientist from nearby TRE.

The English Channel was placed off-limits to destroyers in daytime as a result of the attack on HMS *Delight*. There had been an unsustainable rate of losses to Royal Navy destroyers in the English Channel and southern North Sea in July – the others being HMS *Brazen* (in the Strait of Dover), HMS *Codrington* (Port of Dover) and HMS *Wren* (Aldeburgh). The burnt-out hulk of HMS *Delight* sank in Portland Harbour.

Air Chief Marshal Sir Hugh Dowding, Air Officer Commander-in-Chief at Fighter Command, visited the Special Duty Flight at Christchurch Aerodrome on 30 July for a briefing on their top-secret work for scientists from TRE.

As an example of the extent of efforts made to deny the enemy landing space on vulnerable South Coast beaches, a total of 3,500 mines were laid along just one mile of beach and low cliffs at Ringstead Bay. Similar quantities were buried in the shingle and sands of Kimmeridge, Worbarrow, Swanage, Studland, Bournemouth, and Barton-on-Sea.

Home Guard volunteers dragged scrub and branches across the hillside north of Cerne Abbas to conceal the famous 180-feet high chalk-cut figure of a naked man etched into the turf of the Dorset Downs. It was considered that this ancient curiosity, known as the Cerne Giant, might be of practical use as a navigation marker for German aircraft, particularly any making northward across the Dorset coast from Portland towards Bristol. Likewise the prominent Cornish marble obelisk on Ballard Down, above Swanage, was toppled.

Local authority workmen dug up milestones and took down road signs so that German invaders would not find routes spelt out on the ground. At Hazelbury Bryan the village name was erased from a charity-bequest panel in the church porch. It remained relatively easy to identify the major conurbation as it was impractical to remove all clues, such as hundreds of cast-iron drain covers proclaiming 'County Borough of Bournemouth'.

The Air Ministry turned down requests from Dorset County Council for the camouflaging of prominent buildings in Poole, saying that this could make attacks more likely:

'Low flying aircraft would easily see these buildings even if they were camouflaged, and, if they were seen to be camouflaged they would be taken to be more important targets than they really were. Thus camouflaging them would attract attack rather than avoid it.'

Thirty-two underground hideouts were secretly established by the Royal Engineers in woods and commons scattered through the Dorset countryside to conceal the weapons, explosives, and food necessary for Auxiliary Units of British Resistance to operate behind German lines in the event of an invasion. This was considered most likely to take place on the sandy beaches between Studland Bay and Hurst Castle, with secondary landings to the west, in Lyme Bay.

The plan for guerrilla resistance was that elite units of the Home Guard, with local knowledge and connections, could sustain a campaign of harassment against the occupying forces. Each unit was under the control of regular Army officers to ensure the necessary level of expertise and professionalism. Operational Bunkers of these Resistance Units were underground Nissen huts, set in holes dug by the Pioneer Corps and covered with timber, earth and camouflage. Guerrilla warfare training took place at Duntish Court, Buckland Newton, and in the nearby wilderness of Melcombe Park.

A major Dorset landowner was arrested and imprisoned in the round-up of pre-war members and supporters of Sir Oswald Mosley's British Union of Fascists. Captain George Henry Lane Fox Pitt-Rivers of Hinton St Mary was previously in the news when he opposed billeting city children in rural Dorset. Pitt-Rivers was held under Defence Regulation 18b among 1,600 detained in prison without trial. All but 400 would be released that winter. Pitt-Rivers remained interned.

BOAC flying-boat *Clare* on her return to Poole (shoreline details censored) having re-established the transatlantic air link in August 1940

Early on Saturday 3 August the Short 'Empire' flying-boat *Clare* took off from the 'Trots' in Poole Harbour – as the water runways were known – to land on the east coast of the United States the following day, and thereby resumed the Trans-Atlantic air service. She carried three American government VIPs and returned with ferry pilots on 14 August. *Clare*'s pilots were Captains J. C. Kelly Rogers and G. R. B. Wilcockson, with crewmen Burgess, Rotherham and White.

Sister flying-boat *Clyde* left with Colonel Rene de Larminat to arrange a coup d'etat in the Vichy-controlled French colonies of the Congo basin. They flew via Lagos, Nigeria, to Leopoldville in the Belgian Congo from where the general and his staff officers began repossession of French Equatorial Africa. The Free French Army, led by General Carretier, walked back to power after taking Brazzaville by complete surprise. It was of practical as well as strategic significance, enabling the resumption of the Empire flying-boat services, from Poole to South Africa, India, Malaya and Australia.

Things continued to be difficult at sea. Channel shipping lanes were subject to further German minelaying. Raumboote – armed motor minelayers – of the enemy's 3rd Mine Laying Flotilla were protected by Schnellboote of the 5th E-boat Flotilla.

Convoy CW9 broke through the enemy's blockade, westwards from the Thames, but with severe losses. Three ships were sunk and one damaged by E-boat attacks off the Isle of Wight. Two Royal Navy destroyers were called out from Portsmouth to give help. An air attack by 60 planes on 8 August was intercepted and driven off but the convoy fell victim to a second wave of more than 130 aircraft off Bournemouth. Three more ships were lost and 13 damaged. The Germans lost 14 aircraft.

Spitfire K9894 of 152 Squadron from RAF Warmwell was damaged in the dog-fight, after running out of ammunition, and headed for home. It force-landed at Bestwall, on the east side of Wareham, where Sergeant-Pilot Denis Norman Robinson made a dramatic escape. After bouncing across a meadow he struck a ditch, where the propeller ploughed into the soft ground, and the fuselage ended up standing vertically. Robinson jumped down on to grass.

Spitfire K9894 of 152 Squadron from RAF Warmwell at Wareham, in a crash-landing from which Sergeant-Pilot Denis Robinson walked away unhurt on 8 August 1940

A damaged Hurricane of 87 Squadron from RAF Exeter was successfully brought down by Flying Officer Roland Prosper Beamont (20) at Spyway Farm, on top of the Purbeck cliffs at Langton Matravers. He landed safely but the machine was destroyed by fire. Tommy Suttle reported the incident, in time for the fighter to be saved, but Swanage firemen went to the wrong field.

Bombs fell on Bournemouth. As 47 Alyth Road was demolished at 23.24 hours on 9 August, the disrobed lady of the house fell back into the safety of her bath, with the roof and ceiling collapsing around her. Less fortunate was a cyclist in Meon Road where five high-explosive bombs dropped at about 06.30 on the 10th. He was killed.

(Left) Southampton evacuees leaving the city for relative safety in Dorset

(Right) Bombed-out Southampton residents heading for Wimborne

Then on Sunday 11 August a massed formation of Luftwaffe bombers and fighters, comprising more than 150 aircraft, was plotted by Ventnor radar as it gathered over the Cherbourg peninsula at 09.45 hours. Two other Chain Home radar stations confirmed a strength of '100 plus'. By 10.07 they were in mid-Channel, with some 90 Messerschmitt Bf.109s and Bf.110s sweeping towards Portland from the south-east, to clear the way for following formations of 50 Junkers Ju.88 and 20 Heinkel He.111 bombers. The Junkers – of I Gruppe and 2 Gruppe of Kampfgeschwader 54 – attacked from 10,000 feet at around 10.30, dropping 32 bombs inside Admiralty property at Portland and three bombs on the Royal Naval Torpedo Depot at Bincleaves, Weymouth. A total of 58 bombs fell on the borough. Quite a number dropped harmlessly into open sea as well as in Balaclava Bay and Portland Harbour.

Almost everywhere it was the same story of near misses and lucky escapes. Though serious, a fire beside No. 3 oil-tank at Portland was contained, and the blaze that blocked the beach road was due to burning grass. The main pipeline was fractured in three places with the loss of about 200-tons of oil. About the only significant damage was to the shipwright's shop at Bincleaves which received a direct hit.

Five Bf.110s were claimed during the morning by 609 Squadron in a fast-moving action that swirled high above Portland from 10.10 to 10.35. Pilot Officer David Moore Crook, flying R6986, recorded in his log:

'We took off at 09.45 and after patrolling round Warmwell saw some smoke trails out to sea. Investigated and found a large force of Bf.110s flying round in circles at 25,000 feet, Hurricanes already engaging them. We all attacked separately. I climbed well above the scrum and then saw a Bf.110 some distance from the others. I dived on him and fired a burst from the rear quarter which missed as I could not get sufficient deflection. I then came into very close range and fired. I hit him and he did a climbing turn to the right, stalled, and started to turn over. I narrowly missed colliding with him and did not see him again. Found myself with Messerschmitts all around so dived away as hard as I could and returned to Warmwell.'

Most of the kills fell into the sea, including one shot down by Pilot Officer Noel le Chevalier Agazarian of 609 Squadron, but one crashed on land near Swanage. It was credited to Flying Officer John Dundas, whose Spitfire, R6769 of 609 Squadron, took shots through the starboard wing and rudder from the gunner of the stricken Bf.110.

THE BATTLE OF BRITAIN

Pilot Officer John Sinclair Bucknall Jones (21), in Spitfire R6614 of 152 Squadron from Warmwell, was shot down at 10.50 hours by Bf.109s, over the sea off Lulworth Cove. He was the second flyer from 152 Squadron to be lost in combat since they arrived at Warmwell and the station's sixth Spitfire pilot to be killed. His body was washed ashore in France.

Hurricanes of 601 Squadron from RAF Tangmere, Sussex, lost four pilots in the intensive aerial combat off Portland Bill. The first to fall into the sea was Pilot Officer Julian Langley Smithers (24), a stockbroker from Knockholt, Kent. Next was Pilot Officer Richard Stephen Demetriadi (21). Just a minute later, the Bf.109s claimed Pilot Officer James Gillan (26). The fourth victim was Pilot Officer William Gordon Dickie (24).

There were also serious losses for the Hurricanes from RAF Exeter. Three were lost, with their pilots, into the English Channel. Flight-Lieutenant Ronald Derek Gordon Wight (22), in N2650 of 213 Squadron, was shot down by Bf.109s at 10.23 hours. Sergeant Pilot Samuel Leslie Butterfield (27), also with 213 Squadron, was killed in the same engagement. Flying Officer Robert Voase Jeff DFC (27), was last seen taking V7231 of 87 Squadron into a dive towards Messerschmitt Bf.109s, ten miles south of Portland Bill, at 11.00 hours. At the same time, Pilot Officer John Reynolds Cock (22), an Australian in 87 Squadron, baled out of V7233 as he was shot down off Portland Bill. Though wounded he swam ashore. Minutes later, Pilot Officer Andrew Crawford Rankin McLure (22) of 87 Squadron, limped from his gun-damaged Hurricane after it finished upside down in a crash-landing at RAF Warmwell. He nursed a relatively minor leg wound.

New Zealander Terence Lovell-Gregg led 87 Squadron against impossible odds, was shot down and killed at Abbotsbury Swannery, and lies in the RAF plot beside Warmwell Church

Hurricanes of 87 Squadron scrambling from RAF Exeter in the summer of 1940

Robert Jeff had the distinction of having destroyed the first enemy aircraft to fall on French soil – a Heinkel He.111 bomber on 2 November 1939 – for which he was awarded the Croix de Guerre and the DFC. John Cock also survived a mid-air collision, on 24 October 1940, and left the RAF as Squadron Leader in 1948. From retirement in Renmark, South Australia, he returned to Britain to see wreckage of V7233 recovered by Portland divers in 1983.

Hurricanes from Middle Wallop suffered multiple losses as well. At 10.45 hours, three members of 238 Squadron were shot down and killed, by Bf.109s off White Nothe and Lulworth Cove. The flyers were Sergeant Pilot Geoffrey Gledhill (19), Flying Officer Michal Jan Steborowski (31), of the Polish Air Force, and Flight-Lieutenant Stuart Crosby Walch (23), a Tasmanian.

DORSET AT WAR

Flying Officer James Murray Strickland in a Hurricane of 213 Squadron from Exeter bagged a Ju.88 (B3+DC) in style over Portland that afternoon. The German pilot almost succeeded in bringing his crippled bomber safely down on the flat top of 275-feet cliffs beside Blacknor Fort but then ran into telephone wires. These retracted the undercarriage. He was badly hurt but his three comrades had only superficial injuries. The markings 'B3' indicated that the Junkers belonged to Kampfgeschwader 54, a bomber wing whose death's head emblem – Totenkopf, as a tribute to the 2nd SS Division – appeared on the fuselage.

A Heinkel He.111 bomber (1G+AC), heading homeward via Dorset's Stour valley from a raid on Bristol docks, was intercepted at 02.00 hours on 12 August by a British night-fighter. The bomber was raked with cannon fire and the pilot, identified as a 'Gruppenkommandeur', parachuted to captivity along with his four crewmen. Their aircraft crashed in flames at Sturminster Marshall. '1G' markings indicated it belonged to Kampfgeschwader 27.

Two more Warmwell Spitfire pilots from 152 Squadron were killed in action on the 12th, over the Channel off St Catherine's Point, bringing the squadron losses to four and those for Dorset's front-line RAF station to eight. Australian Flight-Lieutenant Latham Carr Withall (29), in P9456, was shot down and killed by the gunners of Ju.88 bombers, within sight of the Isle of Wight. Almost simultaneously, return gunfire accounted for Pilot Officer Douglas Clayton Shepley (22) in K9999.

The same action, ten miles south of Bognor Regis, destroyed two more Hurricanes and killed their pilots, from 213 Squadron, who flew across Dorset from RAF Exeter to operate at long-range against massed enemy formations. Sergeant Pilot Sidney George Stuckey, in P2802, and Sergeant Pilot Geoffrey Wilkes, in P2854, fell into the sea.

Surviving pilots were shocked into arguing about faulty tactics. Replacement pilots were inevitably inexperienced and the flaw was in sending them to sea to meet the enemy. Those who had survived weeks of combat urged that the Luftwaffe should be left 'to come to us'. The other essential element for survival was to get as high as possible before going into action. 'This is the whole secret of success in air fighting,' wrote Pilot Officer Crook.

The badge of the Royal Air Force – defending front-line Dorset with Spitfires from Warmwell and Hurricanes from Devon, Hampshire and Wiltshire airfields

The death of Douglas Shepley was avenged by his mother, who raised £5,700 in south Yorkshire to buy Mark Vb Spitfire W3649, for 602 Squadron in 1941. Famously, it was flown by Wing Commander Victor Beamish (38) when he spotted the German warships *Scharnhorst* and *Gneisenau*, as they made their Channel Dash on 12 February 1942. The memorial to both aircraft is the Shepley Spitfire public house at Totley, Yorkshire.

In contrast, Tuesday 13 August was Eagle Day, on which none of the enemy planes reached its target. The Luftwaffe's Adlertag attack of nearly 300 aircraft against military targets in southern England was routed. At noon, Bf.110 (L1+FZ) crashed in flames at Swalland Farm, Kimmeridge. 'L1' showed that it belonged to Lehrgeschwader 1, a specialist unit formed to test new and adapted aircraft of all types, and innovative tactics, under operational conditions. The two crew baled out and were taken prisoner. Both Spitfire squadrons at Warmwell were scrambled at 15.30 hours. 'Achtung, achtung, Spit und Hurri,' Pilot Officer Crook of 609 Squadron heard repeatedly as he approached the German formations.

'Victor and the Vanquished' showing Spitfire pilot David Moore Crook of 609 Squadron from RAF Warmwell with the remains of a Stuka he shot down near the Hardy Monument

One of the 27 Stukas of II Gruppe Stukageschwader 2 that had been targeted on Middle Wallop Aerodrome, was shot down between Portesham and Rodden at 16.00 hours. Its crewmen, Feldwebel Linderschmid and Gefreiter Eisold, died in the crash. The kill was been claimed by Flight Lieutenant Derek Boitel-Gill (31) of 152 Squadron.

At the same time, Pilot Officer Crook sent a Bf.109 smoking into the cloud and descended to see the debris of a crash which he thought was near the Hardy Monument. This, however, was that of another enemy aircraft, which came down 'just outside a small village' according to Crook's description. This crash-site lay 200 yards from the railway station at the hamlet of Grimstone, near Stratton. Two dead crew and the discovery of an unexploded 250-kilogram bomb in the wreckage confirmed it was a either a Stuka or Bf.110.

As for the Bf.109 escort fighters that were being chased by 609 Squadron, as they turned for the coast short of fuel, Crook's crippled claim ended up in Poole Harbour. The pilot, Unteroffizier Wilhelm Hohenseldt, was rescued and made prisoner of war. Another Bf.109 was shot down off Weymouth. Its pilot, Leutnant Heinz Pfannschmidt, was also saved and taken prisoner. This kill was claimed by Pilot Officer Tadeusz Nowierski, who was avenging the rape of Poland. His compatriot, Flying Officer Piotr Ostaszewski-Ostoja (30), returned to Warmwell to claim two Ju.87s 'probably destroyed'.

There were few lucky Germans, but the day's most fortunate Briton was Flying Officer Dundas of 609 Squadron. His Spitfire narrowly pulled clear from a collision with a Stuka and in the process he found his oil system ruptured by a bullet from its gunner. His propeller stopped. Dundas skilfully used his height, from over the sea off Portland, to glide down to Warmwell Aerodrome.

Hard-pressed 213 Squadron, flying Hurricanes from Exeter, lost another pilot off the Dorset coast on 13 August. Contact ceased with P3348, being flown by Sergeant Pilot Philip Purchall Norris (22), over the sea near Portland, at 15.42 hours. He was shot down during combat and his body washed ashore in France. Hurricanes of 238 Squadron from Middle Wallop also took part in the dog-fights. One of the flyers, Sergeant Pilot Ronald Little (22), was driven away unhurt after P3805 had crash-landed at Bredy Farm, Burton Bradstock. Little's luck ran out on 28 September 1940 when he was shot down off the Isle of Wight.

The following is an entry from Dorchester Observer Corps log for 13 August:

> **'Time: 16.35 hours. Location: Poundbury Camp, Dorchester** [north-west of the county town]. **Area of activity: South of sector R4, Dorchester. Report: Confirmed hostile and friendly pilots approaching the post. Much machine-gun and cannon fire. Fierce contest going on. Plane shot down believed Bf.110, another plane down, much confused sound-plotting and heavy firing for a considerable period. One plane believed friendly, flying low east. Believed forced-landing** [of a Spitfire] **this side of Maiden Castle House and in neighbourhood of the Fever Hospital.'**

The Prime Minister was watching the air battle from the other side of Ridgeway Hill. General Alan Brooke, the newly appointed Commander-in-Chief of Home Forces, had flown down from Hendon – picking up General Claude Auchinleck of Southern Command from Old Sarum – to RAF Exeter. There they were met by Major-General Harold Franklyn and Colonel Charles Allfrey. They drove eastwards, inspecting coastal defences around Lyme Bay, and met with Major-General Bernard Montgomery of 5th Corps and Major-General Giffard Le Quesne Martel, Commander of the Royal Armoured Corps, at Weymouth.

Here the military top brass were joined by Prime Minister Winston Churchill and Lieutenant-Colonel Joseph Charles Haydon who was bringing together Commando forces. 'All work proceeding well,' General Brooke commented, as an air battle proceeded overhead. On the ground they came across a freshly crashed German aeroplane, with its pilot incinerated, but were warned to keep clear due to 'a 500-pound bomb' in its burning debris. Time ran out for further exploration of anti-invasion defences and the party dispersed. General Brooke flew back to Hendon from RAF Warmwell and arrived in London at 18.00 hours.

The Air Ministry Under-Secretary, Harold Balfour MP, flew from Poole to the United States on 14 August on the second wartime transatlantic flying-boat crossing by *Clare*. The flying-boat was back in Poole on the 18th. Balfour had bought three Boeing 314s – 'Clipper' flying-boats – from the Americans. These long-range boats would be delivered to British Overseas Airways at Poole early in 1941.

The destruction of a Heinkel He.111 bomber, shot down over Lyme Bay on 14 August, was claimed by Pilot Officer Harold Derrick Atkinson (21), flying Hurricane R4099 of

213 Squadron from Exeter. Atkinson was hit by return fire and had shell splinters removed from his arm.

That evening Spitfire N3024 and Flying Officer Henry MacDonald Goodwin (25) failed to return to RAF Warmwell after 609 Squadron again saw coastal combat. He had just come through an eventful couple of days having claimed a Bf.110 on Monday and a pair of Stukas over Lyme Bay in the previous day's dog-fights.

Nine Spitfires of 152 Squadron from Warmwell were at 15,000 feet above Portland at 17.15 hours on 15 August when they heard over the radio:

'Many enemy aircraft approaching Portland from the south.'

Two minutes later a cloud of black specks became visible in mid-Channel, at about the same height as the British fighters. There were an estimated 100 or more German aircraft in tight V-formations comprising a cluster of Stukas surrounded by Bf.110 fighter-bombers.

The Spitfires climbed to 18,000 feet in a wide circle across Lyme Bay that brought them out of the south-western sun to descend through the German ranks about five miles south of Portland Bill. The resulting melee, which was joined by Hurricanes from RAF Exeter, had a mixed outcome. Ralph Wolton of 152 Squadron was shot down in the engagement with the Stukas and fell out of his Spitfire seconds before it crashed into the sea. He managed to swim to one of the offshore marker buoys of the Chesil Beach Bombing Range, from which he was rescued by an RAF launch from Lyme Regis.

Pilot Officer Harold John Akroyd (26), also of 152 Squadron, limped home to Warmwell with a jammed rudder, following an engagement off Portland in which he accounted for a Ju.87. Sergeant Pilot Robinson shot down a Bf.110. Flight-Lieutenant Howell of 609 Squadron returned to Warmwell Aerodrome with the claim of a Ju.88 bomber kill. 'How many Huns shall we get tomorrow?' they dared to ask.

Things were very different for the surviving few of 87 Squadron when they returned to RAF Exeter. Squadron Leader Terence Lovell-Gregg (27) failed in a desperate attempt to make a crash-landing in The Fleet lagoon. Hurricane P3215 came in blazing from over the sea but was brought into a controlled descent for a forced landing. It then clipped a tree beside Abbotsbury Swannery and its wounded pilot fell to his death at 18.00 hours on 15 August.

Flying Officer Beamont, one of the Exeter pilots, returned with the story of how Lovell-Gregg had led his squadron into the midst of a mass of German aircraft at 18,000 feet over the English Channel:

'We saw the "Beehive" almost straight ahead at the same height, and with his Hurricanes, Lovell-Gregg flew straight at the centre of the formation without hesitation or deviation in any way.'

One hundred and twenty enemy aircraft were heading towards Portland. Lovell-Gregg was a quiet pre-war professional, from Marlborough in New Zealand, who had taught many of the emergent generations of flyers. His courage was never in any doubt, though he had led his squadron for only a month. The pilots knew him as 'Shovel'. There were only four of them with him when they scrambled at 16.00 hours. Those five Hurricanes were all the air-worthy machines that 87 Squadron could muster.

Undaunted by the adverse odds of 15-to-one that loomed in front, Lovell-Gregg asked the impossible of himself and his men:

'Come on chaps, let's surround them!'

Only one of the five returned to Exeter on his own wings. The second fatality at 18.00 hours was Pilot Officer Peter Woodruff Comely (19) in P2872 who was shot down into the sea off Portland. Moments before he had accounted for a Bf.110. Sergeant-Pilot James Cowley recovered in Bridport Hospital from minor injuries caused in a crash-landing at Symondsbury which has wrote-off P3465. Pilot Officer Dudley Trevor Jay, in claiming two Stukas and a Bf.109, ran out of ammunition and suffered crippling damage from return fire. He barely topped Weymouth's rooftops before making a forced-landing on soft ground at Field Barn Farm, Radipole. He stepped out of R2687 unhurt but the fighter was a write-off.

Lovell-Gregg was buried in the RAF plot at Warmwell churchyard. Ironically, in St Nicholas's Church at Abbotsbury, there is a plaque recording with thanks that no one from the parish died on active service or from enemy action in the Second World War – without any mention of their heroic defender from the other side of the world.

The eastern side of the Middle Wallop Sector also saw action on the 15th with a formation of bombers approaching Bournemouth. The Spitfires of 234 Squadron were scrambled from RAF Middle Wallop at 17.05 hours and intercepted the bombers, which were heading homeward, over the town. A sustained air battle took place at 4,000 feet, during which Spitfire R6988 was hit by return fire from one of the German rear gunners. It spiralled into Leven Avenue, leaving a crater and wreckage across a wide area, with one of the wings falling on a hedge in Walsford Road. The pilot fell from the aircraft but his parachute did not open.

Pilot Officer Cecil Henry Hight, aged 22 from Stratford, New Zealand, had been seriously wounded and apparently passed out before he could pull the rip-cord. His body was found in Mr and Mrs Alfred Hoare's garden at Hambledon in Leven Avenue. The pilot's stomach had been ripped open by machine-gun bullets.

Mr and Mrs Hoare's house was to be visited again by the war. Ian McQueen records in *Bournemouth St Peter's* that it was hit by a German bomb. Canon Hedley Burrows recalled that it was the house where Hight's Spitfire had crashed. 'The dear old man, Mr Hoare, died,' Canon Burrows said, but then they heard Mrs Hoare. 'Who is that?' she asked. 'I am Canon Burrows. Keep still – they are going to get you out.' 'Canon Burrows,' she replied, 'how kind of you to come and see me today.'

Pilot Officer Walter Beaumont (26), flying a Spitfire with 152 Squadron from RAF Warmwell, scored his squadron's first double kills on 16 August with two Bf.109s brought down over the Isle of Wight at lunchtime. In the evening, as 152 Squadron's second patrol of the day was about to head for home, two Heinkel He.111 bombers were spotted below, at 3,000 feet over the Solent. The rear one was attacked at 18.15 hours by Pilot Officer Eric Simcox 'Boy' Marrs (19) who was given his nickname for his young looks.

As the Heinkel came out of a bank of mist he shot it up. 'I left it with smoke coming from both engines and my own machine covered in oil from it. I don't think it could have got home and I'm pretty sure it didn't.' His claim was not accepted, however, because a radio transmission was misunderstood, and no one else in the squadron saw the action. Marrs, however, was in no doubt, as he wrote to his father: 'I am counting it as my first.'

Canadian Pilot Officer Joseph Emile Paul Laricheliere (27), flying a Hurricane of 213 Squadron from Exeter, failed to return from combat off Portland on 16 August. Sergeant Pilot Robinson, in a Spitfire of 152 Squadron, returned to RAF Warmwell on 17

The bombing of Newstead Road, Weymouth, with three houses destroyed and others damaged, in August 1940

Squadron Leader Peter Devitt of 152 Squadron at RAF Warmwell was an Old Shirburnian

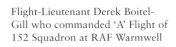

Flight-Lieutenant Derek Boitel-Gill who commanded 'A' Flight of 152 Squadron at RAF Warmwell

Sergeant- Pilot Howard Marsh (left) and Flight-Lieutenant Derek Boitel-Gill beside 152 Squadron's Dispersal Hut – waiting for the order to scramble – at RAF Warmwell

Sergeant-Pilot George White with 152 Squadron's collection of road signs 'lifted' from the Dorset countryside (that for 'Joe Guppy's Camp' being above the door)

Sergeant-Pilot Edmund Shepperd with Pilot Officer Pooch, mascot of 152 Squadron, at RAF Warmwell

Spitfire R6915 of 609 Squadron from RAF Warmwell, which saw repeated action over Dorset in the Battle of Britain, now in suspended animation at the Imperial War Museum

August from a sweep over the English Channel with the claim of a Stuka successfully shot down into the sea.

On Sunday 18 August, more than 100 Stuka dive-bombers, escorted by Messerschmitt Bf.109 fighters, crossed the Channel to attack the radar station at Poling, Sussex, and aerodromes at Ford, Thorney Island, and Gosport. Eleven Spitfires of 152 Squadron were scrambled from Warmwell. They dived from 4,000 feet on the Stukas as they swept back to sea after dropping their bombs. Pilot Officer Marrs claimed a kill – his first to be confirmed.

> 'We dived after them and they went down to about a hundred feet above the water. Then followed a running chase out to sea. The evasive action they took was to throttle back and do steep turns to right and left so that we would not be able to follow them and would overshoot. There were, however, so many of them that if one was shaken off the tail of one there was always another to sit on. I fired at about six and shot down one. It caught fire in the port wing petrol tank and then went into the sea about 300 yards further on.'

The Stukas were from I and II Gruppen of Stukageschwader 77 (the same unit as Von Dalwigk's dive-bomber, shot down on 9 July). They suffered 16 losses as 43 Squadron, 601 Squadron, and 602 Squadron joined 152 Squadron in the action. The Bf.109 escort fighters were routed by the Spitfires of newly-arrived 234 Squadron from Middle Wallop.

As defending Hurricanes tangled with Messerschmitts over Bournemouth and Christchurch, the Special Duty Flight from Christchurch Aerodrome found itself uncomfortably close to the action. Flight-Lieutenant Douglas L. Rayment was unhurt but he brought back his Blenheim flying test-bed with bullet-damage to the starboard mainframe.

Pilot Officer Marrs was scrambled again at 17.25 hours for his second combat patrol of the day. He led the three Spitfires of Blue Section in a 'Tally-ho' after a German Dornier Do.17 which was flying towards Portland. The interception took place from 16,000 feet and the bomber dropped into cloud at about 5,000 feet. Marrs had emptied his guns and the third Spitfire claimed a share in the kill, though it could not have been that decisive as the bomber managed to return to France.

On Monday 19 August there was an example of the importance and accuracy of Enigma decrypts from Bletchley Park and how the information was relayed to the bases concerned:

'01.52 hours. From a reliable source, information has been received of an impending attack on Warmwell Aerodrome this morning. Aircraft are to be ready to leave at 07.00 hours.'

Pilot Officer Noel le Chevalier Agazarian was among those who flew R6915 from Warmwell

Mrs Pauline Fairbrother and Frederick Landrey were killed on the afternoon of 21 August when a single German raider, a Junkers Ju.88, came in low over the Old Town area of central Poole from Sandbanks direction. It dropped six bombs. The one that killed Mr Landrey destroyed the National School air-raid shelter, thankfully unoccupied, and the others hit shops and timber stores.

A lone German raider attacked Lulworth Camp on 23 August just minutes after the 'All Clear' sounded. Recruits had resumed infantry training and were back in the open as the aircraft approached. Sergeant J. Thompson shouted to them: 'Get down and stay still.'

Eight bombs dropped on the sports-field, the ranges, and at St Andrew's Farm which is inside the camp complex. Two men were killed and seven injured. The latter included quick-thinking Sergeant Thompson who received severe leg wounds. He had been in the stores when he heard the aircraft approaching and but for his instant and brave response, when he put himself into the line of fire to warn the men, there would have been a greater number of casualties.

Twenty-four people were killed and many injured on the evening of 23 August when Junkers Ju.88 bombers devastated Station Road, New Milton. The main street of the New Forest seaside village had numerous flats above the shops and was surrounded by a residential area. Train services into Dorset were diverted from Brockenhurst to Poole, northwards via Ringwood and Wimborne branch lines, though the railway escaped damage.

On Sunday 25 August, decoded signals intelligence which originated from Enigma decrypts at Bletchley Park roused Warmwell to a day of action:

'07.40 hours. It is reliably reported that air attacks are to be expected during the course of today 25th August at Warmwell, Little Rissington, and Abingdon aerodromes, and reconnaissances by a single aircraft in the area Southampton-Aldershot-Brighton.'

For RAF Warmwell, radar confirmation of approaching aircraft came at 16.45 hours and by 17.00 the twelve Spitfires of 152 Squadron were airborne. Half an hour later the station was rocked by 20 bombs, which destroyed the sick quarters and damaged hangars.

The Spitfires met Luftflotte 3 over Portland but despite the advance warning it was a more or less even match. Delayed action bombs went off over the next couple of days.

Hurricanes of 87 Squadron and 213 Squadron from RAF Exeter joined dog-fights over Portland. Sergeant Pilot Sidney Richard Ernest Wakeling (21) of 87 Squadron was killed at 17.25 hours when his fighter, V7250, plunged in flames at New Barn, Bradford Peverell. Then 213 Squadron lost two fighters – to Messerschmitt Bf.109s – into Lyme Bay. The missing flyers were Pilot Officer Harold Derrick Atkinson (22), in P3200, and Pilot Officer Jacques Arthur Laurent Philippart (31) who escaped in May from the invading Germans, by air and sea, and became the first Belgian ace of the war. He was shot down off Portland by Hauptmann Mayer of I Gruppe, Jagdgeschwader 53.

German aircraft fell all over Dorset. A Messerschmitt Bf.109 crashed on the Chesil Beach at Chickerell and its pilot, Hauptmann Maculan, fell out and drowned. To the north, a Bf.110 exploded at Tatton House, between Langton Herring and Buckland Ripers, killing both crew. A Bf.109 belly-landed in an adjoining field, beside woodland at Tatton Farm, and its pilot escaped with wounds as it was engulfed in flames. Gefreiter Josef Broker of Jagdgeschwader 53 was taken prisoner and survived his burns. Credit for that kill was claimed by Pilot Officer Beaumont of 152 Squadron who drove across the hill from Warmwell to arrive 'in shirtsleeves and sweat' at the scorched scene of his triumph.

Shortly after 18.00 hours, a Bf.110 was reported crashing at Creech Barrow, the conical-shaped summit of the Purbeck Hills south of Wareham, and another Bf.110

(3M+KH) came down at Priory Farm, East Holme. Both sets of crew parachuted into captivity.

A third Bf.110 (3M+CH) was taken on by two Spitfires of 609 Squadron from RAF Warmwell. Squadron Leader Darley and American volunteer Pilot Officer Eugene Quimby 'Red' Tobin (23) gunned it down at East Chaldon, to the west of Lulworth. It became a fireball and the crew died in the explosion. '3M' indicated that these aircraft belonged to the 1st Staffel of II Gruppe, Zerstorergeschwader 2.

Darley also accounted for the first Messerschmitt to be brought down. In all, 609 Squadron claimed eleven kills, and certainly several Bf.110 fighter-bombers from II Gruppe Zerstorergeschhwader 2 and V Gruppe Zerstorergeschwader 1 were destroyed, and Bf.109 fighters from II Gruppe Jagdgeschwader 2 – a fighter wing named Richthofen – though these escorts had succeeded in keeping the Spitfires from the Ju.88 bombers.

Two more Spitfire pilots from Warmwell's 152 Squadron were lost in the intense early evening combat off Portland. Both crashed into the sea. Pilot Officer Hogg was shot down by Messerschmitt Bf.109s at 17.22 hours. Minutes later, at 17.50, Pilot Officer Timothy Seddon Wildblood (20) joined him in being posted 'Missing in Action'. Their demise brought the squadron's losses to six pilots, and those for the station to eleven, since the start of the aerial onslaught in July.

609 Squadron just about scraped through the day with their numbers intact. The closest call was for Flying Officer Piotr Ostaszewski-Ostoja (20) in R6986. The Spitfire was riddled by cannon fire from a Messerschmitt Bf.110 he engaged over Swanage. Though his flaps were damaged, the Pole succeeded in bringing the fighter and himself back to Warmwell Aerodrome, though the machine was written-off when he overshot the runway and crashed through the perimeter hedge. Damage to the pilot was confined to a minor arm injury. Piotr Ostaszewski-Ostoja continued to have a reasonably good war. He left the RAF in 1946 as Wing Commander and changed his name to Peter Raymond on deciding to stay in England.

On 27 August, Pilot Officer Beaumont baled out of Warmwell Spitfire R6831, belonging to 152 Squadron, as it was hit by return fire from a Junkers Ju.88 bomber. His fighter crashed into Lyme Bay, eight miles west of Portland. Beaumont, who survived to fight another day, had just shared the honours in the destruction of a Heinkel He.111 bomber.

Though no one was injured, high explosive and incendiary bombs caused considerable damage to buildings in the Longfleet, Oakdale, and Parkstone suburbs of Poole at 04.00 hours on 29 August. Around the same time incendiaries landed in Christchurch near the Priory, Millhams Street, and at Queens Avenue. One was on the roof of the air-compressing station. There were also the thuds of high explosive bombs but daylight revealed they had dropped on the northern side of the town into heathland and woods at St Catherine's Hill. Ten had gone off and one had failed to explode.

Writing in *The Two Edged Sword*, Adela Curtis, leader of the Christian Contemplatives' Community at St Bride's Farm, Burton Bradstock, advised on methods of furthering the war effort through positive prayer:

> **'We are to summon each enemy leader by name. For cumulative effect the message should be spoken three times – Adolf Hitler! Adolf Hitler! Adolf Hitler! Hear the Truth!'**

The 4th Battalion of the Royal Northumberland Fusiliers were reorganised as a motor-cycle reconnaissance column at Blandford Camp. Their sidecar patrols became ubiquitous in the chalkland villages of Cranborne Chase. The 2nd and 8th Battalions of the Northumberlands were also in Dorset, dispersed on anti-invasion duties, across the dairying country of the Blackmore Vale.

Sergeant Pilot John Keeth Barker (23), in a Spitfire of 152 Squadron from RAF. Warmwell, failed to return on 4 September from an operational sortie over the Isle of Wight. He was last seen approaching a Dornier Do.17 bomber. The squadron's seventh fatality, Barker's body was washed up in France.

Druitt's House, the Christchurch solicitor's offices and former residence of one of the town's leading families – which produced Montague John Druitt who was a suspect for Jack the Ripper, the Whitechapel murderer – was destroyed by a German bomb at 01.30 hours on 5 September.

Ralph Wolton, flying at the rear of a flight of Spitfires with 152 Squadron from RAF. Warmwell, lost control of his fighter whilst attempting a sudden dive on Saturday 7 September. He jumped from the falling plane at 13,000 feet though he estimated it was not until nearly a thousand feet from the ground when he managed to sort out the cords and activate the chute. The Spitfire crashed at Higher Kingston Farm, Stinsford.

It was the day of the great invasion scare. Reports circulated of a seven-mile convoy heading towards the Dorset coast and there was a general flap that Operation Sealion was taking place and Field-Marshal Fedor von Bock was on his way with the victors of Poland, the Wehrmacht's Army Group B. The order was given for fuel tanks to be fired, to set the beaches ablaze, and an aircraft from Gosport dropped incendiaries to start them off. Troops manning the cliffs at Bournemouth insisted that 'this is not an exercise'.

That was confirmed at 20.07 hours. A national alert was issued by the War Office for 'Condition Cromwell'. An invasion was 'imminent and probable' within 12 hours. Nothing happened! One set of 'Fougasse' tanks ignited a beach but the plane was recalled before it set alight to any more. There was no landing in Dorset or anywhere else. Despite that, invasion fears reached fever-pitch – not without reason – as aerial reconnaissances showed concentrations of ships and barges in harbours from Brest to Calais.

Hurricane pilot Wing Commander John Scatliff 'Johnny' Dewar (33) was reported missing on 12 September while on a coastal flight across Dorset and Hampshire from his home base at Exeter to RAF Tangmere in Sussex. Dewar's body would be washed up on Selsey Bill at the end of the month. He was the highest ranking Royal Air Force officer to be killed in the Battle of Britain.

Flight-Lieutenant Frank Howell of 609 Squadron claimed his fourth enemy aircraft destroyed – a Stuka – on 13 September. Next day, Flying Officer C. O. Hinks was killed in a flying accident at RAF Warmwell.

The Spitfires of 609 Squadron from Warmwell were drawn into the air defence of London on Sunday 15 September as what was now being called the Battle of Britain reached its climax. Claims for the day totalled 186 enemy aircraft destroyed. Among them were a Dornier Do.17 bomber shot down by Flight-Lieutenant Howell and a half-share in another Dornier, claimed by Pilot Officer Tobin, a lanky and laconic American volunteer whose neutral Embassy in London tried and failed to send back to the States. He pointed to the wings on his tunic:

Warmwell's American was Pilot Officer Eugene Quimby 'Red' Tobin of 609 Squadron

'I reckon these will be a one way ticket, pal.'

The Air Ministry was warned by its own intelligence department that kill claims were being overstated and that no more than 76 planes could have been destroyed on 15 September. Post-war examination of German records showed even that to be exaggerated – the real figure being 62.

For all that it was a victory. Air Chief Marshal Sir Hugh Dowding had handled his forces with precision and economy. They had not been wasted on pointless patrols. A combination of radar and decoded German radio traffic meant that the sectors that were going to have a quiet day – in this case Middle Wallop and Warmwell – could be partly redeployed sideways to provide additional aircraft for an area where resident defenders were about to be outnumbered.

Dowding's achievement, amounting to a triumph, was to deny the Luftwaffe its one prerequisite for winning the Battle of Britain. This was a combination of caution and reaction. Firstly, he insisted that there were always planes grounded in reserve, but used this element of restraint creatively, to ensure that something could always be done to counter the following day's attack. Göring was frustrated by this and had ordered his commanders:

'You must bring the RAF up to battle.'

Dorset's disaster that Sunday was an own-goal. The 1873-built tower of Cattistock parish church was gutted by fire, melting its famous carillon of 35 bells. It was blamed, ironically, on a cigarette discarded by a member of the Home Guard who was up the tall tower as a fire-watcher. The enemy were almost in sight, above Portland Bill, where six Spitfires of 152 Squadron from Warmwell intercepted 30 Heinkel He.111 bombers. They jettisoned their bombs from 16,000 feet and turned back towards France.

Pilot Officer Marrs led Blue Section of 152 Squadron from RAF Warmwell over Portland on the afternoon of 17 September. He was then told to rise to 20,000 feet on a course of 350 degrees, which eight minutes later was revised to 280 degrees, with the other two Spitfires following. This flight-path brought him in sight of a lone Junkers Ju.88 bomber (L1+XC) above Shepton Mallet, Somerset. It belonged to operational test unit Lehrgeschwader 1 and was heading for factories at Speke, near Liverpool.

'Tally ho!' Marrs called over the radio from Blue One, as he led the three fighters in line astern. The first burst from his guns hit the radiator of the bomber's starboard engine and had it streaming white ethylene glycol coolant. The aircraft, which was heading east, descended into thick cloud, and crash-landed near Imber, in sight of Dauntsey's which was Marrs's public school. Marrs then had to contend with his own emergency as 'Old Faithful' suffered engine failure. The machine in which the Dover-born 19-year-old had flown 130 hours was coaxed down from 12,000 feet on to the concrete runways of a training aerodrome at Yatesbury that was partly obstructed to prevent German landings.

For Britain, Tuesday 17 September marked the turning point of the year, as Hitler had postponed Operation Seelowe [Sealion] for the planned invasion of England. Winston Churchill read out a deciphered German Enigma machine-coded radio message to the Chiefs of Defence Staff. The intercept contained a minor order of huge significance – for the dismantling of loading equipment on Dutch airfields. Churchill referred to Sealion as Operation Smith, to lessen the risk of compromising the source of those crucial Enigma intercepts that revealed its name. This was good news that could not be shared with the nation.

It did, however, lead to the standing down of the Bournemouth Garrison, 48 hours later, with the Garrison Commander being replaced by a new posting – that of Officer Commanding Troops, Bournemouth. Routine invasion patrols and counter-measures continued in order to avoid indicating to the enemy that anyone realised the situation had changed. Home Guard expansion brought the strength of Bournemouth's five battalions to 8,000 men.

It was also more of the same for RAF Warmwell as the Luftwaffe kept coming. Sergeant Pilot Kenneth Christopher 'Casie' Holland (20) of 152 Squadron sent a Junkers Ju.88 bomber blazing into the sea off Purbeck. SS *Trito*, a British steam freighter, sank on 20 September after being bombed by German aircraft in Lyme Bay. Warmwell lost its fourteenth pilot on 23 September when 152's Pilot Officer Beaumont was shot down over the sea.

Six sleeping seamen were killed in their bunks at 02.45 hours the following morning when HMT *Loch Monteith*, on an anti-invasion patrol, struck a mine in Lyme Bay. On the morning of Wednesday 25 September a German mass bombing force of 220 attacking planes and their escorts passed northwards over Portland and flew across west Dorset and the Somerset Levels to the Bristol Channel coast. They then turned north-eastwards, between the islands Steep Holm and Flat Holm, to make an approach across the water towards the Bristol Aeroplane Company's works at Filton. This was devastated by 350 bombs from 15,000 feet. The aerodrome rippled with flashes.

On the way home, however, the raiders were harried by the Royal Air Force. Five aircraft were brought down and a further three had to crash-land in France. The two that were shot down in Dorset were claimed by Hurricanes of 238 Squadron from Middle

Wallop. Heinkel He.111 (G1+LR) ploughed into Underwood, a house in Westminster Road, Branksome Park. Four of its crewmen were killed but the fifth baled out into the sea off Branksome Chine:

> 'A short, ugly, broad-chested Nazi airman was hoisted by the military into a truck to be taken away.'

The second Heinkel He.111 (G1+BH) force-landed at Westfield Farm, Studland. Josef Attrichter, the flight mechanic, was taken from the wreckage but died half an hour later. The other four crewmen staggered out with little worse than aching backs. Off-duty wine waiter Theo Janku took them prisoner with the aid of an unloaded Home Guard rifle and relieved them of their Lugers. On seeing there were casualties, the Studland villagers then tried to help the Germans, and provided cigarettes and tea.

'G1' markings to the left of the black cross on the fuselage identified the Heinkels as belonging to Kampfgeschwader 55. Their emblem was the coat of arms of Giessen. The Studland Heinkel was salvaged and reassembled for Cardiff's War Weapons Week.

A document was found in the bomber forbidding the use of explosive ammunition against troop concentrations and other human targets. The burial of the Branksome Park Germans in Parkstone Cemetery, next to the graves of British seamen, enraged the *Poole Herald* into protesting that 'Nazi murderers and British heroes' had been placed side by side. A week later the newspaper felt utterly let down by one of his readers: 'Someone has put flowers on the grave!'

Another Heinkel kill, that of Hauptmann Helmut Brandt's He.111 (G1+EP) belonging to II Gruppe of Kampfgeschwader 55, was credited to a Warmwell Spitfire of 152 Squadron. The wreckage of both aeroplanes lay strewn across fields at Church Farm, Woolverton, Somerset. The crash sites were less than 500 yards apart and occurred within two minutes of each other.

Sergeant-Pilot Holland hit the ground first, in N3173, at noon precisely. An Australian orphan, he also used the name Ripley. He died almost immediately from the effects of the crash and a severe bullet wound in his skull which caused him to lose control of the fighter. Having spotted the pilot baling out he approached the stricken Heinkel to watch it come down. He was then hit at close range by return fire from its gunner who was about to die. The fatal shot penetrated the seal between the rounded port-side top of his toughened windscreen – double sheeted glass, to a thickness of 25 mm – making an exit hole four inches across.

Flight-Lieutenant Boitel-Gill led a section of 152 Squadron from RAF Warmwell into combat against a formation of bombers and escort fighters over the sea to the west of the Isle of Wight on 26 September. One of the bombers was seen to fall into the water, resulting from an engagement by Sergeant Pilot Wolton, but two of the attacking Spitfires were then gunned down in a dog-fight. The loss of Sergeant Pilot Jack McBean Christie (22) in K9882 brought the squadron's losses to eight and the Warmwell toll to 16. Flying Officer Deansley baled out of K9982 and was picked-up by an Air-Sea Rescue launch which landed him in Swanage. The vessel also recovered Christie's body.

Some 60 Heinkel He.111s of Kampfgeschwader 55 wrecked the Vickers Supermarine works at Woolston, Southampton – the main centre for Spitfire airframe assembly – with 70 tons of bombs. More than 30 people were killed.

Pilot Officer Marrs of 152 Squadron started the action on a busy Friday 27 September by finding a lone Junkers Ju.88 at 23,000 feet over Somerset. He followed it in a running fight across Exmoor, flying in places at only 50 feet above the heather and scattering the wild red deer, and had ethylene glycol coolant streaming from both engines of the bomber:

> 'As I expected both engines soon stopped. He made for the south coast of the Bristol Channel and landed about 20 feet from the beach in the water, running his machine up on the beach. I circled round and watched the crew get out. They waved to me and I waved back, and then hordes of civilians came rushing

up. I watched the crew taken prisoner, beat up the beach, and then climbed away.'

The tiny seaside resort treated to this excitement was Porlock, to the west of Minehead, where it is unusual for anything to happen. The town's single claim to fame is 'a person on business from Porlock' who interrupted Samuel Taylor Coleridge as he was recalling and writing down his dream-poem *Kubla Khan* and remains unknown to this day.

Anti-aircraft gunners at Lulworth Camp jubilantly celebrated their first definite kill. The unlucky German aircraft was a Messerschmitt Bf.110 which had come low over the huts. There had been an air-raid warning and a red alert was in force. The stricken fighter crashed to the ground about 1,000 yards from the sea.

German planes crashed all over Dorset on 27 September, plus Pilot Officer Miller in a Spitfire of 609 Squadron. His death brought 609's losses to six and those for the station to 17. The Luftwaffe attempted what became an abortive raid on Parnall Aircraft Limited – makers of gun turrets – at Yate, near Chipping Sodbury. Ten fighter-bombers of Erprobungsgruppe 210, an experimental and proving unit from Cherbourg, led by Hauptmann Martin Lutz, had the support of 89 fighters. The Gruppe's aircraft had as their crest a red map of the British Isles superimposed with a yellow ring-type gun sight. Their objective was to test bomb-carrying on Messerschmitt Bf.109s and Bf.110s.

The German attackers, coming in fast over north Bristol at 11,000 feet, were met head on by Flying Officer Edward Murray Frisby in a Hurricane of 504 Squadron from RAF Filton. He scored a hit that damaged Lutz's leading plane and forced the others to turn sideways from their run towards the Parnall factory. The rest of 504 Squadron rounded on the scattering enemy and caused them to jettison their bombs. Escape was now the only German objective.

One of the Bf.110s was shot down over Fishponds, Bristol. Another came down at Haydon Hill near Radstock. That was at 11.45 hours.

At the same moment, over Bellamy's Farm, Piddletrenthide, there was a similar bang as one of the rearguard manoeuvres went wrong. Pilot Officer Miller was leading the Spitfires which had been scrambled from Warmwell. His machine, X4107, collided with Bf.110 (3U+FT) at 27,000 feet. Miller and the Messerschmitt's wireless operator, Emil Lidtke, were killed instantly. Remarkably, however, the German pilot was blown sideways by the explosion and found himself parachuting (minus his boots) into a field. He was given some lemonade and taken off by police. His dead comrade was treated with less respect, with farmer Ralph Wightman noting that after it had been removed from the wreckage it was left lying in full view for hours, before someone draped it with a sheet.

A fourth Bf.110 (3U+IM) was also exploding at 11.45, at 1,000 feet above Salter's Wood, Middlebere, in the Isle of Purbeck. It had been engaged by a Spitfire of 152 Squadron from RAF Warmwell. In the crashed plane were Arthur Niebuhr and Klaus Deissen; both were killed. Equally unfortunate, at 11.50, were the crew of another Messerschmitt, between Tyneham and Kimmeridge. This was almost certainly Bf.110 (3U+BD) manned by Hans Carschel and Unteroffizier Klose.

Luckier, just a mile away at 11.55, were the crew of Bf.110 (3U+DS). Fritz Schupp and Karl Nechwatal had been attacked by Spitfires and their port engine was hit and burning. Despite the damage, Schupp successfully brought the Messerschmitt down in a forced-landing beside Gaulter Gap. These '3U' aircraft belonged to Zerstorergeschwader 26, the Geschwader named Horst Wessel, for the Nazi writer of a militant anti-Semitic song which became the alternative national anthem.

At noon a second Bf.110 (S9+DU) made a belly landing. It had received engine damage over Iwerne Minster and came down at The Beeches, beside the main road from Blandford to Shaftesbury. There was another noon crash, at Bussey Stool Farm, near Tarrant Gunville, where Bf.110 (S9+DH) finally bit the dust. This was the Messerschmitt of the operation's leader who had been thwarted by Murray Frisby over Bristol. Martin Lutz was still flying at speed but was losing height and then found the ground coming towards him on the top-lands of Cranborne Chase. In the final moments he hit trees before ploughing into the ground.

THE BATTLE OF BRITAIN

As a finale, also within seconds of mid-day, two more Messerschmitts were put down into the sea off Dorset just as the safety of Cherbourg came into sight. They were Bf.110 (S9+JH), crewed by Gerhard Schmidt and Gerhard Richeter, and Bf.110 (S9+GK) with Wilhelm Rossiger and Hans Marx. They were shot down about 25 miles south of Portland Bill, with one of the attacking Spitfires of 609 Squadron from RAF Warmwell being flown by Pilot Officer Agazarian. 'S9' aircraft belonged to Erprobungsgruppe 210. Pilot Officer Crook joined the chase into mid-Channel:

> 'I saw a Bf.110 about half a mile ahead and went after him on full throttle. He was also going flat out and diving to get extra speed, but my beloved Spitfire rose nobly to the occasion and worked up to over 400 m.p.h., and I caught him fairly easily, though we were about 20 miles out to sea by this time. The enemy rear-gunner, who obviously had the wind up, opened fire at me at rather long range, though I could see his tracer bullets flicking past me. It is an odd thing when you are being fired at by a rear-gunner that the stream of bullets seem to leave the machine very slowly and in a great outward curve. You chuckle to yourself, 'Ha, the fool's missing me by miles!' Then, suddenly, the bullets accelerate madly and curl in towards you again and flick just past your head.'

In this instance, Crook dipped below the enemy aircraft and then came up at it with bursts of fire that killed the rear gunner, and set the aircraft on fire but used his last ammunition. 'OK, OK, help coming,' he heard on the RT. Another Spitfire arrived on the scene and delivered the coup-de-grace to put the Messerschmitt into the sea.

Warmwell's Armenian-French Spitfire flyer, Noel le Chevalier Agazarian of 609 Squadron, scored a hat-trick of kills in three days. That for 27 September – put down in the sea – was Bf.110 fighter-bomber S9+GK of Erprobungsgruppe 210. Agazarian was killed later in the war but he left one of the most evocative of all memorials. His fighter from those Dorset days, R6915 – the earliest to survive the war – is now suspended over the main Battle of Britain display in the Imperial War Museum.

An underwater explosion off Portland at 21.16 hours on 27 September sank His Majesty's Trawler *Recoil*, which as the *Blankenburg* was captured from the Germans. The explosion was heard from sister vessel HMT *Angle* which went to the spot to investigate. No wreckage was found but there was a stench of diesel oil in the vicinity.

Six high explosive bombs and a number of incendiaries dropped at 01.17 hours on 29 September on the Ministry of Supply's Air Defence Experimental Establishment, which manufactured radar components, at Somerford, Christchurch. Damage, however, was slight. By 02.48 all the fires had been put out.

Scrambling at 11.00 hours on 30 September from RAF Warmwell, in Spitfire X4165, Pilot Officer Crook led Green Section of 609 Squadron as they swept in a line seawards across the Isle of Purbeck. Pilot Officer Appleby quickly put a Messerschmitt Bf.109 into the sea, but Crook's action was protracted:

> 'We intercepted some Bf.109s at 23,000 feet over Swanage. The fools tried to escape by diving and we all went down after them. I got to about 600 m.p.h. and easily caught mine, gave it a burst, and he crashed into the sea. I then chased another and put him into the sea about 25 miles from Cherbourg. It took me a long time to get back to the English coast . . . pleased to see the white cliffs.'

Crook was airborne again in the afternoon, against six Bf.109s, ten miles north of Poole:

> 'I had a very enjoyable few minutes dog-fighting with one and though behind him all the time could not get sights properly on him. Finally he dived for cloud, but I chased him to Weymouth and then gave him a good burst. He turned over on his back and spun into cloud streaming glycol and smoke. I could not claim him as definite as I did not see him actually crash but he certainly never got back to France. This was my best day yet.'

Yeovil's barrage balloons were raised at 15.55 hours on the warm but cloudy afternoon of 30 September. In Sherborne the air-raid sirens also wailed. Thirty-seven Heinkel He.111 bombers were attempting to find the Westland Aircraft Company's factory in Yeovil but precision was impossible due to nine-tenths cloud cover at 20,000 feet.

Instead, flying in formation on a north-easterly line that had been set from glimpses of the railway line, they missed their target by five miles. They then began to bomb blind in the vicinity of Lenthay Common and then across the ancient yellow-stone town of Sherborne, raining more than a hundred bombs down on its clustered terraces and between scholastic and ecclesiastical roofs. There were 766 damaged buildings, some ten per cent being virtually destroyed, out of a total of 1,700.

Townspeople insisted that the raid was over in a matter of minutes. Remarkably, the town's famous Abbey and other historic buildings came through it almost unscathed, and casualties were light considering the extensive overall damage to shops, homes, and roads. Fortunately the schools had just gone home. Seventeen civilians were killed and there were 32 hospital cases (one of whom died).

The heroine amongst the debris was the supervisor of the telephone exchange which had been blown apart by a direct hit. She stayed calm and ensured that the town's initial calamity reports were sent out by road. Miss Maud Steele was awarded the George Cross for her pluck. It had been instituted by King George as the 'Civilians VC' only a few days earlier. Sewers as well as the phones were out of action. Blankets had to be brought in by the Red Cross and a council appeal, competing with many others, raised £2,200 including contributions from the community of Sherborn in Massachusetts.

The Heinkel He.111 bombers that jettisoned their bombs on Sherborne had been met by 152 Squadron as they flew at 21,000 feet over Portland. They had apparently been intending to raid the Westland Aircraft factory at Yeovil which manufactured the Whirlwind, though with only 100 produced this was set to be dismissed as a failure. Anyway, the bombers were heading northwards from the coast.

Squadron Leader Devitt could only muster eight Spitfires of 152 Squadron at RAF Warmwell 'and some of these should not have flown by peacetime standards'. He was ordered by Sector Control to proceed as quickly as possible to Yeovil. Devitt found it covered with cloud and there was no sign of the enemy:

Westwards along Half Moon Street to the Almshouse in the heart of historic Sherborne

'Thinking that perhaps they had delivered their bombs and swung round through 180 degrees to starboard, as they had done on a previous Bristol raid, I turned the squadron eastwards in the hope of picking them up. They had obviously

Philips and Son's outfitting department (left) and the Half Moon Hotel, Sherborne, on 30 September 1940

turned this way so as not to be silhouetted against a background of white cloud for our fighters to pick up. It is always more difficult to pick up a camouflaged aircraft from above and with the earth below, but a fighter must have the advantage of height in order to deliver his full weight in the first attack.

'A few seconds after I had spotted them I saw their bombs falling away from beneath their bellies. On looking down to see what the target was, to my horror I saw the old school Courts which I knew so well.'

Devitt was at Sherborne School from 1924 to 1929. He found himself driven off by 'a pack of Bf.109s' which came from above. 'Boy' Marrs briefly engaged the formation and had to limp back to Warmwell with a crippled Spitfire. Only one wheel came down. Then it would not retract, and to attempt a landing on a single wheel is much more hazardous than a belly-flop. Marrs turned off the engine and glided down on to the grass as gently as possible:

'I began to slew round and counteracted as much as possible with the brake on the wheel which was down. I ended up going sideways on one wheel, a tail wheel, and a wing tip. Luckily the good tyre held out and the only damage to the aeroplane, apart from that done by the bullets, is a wing tip which is easily replaceable. I hopped out and went to the Medical Officer to get a lot of splinters picked out of my leg and wrist. I felt jolly glad to be down on the ground without having caught fire.'

Sergeant Pilot Leslie Arthur Edwin Reddington (26) went down into the sea off Portland with Spitfire L1072 of 152 Squadron. His death brought the squadron's combat losses to eleven and those for RAF Warmwell to 18. It was also a lack lustre day for 56 Squadron from RAF Boscombe Down, Wiltshire, which had half its Hurricanes put out of action over Dorset, though without any losing any pilots. Exeter's 87 Squadron lost a Hurricane – over Sherborne itself – but Sergeant Pilot Herbert Walton baled out over Honeycomb Wood and was taken to the town's Yeatman Hospital with minor injuries. The fighter crashed into a hedge between Castle Farm and Burdon's Nurseries in Oborne Road.

Filton's 504 Squadron lost several Hurricanes. Three pilots made forced-landings, writing off two of the fighters, and Flying Officer John Reginald Hardacre (24) was shot down and killed in P3414. He was seen falling into the sea off Weymouth.

A Messerschmitt Bf.109 was shot down at 16.40 hours over Hundred Acres Field, Spriggs Farm, Sydling St Nicholas. It had been flown by Unteroffizier Alois Dollinger, of the 5th Staffel of fighter wing Jagdgeschwader 2 Richtofen from Octeville airfield at Le Havre. He had baled out three miles to the south, over Grimstone near Stratton, but the parachute failed to open and he fell to his death.

The Sydling crash site would later be farmed by escaped British prisoner of war and author George Millar who wrote *Maquis*, *Horned Pigeon*, and *Through the Unicorn Gates*. This was the longest range of all the Bf.109 crashes of 1940. For the month as a whole, September 1940, Warmwell's 609 Squadron claimed 19 German aircraft for the loss of two Spitfires. Even allowing for over-claiming, the result was decisive. The confusion over claims was inevitable in that often several fighters had a part in accounting for the same bomber and it was frequently impossible to follow victims down to the ground. Station morale would have been depressed by continual inquests over dubious claims. What dropped on to the fields showed the trend, but the sea could anonymously accommodate any amount of further hopes.

The most exhilarating flying of the day was enjoyed by 238 Squadron from RAF Middle Wallop. Flight-Lieutenant Michael Lister Robinson (23), in R4099, led the nine Hurricanes south over Poole Bay and turned at Swanage to head towards Portland. They climbed into the cloud at 5,000 feet and rose to 15,000 above St Alban's Head, on a gyro-compass course westwards to get the advantage of the setting sun in Lyme Bay before wheeling into a dive on the German formations that were heading towards Portland.

They saw the enemy 3,000 feet below, to port, and swung into head-on attack. Robinson engaged a Messerschmitt Bf.110 from 300 yards, ripping it to pieces and sending an aerial oil-slick across his cockpit, which cleared sufficiently to give him a view of the Messerschmitt splashing down some ten miles south of Portland Bill.

Still with a smeared windscreen, he then saw another Bf.110, which was at 7,000 feet and heading back to France. Robinson gave chase and came to within 100 yards before opening up with three seconds of fire that pulled the port engine apart and moments later had the Messerschmitt explode. Its remains fell upside-down into the English Channel, 15 miles south of Portland Bill.

Robinson then flew towards Portland, and climbed to 25,000 feet to join a line of what he thought were Spitfires, but turned out to be Messerschmitt Bf.109s. He still continued towards them and took on the closest, giving it a sustained six seconds of fire from 300 yards. Debris, smoke, and white glycol streamed out as it flipped over and dropped seawards. Mike Robinson switched to his gravity tank: 'Landed at Exeter, no petrol.' It was 16.30 hours; he heard that others in 238 Squadron also had something to celebrate, including Pilot Officer Bob Doe (20) who had shot down a Heinkel. Robinson and Doe had joined the squadron only two days before.

The Telecommunications Research Establishment at Worth Matravers requisitioned Leeson House and Durnford School in the neighbouring village of Langton Matravers. Further expansion of its hutted encampment beside Renscombe Farm, on the western side of Worth, had been considered inadvisable. The tall aerials of the coastal radar research station were already attracting the attention of German bombers.

Scientists at Worth and Langton were deeply involved in what became the 'Battle of the Beams'. The Luftwaffe targeted inland English objectives by an intersection of radio pulses – one of synchronised dots and the other of dashes – transmitted from Kleve, in Germany, near the Dutch border south-east of Arnhem, and from Stolberg near the Danish border.

Dr Robert Cockburn developed a Radio Counter Measure codenamed 'Aspirin'. This duplicated the continuous Morse dashes, on a frequency of 30 to 31.5 megacycles per second, which disorientated the German pilots by widening their direction beam.

A more ambitious plan was, in effect, to bend the beam by recording a sequence of synchronous German dots and re-transmitting the signal from a mast at Beacon Hill, near Salisbury. This scheme was thwarted, however, because the telephone land-line that Dr Cockburn was using, from Worth to Beacon Hill, was taken over by the military. The signal was recorded in the Isle of Purbeck but without the telephone link it could not be re-radiated from Beacon Hill. Asynchronous signals, however, had the desired effect without more sophisticated forms of interference being necessary.

Two Hurricanes of 607 Squadron from RAF Tangmere were lost at 11.20 hours on 1 October in combat with Messerschmitt Bf.110s between Swanage and the Needles. Both fighters, and their pilots, fell into the sea. The airmen were Flight-Lieutenant Charles Earle Bowen (24) and Sergeant Pilot Norman Brumby (22).

From 2 October the Mark-1 Spitfires of 609 Squadron no longer flew a daily shuttle from RAF Middle Wallop, on the Hampshire Downs, to Warmwell Aerodrome in south Dorset. They ceased to be day visitors and stayed at Warmwell for the winter months. The change of base was a mixed blessing, as the time saved in flying backwards and forwards had to be spent under canvas, in a dispersal area exposed to the elements. It was soon to make the transition from summertime dust-bowl into winter swamp.

Squadron Leader Robinson left 238 Squadron at RAF Chilbolton, after a week of defending the Dorset coast, to take command of the Spitfires of 609 Squadron at RAF Warmwell. Meanwhile, on 5 October, Sergeant Pilot John William McLaughlin of 238 Squadron from RAF Middle Wallop baled out of Hurricane P3611 on being shot down by Messerschmitt Bf.109s. He was taken to Shaftesbury Hospital, critically injured with multiple burns and eventually received pioneering skin-graft treatment at Queen Victoria Hospital, East Grinstead.

Four died and many were injured when the Southern National bus depot at Weymouth received a direct hit by a German bomb on 7 October. Fourteen buses and coaches were badly damaged. Both 609 Squadron and 152 Squadron from RAF Warmwell clashed with German aircraft on their doorstep, at times over the aerodrome itself, as an enemy force crossed the Channel at Portland to bomb the Westland Aircraft factory at Yeovil where a hundred civilian workers were killed in a direct hit of an air-raid shelter.

Four kills were credited to 609 Squadron but for the loss of three Warmwell Spitfires with fatal burns to Pilot Officer Harold John Akroyd (27), the death of Sergeant Pilot Alan Norman Feary (28) and a serious injury to Pilot Officer Michael Staples. Akroyd was pulled clear of Spitfire N3039, after it burst into flames in a forced-landing at Shatcombe Farm, Wynford Eagle, but he died the following day. Feary was hit by Messerschmitt Bf.109s over Weymouth. He baled out from Spitfire N3238 as it crashed at Watercombe Farm, between Warmwell and Owermoigne, but it was too low for the parachute to open. Staples baled out at 21,000 feet with 'a big hole' in his leg and proceeded to land without further injury as Spitfire N3231 plunged into common land meadows at Netmead, Child Okeford. The deaths brought the squadron's losses in the Battle of Britain to eight and those for RAF Warmwell to 20.

Engaging a defensive ring of 15 Messerschmitt Bf.110s, above Cheselbourne and Dewlish at 16.30 hours on 7 October, Flight-Lieutenant Dundas led Blue Section of 609 Squadron from RAF Warmwell. Guns blazing, he flew over the top of the German aircraft. Then, as he climbed away from the circle of fighter-bombers, he came across a lone Bf.110 at 16,000 feet.

'Too low for Double Deckers' (now stating the obvious) at the Southern National bus depot, Weymouth, after a direct hit in which four were killed on 7 October 1940

Approaching its tail he gave a sustained twelve seconds of fire from his eight guns. Both enemy engines belched smoke and white ethylene glycol coolant. John Dundas closed again on his crippled target but as he approached its gunner hit back with a shell that splintered his leg and sent Spitfire R6915 reeling into a spin. Pilot and aircraft both recovered sufficiently to level out and glide back to Warmwell Aerodrome. This is the machine that now hangs from the ceiling in the Imperial War Museum.

The burning Bf.110 was spotted crossing the coast at Weymouth, at 14,000 feet, and was presumed to have crashed in the English Channel, though Dundas was only given credit for a probable kill. Flight-Lieutenant Howell also claimed the destruction of a Bf.110.

As for RAF Warmwell's other squadron, Pilot Officer Marrs, in Spitfire R6968, led Blue Section of 152 Squadron at 20,000 feet over the eastern Frome valley. They descended upon 50 German Junkers Ju.88 bombers and Messerschmitt Bf.110 fighter-bombers with Bf.109 escorts. Marrs picked on the last Bf.109 in an exposed line. It belonged to II or III Gruppen of Zerstorergeschwader 26 and had the nose section painted white. As glycol coolant streamed from the Messerschmitt's starboard engine, Marrs switched his fire leftward across the fuselage:

'Suddenly the back half of his cockpit flew off and out jumped two men. Their parachutes streamed and opened and they began drifting slowly earth-wards. Their aeroplane, left to itself, dived vertically into the sea, making a most wonderful sight and an enormous splash . . . everything seemed to have cleared off, so I circled round the two Huns. They took an awful long time to come down on land and I watched the Army rush up to capture them.'

Though identified as a Ju.88, the enemy aircraft shot down into Worbarrow Bay on the afternoon of 7 October by Pilot Officer John Urwin-Mann in a Hurricane of 218 Squadron from RAF Chilbolton, was in fact Messerschmitt Bf.110E (3U+DD) belonging to the Stabskette of III Gruppe of Zerstorergeschwader 26. It had been defending bombers engaged in attacking the Westland Aircraft Company factory at Yeovil. Another Bf.110E (3U+FM), belonging to the 4th Staffel of Zerstorergeschwader 26 fell into Ringstead Bay.

Messerschmitt Bf.110 (3U+BT) belonging to the 9th Staffel of Zerstorergeschwader 26 came low across the Frome meadows and flew into the gorse-clad slope of Hyde Hill, south of Stoborough, at about 14.00 hours. The pilot, Leutnant Kurt Sidow, and his navigator, Gefreiter Josef Repik, died instantaneously in the fireball. Bf.110 (3U+JT) became another loss for the 9th Staffel when it force-landed near Corfe Castle. Gefreiter Bernhardt Demmig, the pilot, survived and was taken prisoner of war, but his Bordfunker [radio operator], Obergefreiter Josef Bachmann, was killed. They were shot down by Squadron Leader Robinson in a Warmwell Spitfire of 609 Squadron and Flying Officer Richard Brooker in a Hurricane of 56 Squadron from RAF Boscombe Down.

Junkers Ju.88 (9K+SN), heading for Yeovil, was brought down at 16.20 hours on Tappers Hill, above the hamlet of Up Sydling. The kill was claimed jointly by Sergeant-Pilot Edmund Eric Shepperd (23) in a Spitfire of 152 Squadron from Warmwell and Flying Officer Doe in a Hurricane of 238 Squadron from Chilbolton. All four members of the German crew baled out successfully and were taken prisoner of war, after being rounded up by shotgun, following which the farm labourers performed a victory dance around the wreckage. The bomber belonged to the 5th Staffel of II Gruppe, Kampfgeschwader 51.

Messerschmitt Bf.110C (3U+JP) of the 6th Staffel of Zerstorergeschwader 26 crashed at Brickhills Field, near Kingston Russell House.

56 Squadron, flying Hurricanes from RAF Boscombe Down, Wiltshire, joined in the hectic air activity over Dorset and Somerset. A detachment was sent to Warmwell Aerodrome and scrambled at 16.00 hours. They met an estimated 50 Messerschmitt Bf.110 fighter-bombers over Bulbarrow Hill. Hurricane P3154 was shot down in flames from 25,000 feet above Austral Farm, Alton Pancras. Sergeant-Pilot Dennis Hugh Nichols (19), on his first combat mission, parachuted clear of the stricken fighter but landed badly and was taken to Dorset County Hospital, Dorchester, with a suspected fracture of the spine. He resumed operational flying in 1942, survived the war, and returned to Alton Pancras to see relics of P3154 being excavated from the crash-site in 1994.

Another Hurricane, V6777 of 238 Squadron, was shot down by Messerschmitt Bf.110s and crashed at Great Hill, Winterborne Houghton. Pilot Officer Aubrey Richard Covington baled out over Dorset for the second time in a week – the first being during the attack on Sherborne – though this time he was not quite unscathed, being taken to Blandford Cottage Hospital with minor injuries.

At 21.00 hours on 8 October, Moreton's elegant Georgian church was completely wrecked by a German bomb that fell beside the north wall. This collapsed and all the glass was blown out and destroyed. Though ruined, St Nicholas's Church would be restored and re-dedicated, in May 1950. From 1955 it was enriched by the finest set of modern engraved glass windows in Britain – the creation of Sir Laurence Whistler.

Czechoslovakian flyer Sergeant-Pilot Jaroslav Hlavac of 56 Squadron, from RAF Boscombe Down, was killed at 12.20 on

Moreton Church, blown apart by a German bomb, on 9 October 1940

10 October when Hurricane P3421 was shot down at Manor Farm, Worgret, to the west of Wareham. He was aged 25, had been with the squadron just two days, and was in the process of intercepting a flight of Messerschmitt Bf.109s.

Hurricane P3984 of 238 Squadron, from RAF Chilbolton, Hampshire, crashed at 13.00 hours below Corfe Castle – missing the famous ruins by only 200 yards and plummeting into a roadside quarry just north of the Castle Hill. It came down close to the viaduct that carries the railway across the Studland road. This time the pilot, though wounded, was able to bale out. Pilot Officer Bob Doe (20) landed on Brownsea Island and was taken to Cornelia Hospital in Poole.

The lunchtime problem for the Hurricanes seems to have been a dense cloud-base which extended up to 16,000 feet. As British fighters came up through it they were visible to the enemy formations in the clear sky above. For those potentially fatal final moments the sight of the RAF pilots was still obscured by water droplets.

On 15 October, leading Blue Flight of 609 Squadron from RAF Warmwell in Spitfire P9503, Flight-Lieutenant John Dundas flew through the gunfire of three Messerschmitt Bf.109 fighters at 14,000 feet above Christchurch. One Spitfire reported a bullet hole, but no apparent damage, though the squadron's flight pattern was thrown into disarray. Dundas failed to regroup his flight and soared alone to 18,000 feet where he found some 15 Messerschmitt Bf.110 fighter-bombers. He made two runs at them, giving bursts of fire from only 100 yards, but then broke away as Bf.109s came towards the Spitfire from above. A Bf.110 crashed near Bournemouth as a result of the engagement. It became the squadron's 99th accepted kill.

Cryptanalysts at Bletchley Park, deciphering the German 'Enigma' radio traffic, gave warning of the bombing raid on east Dorset on 16 October which hit Bovington and Poole. The intercepted signal was 'Target No. 1 for Y'. Target No. 1 was known to be the Armoured Fighting Vehicles School, at Bovington Camp, and 'Y' indicated that Y-beam radio direction signals were being used. The Y-Gerat target finding system was deployed by the pathfinding 3rd Gruppe of Kampfgeschwader 26 whose aircraft carried the identification marking '1H' to the left of the iron cross on their rear fuselage.

The British armed trawler HMT *Lord Stamp* sank after striking a German mine in Lyme Bay on 14 October. HMT *Kingston Cairngorm* followed her, off Portland Bill, on the 17th. That coincided with an intended raid on the Dorset and Devon coast to cover the infiltration of fifth columnists, mostly Irish Republicans. This was thwarted by the Royal Navy. Submarine *L27*, an ex-Danish boat, shadowed the attack on the German convoy and many of the enemy drowned, including SS agents. It was the day of the 'False Invasion'.

The German force included the 5th T-boat Flotilla – of 1,300-ton motor torpedo boats the size of a light destroyer – and the destroyers *Karl Galster*, *Frederich Ihrs*, *Hans Lody*, and *Erich Steinbrinck*. They had a running fight to escape from a mixed Allied force of two British cruisers supported by two Free French destroyers, two Norwegian destroyers, and one each from the Dutch and Danish navies.

Sergeant-Pilot Shepperd, flying Spitfire R6607 of 152 Squadron from RAF Warmwell, was killed on 18 October when his fighter plunged into the ground at Tadnoll Mill, two miles from the aerodrome. No other aeroplane was involved and there was no obvious reason for the accident. His was the squadron's twelfth fatality during the Battle of Britain and the 21st loss for the station.

Bournemouth firemen, who were the first provincial reinforcements to arrive in the capital at the beginning of the Blitz in September – being among the 50 pumps at Millwall Docks – instigated an exchange scheme with London firemen. Forty members of the Auxiliary Fire Service from Bournemouth – divisional area 16C of No. 6 Region – left on 19 October to swap duties for a week with some of the city's exhausted heroes. Deputy Chief Officer Ken Devereux, leading the Bournemouth team, said they expected to gain valuable experience in tackling major bomb damage.

Pilot Officer Sydney Jenkyn Hill and Flight-Lieutenant Howell shared the credit for the destruction of a Junkers Ju.88 bomber on 21 October. The enemy aircraft was returning from strafing the Army airfield at Old Sarum, Wiltshire, and was approaching the coast,

at 200 feet above the New Forest. The interception was brought about through radar, with Flight-Lieutenant Fieldsend in the Operations Room calling the Spitfires on the RT and arranging the ambush:

'He should be near you now, flying very low.'

Both Spitfires dived to attack and Howell went in first, as the bomber dropped to tree height, then Hill opened fire, and almost immediately a terrific explosion left wreckage scattered across four fields. There was no survivor. The kill was 609 Squadron's 100th victory.

Dorset-born Sydney Hill, a 23-year-old from Ferndown, and Londoner Frank Howell from Golders Green were treated to a boozy party on their return at 18.30 hours to RAF Warmwell.

This was the first Spitfire squadron to be credited with a hundred victories though No. 1 Squadron had done it with Hurricanes, in the Battle of France, four months earlier. Bottles of champagne and brandy had been gathered to await the occasion. Pilot Officer Crook found that everyone felt distinctly pleased with themselves and life in general:

**'We drank to the C.O., we drank to the Poles, we drank to the squadron, and in
fact we toasted practically everything we could think of, in round after round of
champagne cocktails.'**

Pooch, the mascot of 152 Squadron at Warmwell Aerodrome, was reputed to have sired most of the bull terriers that were currently in RAF service. He carried the honorary rank of Pilot Officer and guarded 152's dispersal hut. This was adorned with a growing collection of signs 'lifted and borrowed' by MG-driving Spitfire pilots from the farms and countryside around Weymouth and Dorchester, such as 'Joe Guppy's Camp' and 'Safety First Beware Cattle'.

Grain production for Dorset might well have been a record in any case, given the hot summer, but it was way beyond anything in living memory as a result of 31,000 acres of pasture being hastily turned over to arable food production. The familiar greens of downland sheep walks and dairy vales gave way to golden expanses of wheat and barley.

More ephemeral, exotic even, were the dusky fields that suddenly turned into splashes of vivid cyan blue as the sky brightened. This crop was flax – the flowers of which open only for the sun. T. R. Ferris, executive officer of Dorset War Agricultural Committee, announced that he intended 'ploughing out of grass a further 22,000 acres of land for the 1941 harvest'. Gardeners and allotment holders were urged 'to do their utmost to increase food production by growing vegetables in all parts of the county'.

Captain Eric Wilson (28) of Long Crichel officially came back to life in October. He had been seconded to the Somaliland Camel Corps and was posthumously gazetted for the Victoria Cross as a result of his part in the heroic defence of the British colony in the

Horn of Africa, during the Italian invasion of 4-19 August. He commanded a series of Bren gun positions that were blown to pieces in a sustained attack over four days during which he held out until the end.

The award was cited in the *London Gazette* but the story did not end there as three days later news reached the British that Captain Wilson had survived and was prisoner of war. Neither was that the final chapter. As the war turned against the Italians he was liberated and then fought with the Long Range Desert Group. Lieutenant-Colonel Wilson retired from the Army in 1949 and became an administrator in Tanganyika, until 1961, before returning to a West Country cottage, at Stowell near Sherborne. He died in 2008.

An animal shelter opened by Nina, Duchess of Hamilton, on her estate at Ferne, near Shaftesbury, became a refuge for hundreds of city pets, made homeless by the bombings and the general upheavals of war. As far as possible they were cared for as if they were still at home, with freedom and exercise, rather than being permanently impounded in cages. Larger animals, such as horses, ponies and goats, also found a refuge. In reply to criticism that it is a waste of resources to care for animals in wartime, the Duchess quoted a Regional Commissioner of the Ministry of Home Security:

> **'Experience shows that effective arrangements for dealing with animal casualties and for caring for the domestic pets of homeless people plays an important part in the maintaining of public morale after air-raids.'**

Nina was the widow of the 13th Duke of Hamilton who died on 16 March 1940. Three of their four sons – Lord Douglas Douglas-Hamilton, Lord C. N. Douglas-Hamilton, and Lord Malcolm Douglas-Hamilton – were serving with the RAF at the outbreak of war. The first, who succeeded his father as 14th Duke of Hamilton, had been the chief pilot of the Mount Everest flight expedition in 1933. Ferne Animal Sanctuary survives, but has since moved to Wambrook, Somerset.

On 1 November two 12-inch Mark II railway-mounted howitzers of Great War vintage arrived in the Isle of Purbeck from the Ordnance store at Chilwell, Nottingham. A gun-spur siding was made ready near Furzebrook by the 14th Super Heavy Battery of 5th

Nina, Duchess of Hamilton, turned Ferne House, near Shaftesbury, into a refuge for bombed-out pets

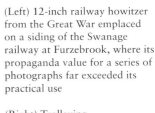

(Left) 12-inch railway howitzer from the Great War emplaced on a siding of the Swanage railway at Furzebrook, where its propaganda value for a series of photographs far exceeded its practical use

(Right) Trolleying

(Left) Cradling

(Right) Hoisting

(Left) Loading

(Centre) Locking

(Right) Elevating

Corps of the Royal Artillery. The massive guns fired 750-pound shells, which shook the mountings apart, so they were of propaganda rather than practical value.

More significantly, H-Flight of No. 1 Anti-Aircraft Co-Operation Unit arrived at Christchurch Aerodrome, from Gosport. Its varied assortment of older types of aircraft included Avro Ansons, Tiger Moths, a Fairey Battle, Miles Magister and Bristol Blenheim. They were for the use of research scientists working on countermeasures against the German bombers, at the Air Defence Experimental Establishment, at Christchurch.

Early in the morning of 6 November a Heinkel He.111 of Kampfgruppe 100 (identification '6N') suffered a compass failure. This unit comprised the elite two per cent of German bombers operating from Vannes, Brittany which acted as pathfinders for the attacking formations. The crew were confused by the British masking of German radio direction beacons into thinking they were back in France. In fact they were over Dorset and running out of fuel.

The pilot force-landed on the shingle beach at West Bay, Bridport, and three of the four crew survived – though they soon had their locational illusions shattered and found themselves in captivity. Troops guarding the aircraft had a difference of opinion with a naval detachment who came to drag the aircraft up the beach. The soldiers followed orders not to let anyone touch the bomber and as a result it was engulfed by the incoming tide. The bomber had three vertical aerials and related radio equipment. The sodden apparatus was salvaged for inspection by Air Ministry boffins and will return to our story.

On the morning of 14 November, No. 10 Group Fighter Command plotted a single German reconnaissance aircraft crossing into the Middle Wallop sector from France. Pilot Officer Marrs, flying Spitfire R6968 with 152 Squadron, and Sergeant-Pilot Albert Wallace 'Bill' Kearsey (20), in Spitfire P9427, scrambled from RAF Warmwell to investigate. They found the Junkers Ju.88 at 24,000 feet over the River Stour, between Blandford and Sturminster Newton, heading on a course for Yeovil or Bristol. Both Spitfires attacked and the intruder tried to escape towards the English Channel. It crashed in flames beside Ringwood Road at Poole.

On the night of 14-15 November a massed formation of some 150 German aircraft flew across the Channel on a directional radio beam from the Cherbourg peninsula and crossed the coast at Christchurch and New Milton. They then headed up the Avon valley and passed two miles to the east of Salisbury.

Their code name for the operation was 'Moonlight Sonata' and they were one of the three streams of German aeroplanes – totalling 449 aircraft – aiming for Target 53, which turned out to be Coventry. The other streams crossed the English coast over Dover and the Wash.

The distinctive landmark of Coventry Cathedral was targeted by the pathfinders of Kampfgruppe 100. The city was devastated by 1,500 bombs (503-tons), leaving 568 dead and many more injured. The cathedral and a third of the factories were destroyed and 60,000 houses damaged. Only one German bomber was lost, over Loughborough.

That day two officers escaped from Normandy in a light aeroplane which they took from an airfield near Dinan. They flew directly across the English Channel and landed in the Dorset countryside at 14.00 hours, at Stinsford Farm, near Dorchester. One man was Belgian and the other French. 'Many thanks for the welcome,' pilot A. Devreux wrote in the autograph book of 19-year-old farmer's daughter Daisy Wyndham Hull.

German bombers attacked Bournemouth in the early hours of 16 November and left major destruction in three suburbs. At about 03.30 hours six parachute mines floated down on Westbourne, Malmesbury Park Road, St Leonard's Road, Turbary Common, and Alma Road Schools. High explosive bombs and incendiaries fell at Gervis Road East, Meyrick Road, Knyveton Road, Groveley Manor, Terrace Road, Leven Avenue, Montague Road and Southern Avenue. Fifty-three people were killed and 2,321 properties damaged. Among them was Skerryvore, which was Robert Louis Stevenson's house at Westbourne – near the head of Alum Chine – where he lived from 1885 until he left for the Pacific in 1887.

Twelve people, including a number of children who had just gone to bed, were killed in Weymouth at 21.00 hours on 17 November. The Jack Buchanan programme had just finished on the wireless as a German raider glided over Weymouth – he is said to have cut his engine – and dropped a parachute mine. The explosion destroyed 77 tightly-packed terraced houses at Chapelhay and damaging a further 879 properties. The device had been intended for the harbour – investigation of its remnants showed it was a sea mine.

During the month, scientists at the Royal Aircraft Establishment, Farnborough, reassembled radio beam-flying equipment removed from the Heinkel He.111 bomber which crash-landed at West Bay. The aircraft had three vertical aerials and an intact X-Gerat radio receiver, also known as Wotan I, which was used for precision bombing by enabling the aircraft to follow a radio direction beam emanating from the Cherbourg peninsula.

What surprised Air Ministry boffins was that the apparatus was tuned to 2,000 cycles per second (approximating to the 'C' which is two octaves above standard-pitch middle 'C'), whereas British jamming countermeasures had assumed a note of 1,500 cycles (approximating to the 'G' below this 'C'). Therefore the pilot, receiving audio notes through his headphones, could filter out the British interference and continue to follow the correct beam.

The revelation came too late to prevent the Coventry raid but it did ensure that radio countermeasures were perfected by the Telecommunications Research Establishment in time to save the vital Rolls-Royce aero-engine plant at Derby. On the night of 8 May 1941, in moonlit conditions similar to those of the Coventry raid, successful distortion of their signal caused Derby's bombs to fall on Nottingham – and those intended for Nottingham fell into open fields.

One flyer's story from the height of the Battle of Britain could now be told. Flight-Lieutenant James Brindley Nicolson (23), leading Red Section of 249 Squadron on a sweep from Southampton to Poole, found himself immobilised by a Messerschmitt Bf.109 during a dogfight over the New Forest. Injured by a cannon shell, causing serious injuries to his hands, face, neck and legs he struggled to bale out as the Hurricane caught fire.

Then another German fighter crossed the sky immediately in front of his crippled aircraft. Despite its damage, and with skin peeling off his burning left hand, he pressed home an accurate broadside into the fuselage of the Bf.109. 'I'll teach you some manners, you Hun,' Nicolson recalled shouting at the time, as he levelled the score.

He then resumed the difficult task of baling out – at 12.55 hours on 16 August – and was relieved to find his parachute was undamaged. His ordeal was not over, however, as he floated down in intense pain from his wounds and burns. On approaching the ground he sustained further injuries as his buttocks were peppered by shotgun pellets from a trigger-happy member of Hampshire Home Guard.

After spending three months recovering in Southampton Hospital, he was the special guest in Buckingham Palace, to receive the Victoria Cross from King George. His medal, the RAF's single VC from the Battle of Britain, was regarded as a representative award to 'The Few'. The battle, however, was not yet over. Or, if it was, 'will someone tell the Luftwaffe', pilots joked.

Though denied permission to intercept a Junkers Ju.88 that was heading south-west from Southampton, Flight-Lieutenant Dundas was allowed to take up his section of 609 Squadron from RAF Warmwell for a 'practice flight' on 27 November.

The two Spitfires climbed rapidly and found the bomber at 22,000 feet over Poole Bay, flying southwards into the sun. Throttling to 2,600 revolutions the Merlin engine of each fighter gave 280 miles per hour as the Spitfires closed on their target in its descent towards the Cherbourg peninsula. Dundas put Spitfire X4586 into an attacking glide at 14,000 feet, firing with five-second bursts at 400, 300, and then 200 yards. Flames shot out of the Ju.88's port engine and it lurched out of control as the three aircraft crossed the French coast. There being a German aerodrome visible below, the Spitfires did not follow their quarry any further towards the ground, and turned north-west for the 80-mile return flight to Dorset.

'Whoopee! I've got a 109.' Those were the last words received by radio transmission from John Dundas, flying Spitfire X4586 with 609 Squadron from Warmwell on 28 November. 'Good show, John,' Squadron Leader Robinson replied, after which nothing more was heard or seen of Dundas.

He had scrambled at 15.50 hours. Missing with him was Pilot Officer Paul Abbott Baillon (26), a solicitor, in Spitfire R6631. Both were lost over the sea off the Isle of Wight, bringing the losses for 609 Squadron to ten, but John Dundas did not die in vain. That night German radio announced that the Luftwaffe had lost one of its ace fighter pilots, Hauptmann Helmut Wick, who had 57 white kill-bars painted on the rudder of his Messerschmitt Bf.109E. He was leading Jagdgeschwader 2.

Having congratulated itself on an 'unusually quiet most of November' the month was also marred for 152 Squadron with loss of two pilots. Polish Sergeant Pilot Zygmunt Klein's Spitfire, K9427, fell into the sea and Pilot Officer Arthur Roy Watson, flying Spitfire R6597, crashed near Wareham, as a result of dog-fights with Messerschmitt Bf.109s over Poole Bay and off the Needles. Watson's death was avenged almost immediately by Pilot Officer Marrs in Spitfire R6968. He crept up slowly on the culprit Bf.109, staying in his blind spot, until he was within 100 yards. Then he fired for just one second, unleashing 55 rounds of .303 ammunition from each of his eight guns, to score 'the easiest victory I've had'.

Next day, at 15.14 hours, a flight from 152 Squadron – including Spitfire R6907 flown by Pilot Officer John Woodward Allen – was scrambled because of a suspected enemy fighter sweep. They were instructed to patrol a circuit of RAF Warmwell at 25,000 feet. Allen sent a radio message but it was unintelligible and nothing further was heard from him. His Spitfire was then seen to break away and dive shallowly, though under control. Suddenly it plummeted vertically towards the ground and disintegrated on impact at Field Grove on the downs above Durweston. He had been flying Spitfires for three weeks and was the squadron's 15th fatality. Those for the station had reached 26.

Unteroffizier Paul Wacker of Jagdgeschwader 27, flying a Messerschmitt Bf.109 belonging to the 4th Staffel of Lehrgeschwader 2 – a specialist unit testing improvised aircraft under operational conditions – suffered engine failure whilst on a weather reconnaissance over Swanage on 30 November. He was fortunate to belly-land on fields at Woodyhyde Farm, beside the railway between Swanage and Corfe Castle, having narrowly avoided heavily wooded countryside. The tail section of his fighter survives as it was used to repair another captured test-flown Bf.109 now displayed in the Royal Air Force Museum at Hendon.

One of the more remarkable aeronautical feats of the war has solved a Dorset puzzle. Four German airmen baled out and walked into a village near Shaftesbury to give themselves up in November 1940. 'But where is their aeroplane?' everyone was asking. Meanwhile, 130 miles away, a Dornier bomber made a perfect belly-landing in mud flats at Ipswich. 'Where are the crew?' people were asking in Suffolk.

The bomber, from the Cherbourg peninsula, was en route for Liverpool when it experienced an electrical storm near Shrewsbury during which its compass had flipped. They reached France but then feared, wrongly, that they were flying north into Britain, and turned back across the Channel for the third time, where they failed to find an airfield and decided to abandon the aircraft. It, however, continued on its automatic pilot and landed safely at Ipswich when the petrol ran out.

Bournemouth anti-aircraft gunners claimed two enemy aircraft on 1 December with one being seen dropping into the sea off Hengistbury Head. The following day Warmwell's flying partnership of 609 Squadron's two eastern Europeans, Pilot Officers Noel Agazarian and Tadeusz Nowierski, achieved a double kill. They intercepted German aircraft off Thorney Island, Hampshire, and shared the destruction of a Messerschmitt Bf.110 fighter-bomber and a Dornier Do.17 bomber. The Spitfires broke up an attacking formation heading for Portsmouth.

The new aerodrome being built at Hurn, north of Bournemouth, had its first air-raid on 3 December. Five high explosive bombs and a number of incendiaries fell at 18.50

(Left) The 5th Battalion, the Northamptonshire Regiment, on manoeuvres at Holdenhurst Farm, Bournemouth

(Right) Bren gun carriers among the turkeys at Holdenhurst, Bournemouth, in the winter of 1940

Mortar firing at Holdenhurst

Northamptonshire Regiment on the march

hours. The site had previously been recommended by Sir Alan Cobham to Bournemouth Corporation for a municipal aerodrome, but in the event – a war – it was the Air Ministry that took the initiative, on behalf of the Royal Air Force.

For several Christchurch families, Friday 13 December turned into a lucky day, as they were evacuated from their homes just in time. A crater with an unexploded bomb, outside 1 Kings Avenue, had been reported at 09.25 hours but the decision to clear the area was delayed until 17.25. A bomb disposal team decided to leave the bomb for 96 hours. Then, at 18.55, it went off – damaging three houses and rupturing gas and water pipes.

General Harold Alexander, General Officer Commanding-in-Chief of Southern Command, and Major-General Bernard Montgomery of 5th Corps, stood on the cliffs between Redend Point and Old Harry Rocks, Studland, on 20 December to watch the sea being set on fire. Pipes were laid from the beach in Project Fougasse to release oil in a

Clearing out 'Invaders' from the Stour meadows

Bournemouth's last-ditch defences

Key apparatus in the secret war, being a Type 15 mobile radar antenna devised at Worth Matravers and Christchurch, and deployed in the field at Sopley on Christmas Day 1940

General Harold Alexander (far left) and VIPs watching oil pools being released in Studland Bay, in December 1940

series of slicks to form a continuous strip that was then ignited. The intention had been to repeat the exercise at night – because British intelligence suggested that German troops feared a conflagration on the beaches – but the second attempt failed due to waves lashed by a cold on-shore wind.

On Christmas Eve, Convoy FN 366, sailing between Portland and the Isle of Wight, was attacked by the German 1st Schnellboot Flotilla. This comprised six large motor torpedo boats; *S26*, *S28*, *S29*, *S34*, *S56* and *S59*. The E-boats sank a Dutch ship, the *Maastricht*, and a Royal Navy armed trawler, HMT *Pelton*.

A trailer-mounted ground-to-air radar antenna, developed by the TRE in Purbeck and built at Somerford, Christchurch, by the Air Defence Experimental Establishment, was tested for the first time on Christmas Day. Known as Type 15, the mobile unit was towed into the countryside, and placed on a flat part of Lord Manners's estate at Sopley, between the River Avon and the New Forest. The scientific war was growing in sophistication.

The sea burning at Studland as an anti-invasion measure

1941

Radar rather than raids

THE AIR WAR eased during 1941. Sustained daylight attacks virtually ceased though bouts of night bombing continued. Reconnaissance aircraft kept coming but were now given individual attention. Most were tracked by radar and a high proportion intercepted by fighters, such as the Dornier Do.17 reported entering Middle Wallop sector on 4 January. Pilot Officer Eric "Boy" Marrs led the Spitfires of Green Section of 152 Squadron from RAF Warmwell at 13.00 hours on a sweep across Weymouth Bay. He found the enemy aircraft over Ringstead Bay:

> 'I approached from the sea and opened fire at about 400 yards from the port rear quarter. He then turned south and dived like stink for the clouds. I turned in behind him, and closing to about 250 yards, fired at the fuselage and two engines in turn. Black and white smoke came from the engines and all return fire from the gunners ceased. I was overshooting and just before he reached the clouds I had to break away.'

The Dornier was spotted from the ground at Lulworth Cove, as it came out of the cloud, trailing smoke and losing height. Its attempted return to France ended in the English Channel, off Portland Bill. No one survived.

On land, home-grown crime could sometimes displace the war news. Private David Jennings (20) was charged on 27 January with the midnight murder of Dorchester tailor Albert Farley of The Grove. What started as a burglary had turned tragically wrong. Jennings was breaking into what he assumed was an empty licensed club and did so in the style of American gangster films. He shot the lock off the door. Unknown to

Overhaul for *Clare*'s four Pegasus engines in January 1941, prior to the transatlantic flying-boat returning to Poole Harbour for BOAC's Empire route to Africa

Jennings, however, the premises were still occupied and Farley was about to unlock the door from the other side. The tailor was shot dead.

Jennings was hanged in Dorchester Prison. Such homicides ceased to be murder under the Homicide Act 1957 and the Criminal Justice Act 1967, in that the jury could now decide whether the accused intended or should have foreseen the results of his action. Clearly he did not, in this case, as the object was theft from a building that was locked-up and apparently unoccupied. The present definition would be manslaughter, though the original jurymen had little patience with such niceties. High East Street grocer Douglas Parsons said:

'We didn't think of things like that. We were at war.'

In January, Christchurch Aerodrome was selected as a shadow-factory for plane-makers Airspeed (1934) Limited who were best known for the Envoy and the twin-engine Oxford. A total of 550 of the latter would be made at Christchurch. Most went into service use as trainers. Dorset-inspired developments also continued in the most-secret electronic war.

Dr Robert Cockburn of the Telecommunications Research Establishment, from Worth Matravers, commandeered the BBC's pre-war television transmitter at Alexandra Palace. It went off the air in mid-cartoon on the outbreak of war because of concern that the straight, horizontal, programme signal would be utilised by enemy bombers as a navigation aid to find the capital.

The powerful aerial, on Muswell Hill in north London, was brought back into action on the very night that the Luftwaffe refined its blind-flying system of following radio beams to English targets. The bombers had changed to a frequency of 42.5 megacycles per second. This was successfully jammed by Cockburn in Countermeasure Domino. He re-radiated the German signal back to the attacking aircraft, from Alexandra Palace, at 46.9 megacycles per second. A second transmitting station, constructed on Beacon Hill near Salisbury, then extended Cockburn's jamming over the whole of southern England.

Across the Dorset countryside, Londoners displaced by the blitz were experiencing their first rural winter. One such family was that of Mrs Alice Stone and her sons Brian (born 1935) and Barry (born 1938). They arrived at thatched Rookery Farm, West Creech, in December. It was their third attempt at finding a place of safety.

Lambeth evacuees Mrs Alice Stone and sons Barry (left) and Brian whose third attempt at escaping the bombs took them into deepest Dorset

Rookery Farm at West Creech, where the Stone family found refuge, in a typical Purbeck winter

Originally from the Lambeth, they were evacuated to Folkestone on the outbreak of war, but found that far from escaping from danger they were on the new front-line. Having then moved to Catford, in time for London's bombs, they were resettled to deepest Dorset. West Creech lies among a cluster of small fields between heaths and downs on the northern side of the Purbeck Hills. The hamlet no longer had its own school, with the nearest being a couple of miles away, at Stoborough.

From there the Stone boys heard and saw the arrival of the first Catalina flying-boat to land on Poole Harbour. *Guba* (G-AGBJ) was the graceful arrival, on 1 February, for the BOAC service across the Bay of Biscay to neutral Portugal. She brought a new sound. Pratt and Whitney's Twin Wasp engines were much louder than the familiar Bristol Pegasus 9-cylinder radial engines of the Empire flying-boats.

Bournemouth War Savings Committee organised the town's War Weapons Week, which was launched by the Mayor, Alderman A. H. Little, beside a thermometer-style proceeds board mounted on the bus-shelter in the Square. Mayor Little rode around the town on top of a tank which displayed progress being made towards the £1 million target.

He announced that £250,000 had been raised on the first day – including £100,000 from Bournemouth Corporation – and said that the money would be safe and secure in National Savings. It was not a gift to the Government, he emphasised, but a timely investment in the future that would yield 3 per-cent interest per annum, free of tax. The town's wartime savings rate had run at nearly £100,000 per week but the campaign committee sought to increase this to an average of £150,000. It spawned 525 savings groups, of which 262 were in places of employment, 155 based on streets, and the remainder including clubs and schools.

A Lysander flew low over Bournemouth and showered the town centre with leaflets:

> **'A message to Bournemouth from the Royal Air Force. To the citizens of Bournemouth – the Royal Air Force is watching with great interest your War Weapons Week. Lend your money to the utmost as we are lending our full support to you. We are banking on Bournemouth, too!'**

Three Spitfires had thrilled the crowd with a display of V-shaped formation flight and aerobatics. Then there was a tragic accident. A Czech pilot of 32 Squadron from RAF Ibsley failed to pull his Hurricane out of a victory roll and plunged into St Clement's Road.

On 20 February, Robert Menzies, the 46-year-old Australian Prime Minister, and his entourage touched down in Poole Harbour, on an Empire flying-boat. The 'Kangaroo party' had been accompanied from Egypt by Henry 'Chips' Channon MP on behalf of the Foreign Office. Their route from the British Embassy in Cairo to the Dorchester Hotel in London traversed the Northern Hemisphere in a great loop with refuelling and rest stops at Khartoum (The Palace), Wadi Halfa, Lagos, the Canary Islands and Estoril (Palace Hotel).

The Australians held talks with Winston Churchill and British officers on their growing contribution to the progress of the war. Sir Henry Channon recorded in his diary that he read *War and Peace* en route, and arrived at Poole in the cold and dark to the 'blackout again'. Although transport was provided for the Australian contingent he had to charter a car. The 'gaunt woman driver' who 'drove recklessly' to London was Sandbanks horse-trainer and bus operator Mrs Louie Dingwall who ran a long-distance taxi service on behalf of British Airways. She charged £8.

'I was wretched to get back,' Channon continued, 'and I heard the sirens as we approached London.' On reaching his home in Belgrave Square he found that R. A. Butler, the Acting Foreign Secretary, was dining with a friend and 'the warmth and affection of their welcome cheered me'. Mrs Dingwall told of driving through bombs falling on Kensington while returning from this, or a similar VIP journey, during the winter.

Bob Menzies, a convivial and witty raconteur with 'rapier-like intelligence', was treated to a house-party in his honour at Chequers on 9 March. The Prime Minister, who hosted the evening, was suffering from bronchitis and came down to dinner in the ancestral hall dressed in his one-piece light blue romper or siren suit. General Sir Alan Brooke recorded that Churchill was 'in great form' and had entertained them with rifle drill which including a bayonet exercise:

> **'I remember wondering what Hitler would make of this demonstration of skill at arms.'**

Spitfires of 609 Squadron, Dorset's first home-fielded defenders in the Battle of Britain, lifted off the turf of RAF Warmwell for the last time. They moved on to Biggin Hill, Kent. With them went their two odd-job planes, a Puss Moth, and a Magister. Meanwhile, on 24 February, Mark-I Spitfires of 234 (Madras Presidency) Squadron arrived at Warmwell. Their markings were 'AZ' and motto 'Ignem mortemque despuimu' (We spit fire and death).

That day, for the first time, a German radar signal was intercepted at Worth Matravers. Air Ministry scientist Derek Garrard, seconded to the Telecommunications Research

Establishment, succeeded in picking up transmissions on a VHF receiver at the 2.5 metre wavelength. Having failed with the official equipment, he put an ordinary radio set in his car and drove off to St Alban's Head, to point it towards the Cherbourg peninsula, and was arrested as a suspected Fifth Columnist infiltrating a designated 'Defended Area'.

Having established his credentials, he returned to his office in London, with bearings that suggested a source in the area of Auderville, where coincidentally two square-meshed aerials in a field were photographed by Flight Officer W. K. Manifould two days earlier. The 22-feet turntable apparatus was the 'Freya' unit to which the Germans credited the sinking off Portland of HMS *Delight* on 29 July 1940.

As a result, Air Marshal Sir Philip Joubert has called an emergency meeting with one item on the agenda:

'To discuss the existence of German radar.'

More than 50 Freya units would be located by a combination of listening, intercepting messages, and reconnaissance flights, by the end of 1941. British radar advancements also continued. The Type-15 mobile unit in a field near Christchurch celebrated the first kill of an enemy aircraft that it had 'stage-managed'.

Months of invasion nerves were taking their toll. A few days after Derek Garrard found himself apprehended for suspicious behaviour on the cliffs there was a high-profile instance of friendly fire at Corfe Mullen. Second-Lieutenant the Honourable C. S. Vereker of the Grenadier Guards, whose father, Lord Gort VC, led the British Expeditionary Force in France, was shot dead on failing to stop at a vehicle check-point manned by the Home Guard.

Squadron Leader Louis Strange (50) from Worth Matravers, was given responsibility for the training of British paratroops. He was the only pilot still flying on active service in the Second World War who went to France with the first squadrons of the Flying Corps in August 1914. Uniquely, he was still flying operationally with the Royal Air Force on Armistice Day in 1918, holding the MC and DFC, and came out of retirement to return to combat in Europe, coming home in a Hurricane to receive a second DFC on the Fall of France.

Experimental burn-ups continued on Studland beach. 'Sea Flame' was ignited on 9 March for the benefit of General Harold Alexander, Commander 1st Division, as the pipes of Project Fougasse released pools of oil. A landing craft was towed through the flames to show the effect of the scorching. As a result the Petroleum Warfare Department was authorised to install 50 miles of such barrages but shortages of steel piping restricted coverage to Deal, Dover and Rye in the prime potential invasion area of Caesar's Coast, and Porthcurno at the landfall of the vital transatlantic cables in Cornwall.

The 'Glamour Puffer' as it was known – a works train for the Royal Naval Cordite Factory on Holton Heath that brought young ladies from Christchurch, Bournemouth and Poole – attracted the attention of a German raider. Steaming home on the evening of 21 March, as it crossed Rocklea Bridge, a stick of six bombs straddled the embankment beside the harbour backwater and blew out all the windows of the ancient non-corridor 'bird-cage' carriages. The train kept going, into the semi-protected stretch of line through the sandy cutting, and then halted to wait for more of the same. The enemy aircraft did not return and the train was able to draw into the platform at Hamworthy Junction. Apart from severe fright none of the passengers suffered more than minor cuts.

Equally uneventfully, on 26 March, a solitary Junkers Ju.88 crossed the Channel and dropped four high explosive bombs on the RAF station at Warmwell. Damage was limited to holes in the grass.

It was a different story on 27 March at Branksome where the air-raid siren had sounded almost every day for a month, and sometimes more than once. Despite the alarm, business continued as usual at Branksome Gas Works, where the staff gathered in the canteen for lunch. At noon a single enemy aircraft dived out of the clouds towards the viaducts in Bourne Valley. Two bombs fell short of the railway and landed on the Gas Works. The first blew up the stores and the second smashed through the upper storey

Veteran aviator Louis Arbon Strange from Worth Matravers was unique in flying in combat for the entirety of the Great War and again from 1940 onwards

above the canteen and then wedged itself, protruding through the ceiling, to the horror of those seated beneath. There was only a matter of seconds to begin evacuating the crowded tables before the not-much-delayed fuse activated the bomb with deadly effect.

The explosion devastated the hall, killing 34 men, including Home Guard members Leonard Bartlett, Archibald Cherrett and Herbert Williams. A further 23 were injured; some seriously. Anxious wives soon thronged at the gates as Royal Artillerymen helped survivors drag out dead and wounded colleagues.

Wing Commander Edward Collis de Virac Lart (39), who was born in Lyme Regis in 1902 and had served as an RAF pilot since he was 23, failed to return to base on 27 March. He was one of Britain's most experienced flyers.

'Bournemouth has over 17,000 civilian fire-fighters,' boasted the *Bournemouth Times*. Following a mass-meeting on 15 February, the town implemented the Fire Precautions (Business Premises) Order, requiring all healthy men between 16 and 60, not otherwise involved in the war effort, to register for up to 48 hours duty a month as part-time firemen. Stirrup pumps, whistles and steel helmets were widely distributed.

Devastated canteen at Bourne Valley Gasworks in which 33 were killed by a German bomb on 27 March 1941

Six-inch diameter steel piping was laid on pavements along the main roads through the centre of town to ensure a ready and repairable water supply. Underground mains pipes proved much more liable to fracture, and usually impossible to repair, during night-time air-raids. Fire, the Government warned, was the most devastating aspect of aerial warfare.

One of the bombs that dropped on Canford Cliffs in March hit the home of Air Marshal Sir Philip Joubert, nominally the commanding officer of Combined Operations which was being set-up at Poole. The job was something of a blind, for he had been running the RAF's radar and signals intelligence system, right through the Battle of the Beams, and in effect controlled the Telecommunications Research Establishment at Worth Matravers.

Three Heinkel He.111s slipped low across the Dorset coast from Lyme Bay on 1 April and followed the railway eastwards from Dorchester to the aerodrome at Warmwell. They had not been picked up by radar, or spotted by the Observer Corps, and the station had no warning of the attack. Ten were killed by the bombs, shortly after noon, and 20 injured. Among the dead was Sergeant Pilot Fawcett, a Spitfire flyer with 152 Squadron, who was killed by a machine-gun bullet as he sat eating lunch.

A bomb crashed through the room of Eric 'Boy' Marrs but the pilot was elsewhere – having the Distinguished Flying Cross, which was awarded in December, pinned on his uniform in Buckingham Palace by King George. Similarly honoured, also from 152 Squadron, was Pilot Officer Dudley Williams. Pilot Officer Marrs did have a shock at the weekend, however, hearing of the death of his best friend, Flying Officer Charles Davis DFC of 238 Squadron from Middle Wallop. His Hurricane flew into a hill near Winchester, obscured by low cloud, on 26 March.

A British bomber, outward-bound on a mission to attack the German battle-cruisers *Scharnhorst* and *Gneisenau* at Brest, was shot down in the Blackmore Vale on 3 April. Whitley T4299 of 51 Squadron crashed at Connegar Farm, Manston. It had taken off from RAF Dishforth, at 19.00 hours, and was brought down at 21.20. The interception resulted from misidentification and was traced to a Hurricane night-fighter of 87 Squadron from RAF Exeter.

Sergeant W. N. Brindley was killed but the other four members of the crew were unhurt. For Pilot Officer M. E. Sharp and Sergeant L. J. Allum it was the second time they had baled out in two months. The earlier escape was also from a Whitley, returning from a Bomber Command raid over Bremen, on the night of 11 February. They found themselves unable to pinpoint their position in deteriorating weather and abandoned the aeroplane above Bircham Newton, Norfolk.

Pilot Officer Eric Simcox 'Boy' Marrs DFC of 152 Squadron, sketched by war artist Cuthbert Orde, reached legendary status among the Spitfire flyers of RAF Warmwell

Unexploded bomb which fell beside Heathwood Garage, Holton Heath, having missed the Royal Naval Cordite Factory in an air-raid in 1941

An RAF Blenheim of 101 Squadron from West Raynham, returning from Bomber Command's raid on the port of Brest, crashed at Frampton. The three crewmen – Sergeants P. I. Burrows, G. B. H. Birdsell, and H. R. Perry – were killed instantaneously as the aeroplane exploded on hitting the ground on the night of 3-4 April.

A Heinkel He.111 H-8 bomber was left lying on its belly beside the coastal ridgeway east of Weymouth on 5 April. Pilots from Warmwell Aerodrome inspected the stranded aeroplane which had been attacking shipping off Portland. It was fitted with a curved tube which projected forward from the nose and extended from the top of one wing to the tip of the other. This refinement was to push barrage balloon cables aside and prevent them fouling wings and engines. The aircraft came into this predicament through navigational error. Its crew survived and became prisoners.

The familiar 'UM' markings of Mark-IIa Spitfires of 152 (Hyderabad) Squadron disappeared from the Dorset sky on 9 April as they headed across Lyme Bay to their next base at newly-built Portreath Aerodrome in Cornwall. 'Prepare to land on tarmac,' pilots were told at their briefing, before their final take-off from the grass airfield that was RAF Warmwell.

Cumberland Clark, a familiar figure in central Bournemouth with white hair and walrus moustache, was killed in his sleep as a German bomb destroyed his flat in St Stephen's Road at 00.03 hours on 11 April. He was a prolific author with 67 books to his credit, many of them poetry, and his *War Songs of the Allies* proved a tonic for the town's morale:

Bofors anti-aircraft gun, manned by Lance-Bombadier Williams on Arne Heath, brought an authentic touch to the decoy site that drew German bombers away from Holton Heath munitions works

'Down in our Air Raid Shelter
There's no cause for alarm,
It is so sure and strongly built
We cannot come to harm.

Let the bombs bounce round above us,
And the shells come whizzing by,
Down in our Air Raid Shelter
We'll be cosy, you and I!'

The same enemy aircraft dropped an incendiary on Woolworths, in The Square, which burned fiercely for some time. Seven women also died in the attack which destroyed several flats at Hampshire Court and in St Stephen's Road.

A Heinkel He.111 bomber, illuminated by a searchlight between Hammoon and Fiddleford on the night of 12-13 April was then engaged by an RAF fighter. The German aircraft passed low over Manston, heading south-westwards into the Blackmore Vale, where it crashed in meadows near Lydlinch. There was a huge explosion.

Battle of Britain pilot Roland Prosper Beamont (21), who took part in many of the dog-fights over Lyme Bay and Portland in a Hurricane of 87 Squadron from RAF Exeter, was talent-spotted by Hawker Aircraft Company to test-fly its latest aircraft. This machine, the Hawker Typhoon, was destined to spearhead the next generation of dual-function fighter-bombers.

Beamont enlisted with the Royal Air Force at the age of 19 and flew with the British Expeditionary Force in France. He was mentioned in despatches during periods of continuous combat along the Dorset coast through the summer of 1940. His new career as a test pilot was restricted to what he termed 'rest periods' but he went on to become Britain's most famous post-war aviator and eventually retired to Pentridge.

Hurricane L1592, one of three stationed at Christchurch Aerodrome to protect the Special Duty Flight, crashed at 12.20 on 28 April when its port undercarriage failed to lock upon touch-down. The fighter spun across the grass but was not seriously damaged.

RADAR RATHER THAN RAIDS

The pilot was unhurt. This was an unusually lucky aircraft. It survived this accident and the war to become part of the National Aeronautical Collection in the Science Museum.

Later that afternoon, Fairey Battle fighter-bomber K9230 of the Special Duty Flight crashed with its crew of two into the sea off Hengistbury Head. Pilot Officer A. C. James baled out shortly before the aircraft hit the water. His action was spotted by Second Lieutenant Andrew Page Watson of the Lancashire Fusiliers who was on top of the headland.

He immediately scrambled down the steep sandy cliffs, and swam out to sea, ignoring and defying the currents which are notoriously strong around this exposed promontory. Despite the water being bitterly cold and rough the soldier reached the pilot, who was entangled in his sodden parachute, and attempted to extricate him from the harness. His efforts. however, were unavailing, and he was ultimately compelled to release his hold through exhaustion as the pilot died.

In attempting to return to the beach, Andrew Watson was himself nearly drowned, and had to be rescued by two of his comrades who dragged him ashore. Watson was awarded the George Medal.

(Left) German Bücker Jungmann aircraft stolen from the Luftwaffe in France and flown to Christchurch by two young Frenchmen in April 1941

(Right) French escapees Denys Boudard (left) and Jean Hebert (right) with Flight Sergeant Pritchard after their flight from Caen to Christchurch on 29 April 1941

Two young Frenchmen, ex-members of the Armee de l' Air, landed at Christchurch Aerodrome on 29 April in a German biplane, a Bücker Jungmann, which they had stolen from an airfield near Caen. They landed at 12.30 hours, after a flight of 75 minutes, and were spared some rounds of Bofors anti-aircraft fire through the quick thinking of 229 Battery of the Royal Artillery who saw the swastikas on the plane but realised there was something unusual in a short-range aeroplane coming this distance. Messieurs Denys Boudard and Jean Hebert werei debriefed by Free French Forces.

Re-equipped but with their commander, General Bernard Montgomery, calling them flat-footed, the Third Division of the British Army – veterans of the Dunkirk beaches – came to the end of seven weeks' intensive training at a full-scale camp on Batcombe Hill, between Evershot and Cerne Abbas. Biting winds, intense frosts, and the hard-slog of a route march from the Dorset Downs to the Avon valley were the memories that lasted. The distance was 65 miles; being first to the Cerne valley, then crossing the Stour at Bryanston, and on to the River Avon at Fordingbridge, on the edge of the New Forest – then all the way back again. En route the men practised attacks on woods and hills and made assault-crossings of each stream and river. Pre-war tourists among the soldiers teased their mates with descriptions of the Cerne Giant, as the field-force tramped towards Cerne Abbas, but he had disappeared (camouflaged to deny the Luftwaffe a navigation aid).

Under the command of Captain Gustavus March-Phillips, an operational guerrilla unit of commandos known as the Small Scale Raiding Force was formed at Poole in April, with headquarters in the Antelope Hotel. Their role, in Winston Churchill's words, was to create 'a reign of terror down the enemy coasts'.

The Experimental Bridging Establishment of the Royal Engineers, formerly known as the Bridge Company, spanned the River Stour at Christchurch with a prefabricated steel bridge. It took shape almost instantly, taking 36 minutes from commencement, to the first lorry driving across. This 70 feet structure was designed in 1939 by Donald Coleman Bailey. The bridge-building Sappers took over the former Horse Barracks beside the river in Barracks Road.

(Left) Cruiser tanks lining up at Gatemerston, beside Lulworth Camp, to fire into Bindon Hill

(Right) Long-range A13 Cruiser, the first British tank to use Christie suspension, test firing on the Purbeck heaths in 1941

Bailey Bridges would be taken to war in Tunisia and Italy. Then in the Normandy campaign, between 18-21 July 1944, they enabled British armoured divisions to cross the River Orne at five points to the north of Caen. The length of the bridges grew to meet the size of the obstacle, such as 1,200 feet to cross the Chindwin in Burma, and a record 4,000 feet plus at Gennep in the Netherlands. Donald Bailey was knighted in 1946 and retired to 14 Viking Close, Southbourne.

The decoy airfield at Winfrith Heath, rigged with flares and moving lights to draw air attack from Warmwell Aerodrome, claimed a German bomber on 4 May to add to the craters it had successfully attracted. The victim was a Junkers Ju.88 that had apparently been hit by anti-aircraft fire. The crew baled out.

A German bomber crashed into the hillside below Oborne Wood, to the east of Sherborne, in the early hours of 7 May. The pilot baled out and gave himself up but the remainder of the crew, Feldwebel E. Ebert, Feldwebel H. Ottlick, and Unteroffizier T. Kowallik, died in the wreckage.

After the All-clear sounded at Weymouth early on 9 May, Mrs Lilian Adnam and her daughters Dorothy, Margaret, May, Violet, and Vivian left their shelter and returned to bed. Then, at 04.30 hours, a single German bomber slipped over the town and dropped five bombs. The house received a direct hit and all six were killed. Two other daughters escaped with injuries.

Christchurch Aerodrome and the factory buildings of Airspeed Limited, at Somerford, were bombed and machine-gunned early in the morning, between 00.40 and 01.09 hours on 10 May. One of the Heinkel He.111 bombers dived to within 50 feet of the ground and bombs were dropped to within 20 yards of buildings. Of the thirteen that landed within the station, no less than nine failed to explode. No air-raid warning had sounded and the attack, in full moonlight, came as a complete surprise.

Flying-boat *Maia*, sunk in Poole Harbour on 12 May 1941 (seen here giving a piggy-back to a Mercury float-plane)

Hendon to RAF Warmwell on 12 August. The Commander-in-Chief of Home Forces was met by Lieutenant-Colonel James Garnett of the 3rd Division. Inspections took place at Weymouth, Dorchester and Blandford.

Aircraft of the Fighter Establishment from RAF Middle Wallop landed at RAF Hurn on 13 August to re-group as the Development Section of the Air Ministry's newly formed Telecommunications Flying Unit. Another technical research team, the Blind-Landing Detachment from the Royal Aircraft Establishment at Farnborough, also moved to Hurn to become part of the new unit.

152 Squadron, based at Warmwell, lost its top man in August. Squadron Leader Derek Boitel-Gill (32) – affectionately known as 'Bottled Gull' – was killed in a flying accident. The great survivor of the Battle of Britain was among the longest serving fighter pilots. He enlisted in the RAF in 1936. Pilot Officer T. W. Pytlak (22), flying a Hurricane with 302 (Poznanski) Squadron from Warmwell, was also killed in an aviation accident on 9 September. He died four days after the Polish squadron arrived in Dorset

A cross-Channel raid from Poole was foiled by the Germans as No. 62 Commando attempted an attack on the defences of the Atlantic Wall West on the night of 12 September. Though the commandos had killed the seven-man German patrol that came across them, and retreated to their wooden boat, it was then hit by a shell. Three of the men were taken prisoner and one escaped. The others were killed, including their commander, Major Gustavus March-Phillips.

On 25 September *The Daily Telegraph* reported an anecdote about General Sir Archibald Wavell. He had been shooting partridge in Dorset on a Friday and was departing on the Saturday with a couple of brace. As he was leaving the country the following day his hosts asked the Commander-in-Chief India what he was going to do with the birds. He replied:

'Eat them myself, of course. In Teheran on Tuesday.'

Wreckage found off St Alban's Head, including parts of a wing and a wheel, belonged to Wellington X9677 of 218 Squadron which took off from RAF Marham, Norfolk, at 21.51 hours on 10 October. They were to bomb Bordeaux. Three members of the crew were picked up by the St Ives lifeboat but the other three drowned. The Cornish boat had been brought to Weymouth to supplement hard-pressed Air-Sea Rescue coverage in the Portland sector.

Sergeant-Pilot Peter Hutton Fox, flying a Spitfire of 234 Squadron from Warmwell, failed to return from an operation over Normandy on 20 October. He baled out on being shot down, became prisoner of war in Germany, and was liberated on 16 April 1945.

There was a huge explosion at Lulworth on 21 October when a Focke-Wulf 190 flew in low from the sea and crashed into the side of Bindon Hill. The pilot was killed instantly. He had apparently misjudged his position and course.

Twenty-nine-year-old mathematical genius Alan Turing, as dishevelled in wartime as during his time at Sherborne School, used his 'Turing Bombe' to crack the cipher codes of the polyalphabetic German 'Enigma' cryptographic teleprinter-enciphering machines which scrambled their military radio commands and responses. His work at the Government Code and Cipher School, Bletchley Park, Buckinghamshire, provided what Winston Churchill called the 'golden eggs' from geese that never cackled. Having shown Churchill how cryptanalysts function, Turing sent the Prime Minister a personal memorandum of demands on 21 October, stating this was vital if full efficiency was to be achieved. Churchill responded instantly, writing on the list of complaints:

'Action this day. Make sure they have all they want on extreme priority and report to me that this has been done.'

Alan Turing designed the first programmed electronic digital computer in the world. His personal behaviour would also prove to be ahead of his time, a conviction in 1952 for gross indecency with another male causing him to take his life with a cyanide-dipped

Old Shirburnian and Cambridge mathematician Alan Turing was pivotal in cracking the German Enigma codes at Bletchley Park

apple, in 1954. Sherborne School now acknowledges its greatest pupil with the Alan Turing Laboratories.

As the tonnage of 'Enigma' decrypts are reappraised – thousands were produced at Bletchley each day – it has become clear that Alan Turing was the factor, as much as radar, that enabled victory in the Battle of Britain in 1940 and would turn the tide of the Battle of the Atlantic in 1942, at a time when German U-boats were sinking ships faster than America could build them.

On Thursday 23 October, King George and Queen Elizabeth visited Bournemouth, to inspect Dominion airmen assembled at the Pavilion. Leslie Howard, the actor and film-maker, was staying at the King's Arms Hotel, Christchurch, to work on *The First of the Few*. This dramatised the legend of the Spitfire from its creation by Reggie Mitchell whose inspired designs first took to the air from Eastleigh Aerodrome, Southampton, on 5 March 1936. Prototype Supermarine monoplane K5054 was at the hands of Mutt Summers who was watched throughout by an already ailing and constantly stressful Mitchell.

A grass airfield was in keeping with the story, and RAF Warmwell was selected for the film, but Howard – who directed as well as acted – decided upon the new concrete runways of RAF Ibsley, two miles north of Ringwood. This not only fitted the image of modern aviation but gave the film-makers smoother footage – rather than tracking eight-gun fighters as they bounced across the turf. The film also starred Rosamund John and Major David Niven. Its music, the 'Spitfire Prelude and Fugue', was composed by William Walton.

Three died and eleven were injured at about 23.20 hours on 1 November, when four high explosive bombs dropped around Abbotsbury Road, Weymouth. Among the 171 damaged buildings was the Adelaide Arms which received a direct hit. Publican John Goddard had a lucky escape from death but was trapped under the rubble until after midnight. He was the Mayor of Weymouth. His rescue was effected by mayoral mace-bearer Bill Docksey, who also managed to save the first citizen's chain of office and his medals from the Great War.

The Mark-IIb Spitfires of 234 (Madras Presidency) Squadron left Warmwell on 5 November but continued to be regular visitors to the Dorset sky. Their new home was RAF Ibsley Aerodrome, where they were re-equipped with Mark-Vb Spitfires.

That day Wellington T2565, being used by the Telecommunications Research Establishment (though nominally attached to 109 Squadron, Bomber Command) had to be abandoned whilst on a signals probe for the Special Duty Flight over France. The starboard airscrew fell off and the crew baled out. It had taken off from RAF Boscombe

Leslie Howard in Christchurch to co-star with the Spitfire in the film *The First of the Few*

The Adelaide Arms in Abbotsbury Road, Weymouth, was hit by a German bomb on 1 November 1941 but landlord Mayor John Goddard had a lucky escape

Down at 18.30 hours. Contact was lost at 20.46. One of the seven crewmen, Sergeant N. W. MacKenzie, avoided capture.

The Mark-IIb 'Hurribomber' variant of the Hawker Hurricane arrived at RAF Warmwell, with 402 (Royal Canadian Air Force / Winnipeg Bear) Squadron. They carried the code letters 'AE' and had the motto 'We stand on guard'. The Hurricanes were adapted into ground attack aircraft for cross-Channel offensive sweeps over Normandy and Brittany.

The Special Duty Flight moved from Christchurch Aerodrome to RAF Hurn on 10 November to become the Research Section of the recently formed Telecommunications Flying Unit. The section embraced a wide variety of ancient and modern aircraft – 58 in all – with 23 single-engine machines and 33 twin-engine aeroplanes, and two specialised communications aircraft. Among their functions was the provision of aerial test-beds for the radar scientists of the Telecommunications Research Establishment.

The Airspeed Oxford – a trainer for the RAF – was manufactured at Somerford, Christchurch

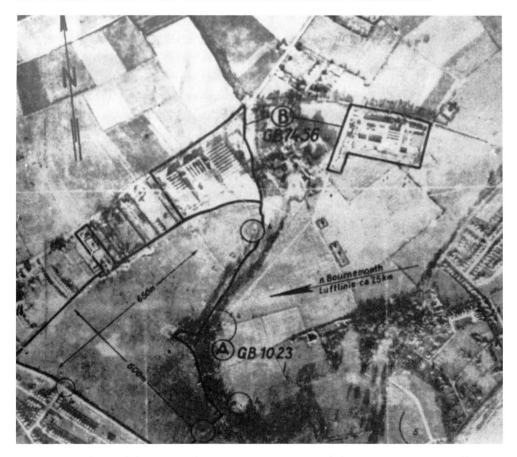

Luftwaffe reconnaissance photograph from 1941 of Christchurch Aerodrome ('A') and its 'Aeroplane Repair Works' ('B'), actually the Airspeed factory at Somerford

Two members of the Dorsetshire Regiment, on guard duty at RAF Warmwell, were killed on 11 November when a Hurricane of 32 Squadron came down out of control and crashed into the station's ammunition dump. The pilot died in the explosions that followed.

Further restrictions on omnibus services came into effect on 17 November and effectively ended the concept of a night out using public transport. The Regional Transport

'Starlight' operational at RAF Sopley with Type 15 mobile radar equipment vectoring fighters to intercept enemy aircraft

Officer ordered that no bus could leave after 21.30 hours. Fuel shortages were blamed. Paper controls were also tightened. There would be no printing of Christmas cards and it was now illegal to use paper for advertising leaflets, posters, or the production of paper handkerchiefs. Efforts to recycle materials, such as waste-paper, scrap-iron, and pig-bin collections, were intensified as the shortages become serious.

There was elation among radar scientists at the Telecommunications Research Establishment in Worth Matravers and its out-stations at Langton Matravers following a discovery made from a Blenheim bomber of the Telecommunications Flying Unit. It took off from Christchurch Aerodrome to test a theory – that it should be possible to devise an airborne radar system that can map the ground. An AI (Airborne Interception) Mark-VII radar set was installed in the aircraft and its centimetric beam tilted towards the ground. The Blenheim climbed to 8,000 feet and the aerial was then spun at 30 revolutions per minute.

As predicted, the apparatus acted as an effective 'Town Finder' for bomber navigation and returned varying signals from across the bay to the streets and roofs of Bournemouth and its adjacent landscape of pinewoods, heath, and cliffs. On receiving a report of the flight, the Secretary of State for Air, Sir Archibald Sinclair, authorised a further six such flights to 'determine whether the signals obtained . . . could be definitely associated with ground objects'.

The experiments were co-ordinated by Bernard Lovell, a young scientist in Professor Philip Dee's section at the Telecommunications Research Establishment. The ramifications of the discovery were considerable. BN (Blind Navigation) would enable bombers to find distant targets in poor weather at night. Bomber Command experienced extreme difficulty in finding the general area of German cities let alone in delivering a significant proportion of the bomb load to any specific location.

In contrast, the crew of Wellington bomber X9785 faced an ordinary naviagatonal problem when their starboard engine failed over Dorset, on the night of 16 December. They were outward bound with 218 Squadron from RAF Marham, Norfolk, on a mission to attack the German warships at Brest. Five men baled out over Chilfrome but the pilot nursed the crippled bomber down to a successful crash-landing in undulating countryside at West Milton, near Powerstock.

Beaufighter R2438 of 307 (Lwowski) Squadron from RAF Exeter force-landed at 15.15 hours on 29 December after its port engine cut out over the Blackmore Vale. The night-fighter, a Mark-IIIF Bristol-made airframe carrying Air Interception radar, landed wheels-up in a field beside Pulham parish church.. Though extensively damaged the machine was repairable. Sergeant Pilot R. Sniezkowski sustained serious internal injuries but his fellow-Pole, Sergeant Observer Z. Domanski, walked uninjured from the wreckage.

1942

Bells ring out but not for invasion

FLAK-DAMAGED Wellington IV bomber Z1312 of 458 (Royal Australian Air Force) Squadron from Holme-on-Spalding Moor, Yorkshire, crashed in the early hours of 9 January at Fifehead Magdalen. It hit power lines as it was attempting a forced-landing. The aircraft, which had its bomb-load intact, exploded on impact, killing Sergeants T. L. Brown, A. I. Hewish, P. H. Smith and D. G. Taylor. The pilot and co-pilot, however, were thrown forward through the windscreen and survived, though seriously injured.

The Wellington had been on a raid against the docks at Cherbourg where it encountered fog and flak. It was hit by anti-aircraft fire and had not been able to release its twelve 250-pound bombs. Four detonated on impact beside Fifehead Wood. The dead were buried in Brookwood Military Cemetery, Surrey. Sergeant-Pilot Garland returned to Australia but came back to Dorset to visit the crash site, at the age of 76 in September 1996, where he was given souvenir rounds from one of the bomber's machine-guns, by wartime local boy Peter Custard.

A naval experimental party demonstrated a Walrus seaplane to Sir Henry Tizard, the scientist on the advisory council of the Ministry of Aircraft Production, who visited the Telecommunications Flying Unit at RAF Hurn and its satellite station at Christchurch Aerodrome on Tuesday 13 January. No. 1425 Communications Flight, which delivered long-range aircraft from the factories to overseas bases, began to ferry out Liberators from RAF Hurn. They were flown via Gibraltar, and across the Sahara Desert, to the Middle East.

The Liberator was the RAF version of the bulky high-wing American Consolidated B-24 bomber which was powered by four Pratt and Whitney 1,200 horsepower Twin Wasp engines. This became the largest single United States aircraft type of World War Two, with 18,482 being delivered, of which the RAF received 1,889.

As a result of the Japanese attack on Pearl Harbor, bringing the United States into the war, the first American contingents arrived in Britain in January 1942, to the tune of *Lilli Burlero*, the lively Ulster Protestant march. The American soldiers found it was a shilling a meal in the British Restaurants, but for what? They were much better fed in camp and for free. The tendency to contrast the public menu with their own was counteracted by a special US Forces newsreel:

> '**The best food in England is GI, but don't keep rubbing in how good your food is . . . And don't say you've come over to win the war!'**

On 18 February, three of the capital ships of the German fleet escaped up the Channel from Brest to Kiel. They were the battleships *Scharnhorst* and *Gneisenau* and the battle-cruiser *Prinz Eugen*. *The Times* was anguished:

Channel dash of the *Gneisenau* (right), *Scharnhorst* and *Prinz Eugen* from Brest to Germany on 18 February 1942

'Nothing more mortifying to the pride of sea-power has happened in home waters since the 17th century.'

The Admiralty assumed that the break-out would start in daytime and pass southern England during darkness. The reverse happened. Admiral Ciliax left at night and sailed up the Channel in daylight, despite the valiant efforts of Commander Esmonde and his Fairey Swordfish torpedo-dropping biplanes.

Friday 27 February was a remarkable day in the secret scientific war. Having practised off Portland and at Redcliff Point, Osmington, 'C' Company of the 2nd Battalion of the Parachute Regiment embarked on an audacious air, land, and sea commando operation to Bruneval, on the coast between Le Havre and Fecamp, to bring back a German Würzburg radar apparatus. The raiding party was led by Major J. D. Frost with technical expertise being provided by Flight Sergeant C. H. Cox.

They jumped from twelve Whitley bombers and landed on a 400-feet clifftop in deep snow to take their objective with complete surprise. The equipment was dismantled for removal by landing craft from the beach below. Its components would be examined by the Telecommunications Research Establishment at Worth Matravers. Only one important piece had to be left behind, despite only ten minutes being available for the technical side of the operation.

(Left) Brunavel target of a German Würzburg radar wanted for evaluation by the Telecommunications Research Establishment in Worth Matravers

(Right) 'C' Company of the 2nd Battalion, the Parachute Regiment practising at Redcliff Point, Osmington, for departure home from the French coast after the Brunavel raid – beginning with a wait on the beach

Würzburg operated at 53 centimetres frequency (between 558 and 560 mHz) and was a coast defence radar apparatus with a range of about 40 kilometres. Its parabolic aerial had shown on air reconnaissance photographs of clifftop fields at Cap d'Antifer. The Biting Plan for the seizure of its aerial, receiver, and cathode-ray tube was organised by

(Left) Approach of landing craft

(Right) Exit begins

(Left) Retreating down beach

(Right) Leaving the beach

Combined Operations headquarters, at Anderson Manor and Poole, under Acting Admiral Louis Mountbatten.

The major concern at the Telecommunications Research Establishment (TRE) that day came from reports that RAF coastal units across the country were losing radar coverage. The fear was that Britain's entire radar network had been jammed by German counter-measures. A scientist, Stanley Hay, then drew attention to the double coincidence that the event took place during daylight, beginning in Essex and Kent, and gradually moved from east to west. To everyone's relief it was linked to the Sun – and in particular a massive sunspot eruption – rather than the enemy.

Part of Hurn Aerodrome was been set aside for No. 3 Overseas Aircraft Despatch Unit. They modified Halifax, Whitley and Stirling bombers into tow-craft and mustered a fleet of gliders for airborne landings. In 1943 the Whitleys were replaced by twin-engine Albemarles; the first British military aircraft with a tricycle undercarriage. The unit would remain at Hurn until D-Day.

'Stop at nothing' was the motto of 175 Squadron which came into existence on 3 March at RAF Warmwell. It was equipped with Mark-IIb Hurricanes and allocated the squadron code 'HH'. They took over from 402 (Royal Canadian Air Force) Squadron, which had also been flying the 'Hurribomber' on cross-Channel ground-attack missions.

German radio on 5 March reported continuous Luftwaffe attacks on England to avenge the RAF bombing of targets in Paris. Initially, the Air Ministry said it had 'nothing to report', but later in the day it was confirmed that bombs had fallen in Dorset at Smacam Down and in Delcombe Bottom.

The national press were encouraged to follow up the reports and, unusually, to publish precise locations. They failed, however, to find Smacam Down (even though it was shown on the Ordnance Survey map as a spur of open grassland near Cerne Abbas). Its only features of note were ancient earthworks. A *Daily Mail* reporter had more success with the second location:

Acting Admiral Louis Mountbatten, commander of Combined Operations, at Anderson Manor and Poole Harbour

> 'After an all-out search I tracked down Delcombe Bottom. At Milton Abbas, a picturesque downland village west of Blandford, I learned that Delcombe Bottom is a valley about a mile away. At the village inn, the Hambro Arms, at Milton Abbas, the 'blitz' was the sole conversation piece. The landlord was despondent. He had slept all night, and was slightly annoyed that the customary crowd of cronies drinking ale and smoking pipes was in its element. George Collis chuckled when told what the Germans were saying. "Armed reckernizing, were they?" he said. A companion interjected: "You know what I reckon, Jarge? We rattled 'ee wi' Warr-ships Week. There be only five 'undred of we, and we got two thousand five 'undred pounds. We 'it 'im 'aard and no mistake. 'Ee were after revenge." "'Never you mind," said Jarge. "Ee missed us and a miss be as good as a mile. One in a field, one in corn-patch, one in the 'ood, and last one – 'ee were in a bit o' field where there used to be potatoes. Not even a rabbit

was ’urt.” One bomb fell a few hundred yards from the famous Church of England faith-healing centre established at the historic landmark of Milton Abbey. But Smacam Down remained a mystery. One farm labourer said: “Reckon ’twas a farmer as told ’em that”.’

At 18.10 hours on Sunday 8 March, two Messerschmitt Bf.109s crossed Wick Hams at low level, and then machine-gunned the Quay at Christchurch. Their single victim was a woman who sat reading on a riverside bench. Josephine O’Reilly of Iford Bridge Hotel was admitted to Fairmile Hospital with a shoulder wound.

There was intense naval activity off Dorset on the night of 13 March as the destroyer HMS *Walpole* and New Zealand destroyer HMNZS *Fernie* tried with 21 motor torpedo boats and four of the larger type of motor gun boats to block the English Channel. They were attempting to prevent the passage of the Nazi raider *Schiff 28 Michel*. She slipped through, however, towards the Atlantic, with the aid of five 1,300-ton light destroyers of the 5th T-boat Flotilla (*Falke*, *Jaguar*, *Kondor*, *Iltis* and *Seeadler*) and nine minesweepers.

A new Halifax bomber – the type had just entered operational service – was delivered to the Telecommunications Flying Unit at RAF Hurn on 22 March. V9977 had been adapted by Handley Page Limited to the requirements of TRE at Worth Matravers, with a Perspex cupola covering the space which would normally house the nose gun-turret. Here the scientists installed the magnetron section of a Mark VII AI (Airborne Interception) radar set, adapted into the first prototype of a version codenamed H2S, which was being developed for ground-mapping.

The 12th Battalion of the Royal Fusiliers arrived at Christchurch in March to guard the top-secret Air Defence Research and Development Establishment, at Somerford and Friars Cliff, against the possibility of the Germans staging a retaliatory Bruneval-style commando raid. The research plant, known locally as the Air Defence Experimental Establishment, worked in conjunction with TRE at Worth Matravers and specialised in radio and radar counter-measures.

On 1 April the 2nd Battalion, the Dorsetshire Regiment, lined up along the Oxford Road at Banbury, Oxfordshire, for inspection by King George. ‘A’ Company then went through a jungle assault course in the trees above the officers’ mess. The battalion was under orders to move to Liverpool from where it sailed to Bombay.

An American B-17 Flying Fortress bomber, returning from a cross-Channel mission, made a successful emergency landing in a field opposite the thatch-roofed Baker’s Arms at Lytchett Minster. The huge aeroplane had been attempting to approach the new aero-

King George VI reviewing the 2nd Battalion, the Dorsetshire Regiment on 1 April 1942

The 2nd Dorsets preparing to depart for India and to meet Japanese invaders

drome at Hurn but lost too much height. There was considerable local commotion as people heard or spotted the B-17's descent. David Pearce (9) said:

> 'I was with a group of boys standing on the pillbox beside the railway bridge at Sterte. We saw the plane getting lower and lower and it came down on Tatchell's Holding at Charity Farm.'

The American crew congratulated their pilot on bringing them to ground outside a traditional English public house. It was a shock, however, for Mrs Joan Hooper, in the final stages of pregnancy at Tatchell's Holding. The excitement induced the birth of a healthy daughter, Wendy, delivered by midwife Margaret Gibson the following day, on 3 April 1942. Then the Americans arrived in force, by road, with outsized earth-moving machinery of an Engineer unit. They flattened the field into a runway. Another team carried out minor repairs and checks on the B-17 which was refuelled and made a smooth take-off for its home base.

Meanwhile, 20 people were killed and 56 injured as Nazi dive-bombers swept across Weymouth. Only one of their bombs hit the central area of the town but this destroyed the *Dorset Daily Echo* offices and printing works. Only a few hours earlier, new hot-metal foundry equipment was being installed, and the newspaper distributed for Maundy Thursday.

The *Dorset Daily Echo* made news at Weymouth on 2 April 1942 with the destruction of its offices and printing works

The staff returned to salvage what they could. Just one item of standing type was found and that, ironically, carried the headline 'Hitler's Nightmare!'

The 8-page paper could miss Good Friday but appeared again on Saturday 4 April, with 12,730 copies printed at Bournemouth. The Richmond Hill plant had already taken on the *Southern Daily Echo* when it was bombed out of its works at Southampton.

The next shock came from across the world. Japanese dive-bombers, coming out of the tropical sun at 13.40 hours on Easter Sunday in waves of seven, sank the cruisers HMS *Dorsetshire* and HMS *Cornwall* in the Indian Ocean. The warships were hunting for surface raiders about 300 miles west of Colombo.

The 1,100 survivors floated in clusters around two leaky whalers in which the worst of the wounded were tended. They were told by the *Dorsetshire*'s captain, Commodore A. W. S. Agar VC, to conserve their strength by making as little noise as possible and cover their heads against the

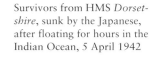

Survivors from HMS *Dorsetshire*, sunk by the Japanese, after floating for hours in the Indian Ocean, 5 April 1942

equatorial heat. Rescue did not arrive for 33 hours, after they were sighted by a 'Stringbag', a Swordfish torpedo-reconnaissance biplane of the Fleet Air Arm.

At home, on Easter Monday, ranks of Churchill tanks – the first to go into service – received their namesake's approval in Arish Mell valley on the Dorset coast. Prime Minister Winston Churchill made an Easter Monday tour of the Gunnery Wing of the Armoured Fighting Vehicles School at Lulworth Camp. Some of the Churchills had been refitted with 6-pounder guns to give them much increased fire-power. The first production version carried 2-pounders.

Churchill and Churchills with the Prime Minister inspecting the British tank bearing his name at Sea Vale Farm, Lulworth, on 6 April 1942

(Left) Churchill tanks on the Bindon Range, East Lulworth

(Right) Valentine tank, with a 6-pounder gun, at Lulworth Camp in 1942

Construction of the Southern 7000 Chain of radio direction stations for RAF bombers being largely complete, installation of technical equipment and arrays could commence. The master station (No. 7211) was on the 900-feet contour overlooking the Blackmore Vale, from Bulbarrow, where a tower of 200 feet had been erected.

Its monitor station, between Tyneham House and Lutton Farm, was named RAF Brandy Bay for the former haunt of smugglers beneath the crags of Gad Cliff. Acting as a receiving station (No. 7231), its 70-feet mast was positioned on a 450-feet ridge above South Egliston. The nearby Nissen hut accommodated three operational receivers and one spare. Slave stations for the signals network were at West Prawle near Kingsbridge, Devon (No. 7221) and on Truleigh Hill at Edburghton, Sussex (No. 7222).

Known as Gee, the system sent synchronised pulses from three locations, with the slight differences in arrival times enabling the navigator of an aircraft to determine his position. Developed by R. J. Dippy, at TRE, it was renamed the 'TR1335' series to imply a radio transmitter-receiver (rather than labelled with a 'R3000' number which would give the Germans an indication of its real purpose). Gee stations were designed and camouflaged – with extra masts – to make them look like ordinary defensive radar posts.

BELLS RING OUT BUT NOT FOR INVASION

The first version of an H2S town-finding radar set, intended for use in long distance bombers, succeeded on 17 April in giving scientists a convincing signal that could be identified as Bournemouth, detected from a height of 8,000 feet at six miles. Halifax V9977 carried the set behind a Perspex dome. That morning's flight over Bournemouth, undertaken by the Telecommunications Flying Unit for the scientists of the Purbeck-based TRE, also proved the apparatus could distinguish between the sea and outlines and land-forms of the adjoining towns of Poole and Christchurch.

Progress on several types of airborne radar had gathered pace. Five important versions were in production or being perfected:

* AI (Airborne Interception) for night-fighters;
* ASV (Air to Surface Vessel), for Coastal Command, to detect submarines surfacing to charge their batteries;
* Gee (renamed TR to indicate Transmitter Receiver, which it is not) formed a grid-lattice map from synchronised pulses on a cathode ray tube in a colour-coded pattern that shows the aircraft's location when superimposed on a chart;
* Oboe (navigation beam) to aid target marking for flare-dropping Pathfinders, as they became known;
* H2S (ground-mapping radar) for Bomber Command to bomb blind, straight through the clouds.

The latter prototype went straight into Halifax V9977 but the operator failed to find a concealed switch and the radar was not turned on. Scientists only spotted the switch after the bomber had landed back at Hurn.

The war brought about a surprise reunion for two of the brightest pupils of recent times from Weymouth Grammar School. A. E. Walkling and R. R. Head had a brief encounter in the Western Desert. Between 1928 and 1937 they had competed at Weymouth for honours with both gaining scholarships and going to Oxford. Lieutenant Alec Walkling wrote to school-friend Norman Windust in Weymouth:

'You will be amazed when I tell you who I ran into the other day. About a month after the campaign started, I was wandering the desert in a truck looking for Jerries. I spotted a large column early one morning and crept up on it as stealthily as an Army truck will allow. It was a friendly column, and out of the nearest vehicle popped a long thin figure with glasses. It was Head. I don't know which of us had the biggest surprise. It seems strange to me, but there was both of us, with more than our fair share of brains, yet we had nothing better to do than chase our fellow men around the desert.'

This would be their last meeting. Head's parents, at Queen's Street, Weymouth, heard that their son had been reported missing. As for Walkling, he went on to Burma where he was mentioned in despatches and not only survived the war but scaled his chosen profession, becoming Major-General and Colonel Commandant of the Royal Artillery, in 1974.

A radar station on the Dorset coast was lost at 08.00 hours on 14 May through natural causes when 300 feet of clifftop subsided in a landslip at Cain's Folly, Charmouth. The concrete building lies partly submerged in the lias clays in the undercliff, 75 feet below the edge, and was half visible in 1985 with its seaward side tilting upwards.

Two of the 1,300-ton craft of the German 5th T-boat Flotilla, *Iltis* and *Seeadler*, were sunk off Dorset in mid-May. They were intercepted by Portsmouth-based motor torpedo boats. The Royal Navy lost *MTB 220* during the action.

Luftwaffe ace Hauptmann Langar, the officer commanding the elite pathfinding Kampf-gruppe 100, was killed on 23 May when his Heinkel He.111 flew into a hillside in low cloud. He had been intercepted by Squadron Leader John 'Cat's Eyes' Cunningham, whose Beaufighter had been scrambled from Middle Wallop on the Hampshire Downs.

Cloud cover was dense and carried heavy rain. Langar dived in an attempt to evade the Beaufighter and then crashed into the hills near Shaftesbury. No shot had been fired.

The intruder was detected by a Type 15 radar antenna in the field near Christchurch that was designated RAF Sopley. Its tented Operations Room directed the Beaufighter, of 604 Squadron, and brought about the interception. Sopley radar station enabled fighters to operate in total darkness, as well as through cloud, and was given the code-name 'Starlight'.

The western end of Brownsea Island rocked to countless explosives in the early hours

Bournemouth's wartime reservoirs provided an emergency supply for fire-fighting

of Whit Monday morning. Pathfinder bombers had dropped incendiaries nearly on target for the new Coastal Command base, at RAF Hamworthy, and many of these landed with some high explosives in Rockley Road, Coles Avenue, and Hinchcliffe Road. Several bungalows were destroyed and five civilians killed, but fortunately for Hamworthy and Poole the fires were extinguished in time for the newly completed 'Starfish' apparatus of the Major Strategic Night Decoy to come to light across the water on Brownsea Island.

Design expertise was provided by the pyrotechnics department at Elstree Studios. The combination of wood, coal, and paraffin, plus flushes of water, produced white-hot flashes just like those of bursting bombs and lured the 55 enemy aircraft to unload 150 tons of high explosive harmlessly on to the uninhabited western extremity of the island. Only one bomb found a military target – a stray made a direct hit on Poole's Home Guard company headquarters in Lindsay Road, causing the unit's first death from enemy action, with the loss of Private W. J. Griffiths. The bombers came from the Pas de Calais and been tracked by radar to St Catherine's Point, Isle of Wight, from where they turned north-westwards.

Street-side water supply – for fighting fires caused by bombing – piped along the gutter beside Beales department store, Gervis Place, Bournemouth, in 1942

The Brownsea decoy saved Poole and Bournemouth from a total of 1,000 tons of German bombs during the course of the war.

On 25 May, the Telecommunications Research Establishment was evacuated from Worth Matravers and Langton Matravers to Malvern College, Worcestershire, because of fears that the Germans might attempt their own Bruneval-style raid on the Purbeck coast. In order to emphasise the danger, Dr. Reginald Jones and Hugh Smith arrived on the Dorset seaboard from Air Ministry Scientific Intelligence in London with revolvers ostentatiously strapped to their belts, when they came to inspect the enemy radar apparatus captured at Bruneval. About 2,000 personnel left Purbeck – ten times as many as had arrived two years before – and the associated Telecommunications Flying Unit departed from Hurn to Defford, near Worcester.

BELLS RING OUT BUT NOT FOR INVASION

RAF Hurn was transferred on 1 June from 11 Group Fighter Command to 38 Wing Army Co-Operation Command. The Air Officer Commanding, Air Marshal Sir Arthur Sheridan Barratt, inspected the aerodrome which was under the command of Group Captain Harold John Granville Ellis Proud. The station would provide transport support for the 1st Airborne Division.

An airstrip to the north of Sherborne, at Sigwells Farm, Charlton Horethorne, which had been used as an emergency landing ground, became a satellite aerodrome for the Fleet Air Arm station at Yeovilton. Flight-Lieutenant H. C. V. Jollef waited on the 600-feet limestone plateau to meet an advance party from Exeter.

Just as the Brownsea decoy saved RAF Hamworthy, the highly explosive Royal Naval Cordite Factory on Holton Heath was spared from a potentially devastating major raid, by the swift ignition of half a ton of waste shell-propellant at its dummy factory on the other side of the Wareham Channel. Inspection of the Arne decoy site on 4 June revealed 206 craters and it was estimated that 50 bombs also fell into Poole Harbour.

Early that morning the Luftwaffe returned to Hamworthy and Poole but the 50 bombers were partly thwarted by heath fires started by the incendiaries of their own pathfinders in the gorse and heather at Rocklea. These drew many of the bombers west-wards from the urban area but nearly created a different disaster.

One of the bombs on Ham Common ruptured a giant tank of 100-octane aviation fuel concealed in the old claypits at Doulting's Pier. A million gallons flowed from it and formed lakes across the wasteland as fire teams could only pray that no one dropped a match, let alone a bomb, as the whole area began to reek with fumes.

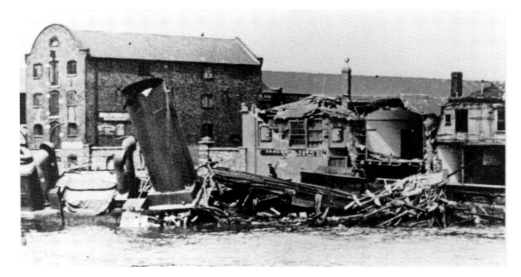

HMS *Sona*, the Royal Navy's headquarters ship at Poole Quay, hit by the Luftwaffe on 4 June 1942 (though the bomb did not explode till the 7th)

Some of the bombs did find the urban areas of Hamworthy and the densely-packed Georgian terraces of the Old Town at Poole. A grocer's shop opposite the parish church was hit, as was Yeatman's Mill on Poole Quay. Bolson's store at their Wessex Wharf shipyard was gutted, in Ferry Road, at Hamworthy. The yard manufactured twin-screw HDMLs (Harbour Defence Motor Launches) which were 72-feet vessels. There a fire-watcher, Louis Pittwood, was fatally injured. Twenty-three others had their wounds tended. Mrs Florence Diffy of Green Road and Victor Park (6) who was staying in Hamworthy, died in Cornelia Hospital.

The Royal Navy's Headquarters Ship for the port, HMS *Sona* – berthed beside Poole Quay – was sunk by a bomb. This dropped through the funnel and buried itself in the mud beneath the hull. As it did not explode – for three days – the sailors were able to escape, by scrambling up the quayside.

High explosive bombs damaged a total of 454 properties in a day-light attack on Bournemouth by Messerschmitt Bf.110 fighter-bombers on 6 June. Only one landed directly on its intended target, the railway sidings beside Southcote Road, east of the Central Station. Others dropped near St Peter's Church, on the Anglo-Swiss Hotel, and at Hill House in Parsonage Road.

Though blown off his bicycle as two bombs exploded, either side of Southcote Road, Stewart Garrett (10) jumped up and dusted himself down. An evacuee from Southampton – to escape the Blitz – he lived in a three-storey house which had been requisition as a billet in Derby Road. There his sister continued playing the piano as broken glass was held in place by a net curtain, which had been glued to the window, as an air-raid precaution. Later in the day Stewart and his mother found a metal cylinder beneath broken branches in Knyveton Gardens. This turned out to be the axle from a goods wagon in marshalling yards on the other side of Southcote Road. It had been blown over the rooftops by the force of the explosion.

Halifax V9977, which operated with the Telecommunications Flying Unit from Hurn, was lost while carrying out a secret experimental test from its new base at RAF Defford. It crashed at 16.20 hours on 7 June, in the Welsh borders, with the loss of all on board. The scientists included 38-year-old Alan Blumlein of Electrical Musical Industries, who revolutionised electronics by filing 128 electronic patents including key discoveries for multiple telephone circuitry, stereo-optical sound, 405-line television transmission, and video waveform.

They were comparing prototype H2S magnetron equipment, being used in ground-mapping radar sets, with a klystron version produced by EMI. Prime Minister Churchill had expressed concern that the magnetron is virtually indestructible, and therefore inevitably bound to fall into enemy hands if used over Germany, whereas a klystron could be destroyed.

Churchill was right. The magnetron was the only piece of equipment to survive the crash of V9977, though this and the death of Alan Blumlein were not announced until after the end of the war. In effect the H2S set had caused the loss of the Halifax. The starboard outer engine of the four-engined bomber failed after an inlet valve fractured, from metal fatigue. This engine was driving a generator to power the H2S apparatus. Rather than feathering the propeller, the crew attempted re-starting the engine, which then caught fire. Extinguishers were found to be empty. Control of the stricken aircraft was lost, at 2,500 feet, and it dropped into the Welsh hills.

On 13 June a full-scale dress rehearsal took place in Lyme Bay, with assault landings on Bridport Harbour at West Bay, to practice for Operation Rutter. The west Dorset holiday town was chosen to represent Dieppe which was selected as the target of a major raid to test German coastal defences with a view to opening a Western Front.

Lessons were learnt from the chaos that attended just about all aspects of the preparations. The attack on Bridport was privately described as 'something between a debacle and a fiasco'. Canadians troops, selected for the assault, were full of enthusiasm but lacked any experience of amphibious operations and had never faced enemy fire.

Repeat rehearsals took place on 23 June, with better results, and authorisation followed for the raid to proceed. The weather, however, refused to co-operate and two key vessels were put out of action by the Luftwaffe. As a result, Operation Rutter was cancelled, but the plan was secretly reinstated (as Operation Jubilee) and went ashore at Dieppe in August 1942.

Mustangs of newly formed 170 (Army Co-Operation) Squadron flew into RAF Hurn from Weston Zoyland, Somerset. They were to provide fast forward-reconnaissance in an Army support role and were both highly manoeuvrable and toughly armed. More Whitleys arrived from Netheravon, Wiltshire, with the redeployment to Hurn of 296 (Army Co-Operation) Squadron. Routine exercises for this and the existing Hurn-based 297 Squadron included paratroop drops over Salisbury Plain.

Coastal forces of the Royal Navy anchored and tied up around the remnants of Bournemouth Pier on 18 June. Its central section was broken in 1940 to prevent it being used by German invaders. The visiting vessels put in for running repairs before leaving for Portland. The damage to the War Programme light destroyer HMS *Albrighton* and two special gun-boats, *SGB 6* and *SGB 8*, was sustained whilst trying to stop an Axis convoy. Four German, Italian and Finnish ships were being escorted by the 1st Schnell-boot Flotilla. One of the four enemy transports was sunk for the loss by the Royal Navy of *SGB 7*.

BELLS RING OUT BUT NOT FOR INVASION

On land, the Navy's cause was championed by the HMS Dorsetshire Replacement Campaign, launched by the Earl of Shaftesbury, which aimed to double the level of War Savings in the county and raise £2,700,000 in the six months to the end of the year. Three new Bangor-class fleet minesweepers, each of 750 tons with a complement of 60, had already been funded by Dorset towns – HMS *Bridport*, *Poole* and *Lyme Regis*.

Tuesday 9 July turned into the Battle of Lyme Bay. The German 1st Schnellboot Flotilla attacked Allied Coast Convoy E/P 91 and caused the loss of 12,192 tons of merchant shipping with the sinking of the tanker SS *Pomella* and four freighters. One of the British escort vessels, the armed trawler HMT *Manor*, also went down.

The E-boats involved were *S48*, *S50*, *S63*, *S67*, *S70*, *S104* and *S109*. The success gave the Germans the confidence to mine the central part of the English Channel through the efforts of Operation Rhein and Operation Stein. The 3rd T-boat Flotilla (*T4*, *T10*, *T13* and *T14*) deposited mines through their torpedo tubes. Operation Maruren followed.

British-made Spitfires returned to Warmwell Aerodrome in July

Blenheim bomber over a ship burning in the Channel which in the early years of the war would have been another British loss

but were flown by a detachment of the 31st Fighter Group of the Eighth United States Army Air Force. A purpose-built VIP hangar was under construction at RAF Hurn to house Prime Minister Churchill's personal Liberator transport and other special aircraft. This hangar had blast-walls at the sides but was left open at each end to avoid containing the blast from any explosion. The hangar survives, plus door but no longer with blast-walls, handling millions of kilos of air-freight each year.

Two Focke-Wulf FW.190 fighter-bombers came out of a clear blue sky and made a hit and run attack on Bridport at 18.33 hours on Sunday 2 August. As they had not been detected by radar it took a couple of minutes for air-raid sirens to wail into action.

By this time the enemy aircraft had slipped in from Lyme Bay and crossed Eype Down. Machine-gun fire and explosions followed as they flew eastwards across the centre of the town. Walls, windows and roofs were blown out along the south side of West Street,

Bomb damage to the Star Hotel (right) and shop-fronts in West Street, Bridport, on 2 August 1942

87

uphill from the taxi rank, opposite the cattle market. The town was quiet, however, as licensed premises as well as the shops were closed at that time on a Sunday.

There were two fatalities from the bombs. Standing at the entrance of the Star Hotel was the landlady's son, George Hecks, on home leave from the barracks in Dorchester. His body was blown some distance across the street. Inside the building, staying as a guest, Mrs Bowerman was also killed.

The Star Hotel was badly damaged and remained closed for some time. Since John Hembrow Hecks, its popular publican, had died suddenly a year earlier, his widow, Mrs Beatrice Hecks, had been running the business.

No. 4 Commando, brought up to full strength and now fielding 1,000 men, returned to south Dorset, where it was formed in July 1940. It was preparing for the Dieppe Raid, with training at Weymouth and coastal landings at Lulworth Cove and nearby bays, in a full-scale rehearsal before being tasked to attacking the German's Atlantic Wall. A concrete mock-up was built in heathland between Bovington Camp and Gallows Hill for assault training by the commandos. Their Commanding Officer was 31-year-old Lieutenant-Colonel Simon Fraser, the 17th Baron Lovat.

A test off Portland on 6 August amplified the enemy's radar echo, from a formation of eight Defiant fighters, causing the Luftwaffe to think that a major attack was in prospect. Thirty fighters were scrambled from airfields on the Cherbourg peninsula to meet the phantom force.

Eight people were killed and 39 injured in a hit-and-run raid by the Luftwaffe that caused considerable damage in seaside Swanage on 17 August. The Westminster Bank suffered a direct hit and was destroyed. Miss Helen Muspratt's photographic studio at 10 Institute Road was badly damaged, as was Hayman's Cafe. Bombs also fell in The Narrows, destroying the southern line of the old terraced cottages that constricted the middle of the High Street, and in Chapel Lane and Church Hill. Cottages opposite the old parish churchyard were ruined and part of the tile roof taken off St Mary's parish church. There was also damage to the nearby Tithe Barn.

That day No. 4 Commando sailed from Weymouth towards a gathering point in the English Channel from which they would proceed toward the enemy shore to land just before dawn on 19 August in an attempt to breach the defences at occupied Dieppe. The purpose of the Operation Jubilee assault reconnaissance was to test the strength of the German West Wall.

Theirs would be the only completely successful operation of that bloody day, as Major James Dunning of the Commando Association reminded me at the 50th anniversary commemorations of the battalion's formation, held in Weymouth on 17 October 1990. They were given the right flank of the attack, codenamed Orange Beach, between Varengeville-sur-mer and Quiberville, where they silenced the Hess Battery.

Frenchmen offered them wine but the celebration was premature as the Canadian sector was being pinned down on the beaches and forced to take cover behind their own dead. No. 4 Commando withdrew as heroes with their Commanding Officer, Lord Lovat, being awarded the Distinguished Service Order, and decorations for his men including the Victoria Cross, to Patrick Porteous. The overall cost was high – of the 5,000 taking part, 2,700 were killed, wounded or taken prisoner.

Five people were killed and nine wounded when German bombs caused extensive damage to commercial buildings around The Square in Swanage on 23 August. The most dramatic casualty was the terracotta cow centrepiece of the facade to Swanage Dairies which was lay in pieces amid the rubble of the collapsed building. The adjoining Ship Inn also suffered considerable damage.

Nine Short S.25 Sunderland Mark III flying-boats of 461 (Royal Australian Air Force) Squadron landed in Poole Harbour from Mount Batten, Plymouth on 31 August. Squadron Leader R. C. Lovelock headed a complement of 132 men. The new base at Hamworthy was established as RAF Poole at the start of the month and renamed RAF Hamworthy only a week later.

Squadron headquarters were established on the north-eastern shore of Poole Harbour in the Harbour Yacht Club buildings at Lilliput. The Australians flew anti-submarine

Military Sunderland flying-boats operated from RAF Hamworthy

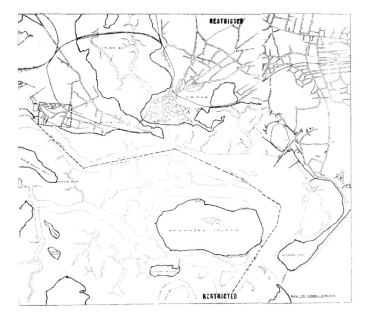

'The Trots' of Poole Harbour with flying-boat runways shown in straight pecked lines across the centre of the map and the on-shore rectangle being RAF Hamworthy

patrols in the Western Approaches and the Bay of Biscay where U-boats had been caught napping by airborne radar and were now under orders to surface only to recharge their batteries.

During August, the old tanks from the Great War that were used as pillboxes around Bovington in the anti-invasion defences of 1940 came back to life for the making of a movie, entitled *Victory*, by the Crown Film Unit. It had realistic scenes, shot on the Dorsetshire heaths at Turners Puddle and Gallows Hill, of British light tanks advancing under heavy enemy artillery bombardment in trench warfare on the Western Front, in 1918.

Captain Willie Meeke DSC completed a series of dummy attacks in Portland Harbour, using a midget X-craft submarine, the *X-3*. Launched in March 1942, the 22-ton boat was 43 feet long and had a crew of three. It could make 6 knots on the surface, and 5 knots underwater, while carrying delayed-action charges of two tons of explosive attached to each side.

The idea for these innovative craft came from Commander Cromwell Varley, a retired submariner of the Great War, who conceived the hazardous plan for miniature submarines to slip through harbour barriers and natural obstacles to lay massive charges beneath anchored enemy warships.

Veteran tanks from the Great War, filmed in action at Bovington in 1942, for the propaganda movie *Victory*

X-3 was loaded on a railway wagon in August for the first stage of its journey to an operational unit, the 12th Submarine Flotilla, established at shore-base HMS Varbel, in the Hydropathic Hotel, Port Bannatyne, on the Isle of Bute. A year later, X-craft of the 12th Submarine Flotilla would carry out Operation Source, in September 1943, and succeed in badly damaging the German battleship *Tirpitz* in her apparently secure refuge in a Norwegian fjord. Two of the Royal Navy's submariners, Lieutenant Donald Cameron in *X-6* and Godfrey Place in *X-7*, won the Victoria Cross for their part in what had been regarded at times as an impossible mission.

The undersea war received a contribution from Poole Commandos. Overnight on 2 September 1942, they surprised a German U-boat signalling station, in the Casquets Lighthouse. This stands in the English Channel eight miles west of Alderney. The attack was undertaken by No. 62 Commando, attached to Combined Operations, which was based at Anderson Manor near Bere Regis and operated from Poole Harbour.

Code-books were captured along with seven German wireless operators, who were taken completely by surprise, and found themselves in Poole at 04.00 hours on 3 September as prisoners of war. The leader of the Small Scale Raiding Force, Geoffrey Appleyard, was promoted to Major and awarded the Distinguished Service Order.

Churches were packed for a national day of prayer to mark the third anniversary of the declaration of war. Services were also held at places of work including the Bournemouth department stores of Allens and Beales.

It had taken a year, but on 9 September an idea suggested by Squadron Leader T. Pugh, was successfully put to the test with the fitting of bomb-racks to Westland Whirlwinds of 263 Squadron at RAF Warmwell. Modifications were made so that a single 250-pound or 500-pound bomb could be carried under each wing. In the trial operation two sections of Whirlwinds were turned into bombers and provided with an escort of Spit-fires, as they crossed the Channel to attack four armed trawlers between Cap de la Hague and Alderney. Two were sunk. No bomb-sight was used and the Whirlwinds dropped their loads from 50 feet, utilising delayed action fuses.

A single German bomber ignored the Bofors guns at Canford Cliffs on 11 September to come in from the bay and drop a stick of bombs that killed five people in adjoining roads at Parkstone. The dead were Revd. William Russell and his son Frank in Marl-borough Road; Mrs Winifred Phillips and her 11-year-old daughter June in Bournemouth Road; Mrs Annie Watts at Earlham Drive; and Lois Millard in Poole Road.

The Empire flying-boat *Clare*, outward bound from Poole Harbour for Bathurst, West Africa, radioed soon after take-off on 14 September to report engine trouble. Half an hour later this had become a fire and she was attempting to make an emergency landing in the English Channel to the south-west of Lyme Bay. The flying-boat, with six crew, was carrying 13 passengers. Nothing more was heard or found.

In the early hours of the morning of 17 September the body of farmworker Louis Aubrey Stickland (42) was found lying beside Chapel Lane at Piddletrenthide. He had a single gunshot wound in the chest. Stickland had enlisted with the Home Guard two months earlier. The previous evening he went to the Golden Grain Bakery for cigarettes but did not return home. His wife was unconcerned because she assumed he was having a long chat, with the baker, Frederick Davis.

Mrs Stickland did not report her husband missing until 00.30 hours. His body was found by the local magistrate, Henry Levi Green, in a spot known to the locals as Darkie Lane. It is called Chapel Lane on the map. The story unfolded later in the year.

RAF Holmsley South, with concrete runways earmarked for the Wellingtons of Coastal Command on anti-submarine patrols, was constructed across the flat expanse of heather and gorse at Plain Heath on the south-western edge of the New Forest. Work was also in progress to make a major military aerodrome on flat-topped sheep downs between Badbury Rings and the valley at Tarrant Rushton, four miles east of Blandford. Its north-south runway was to be 2,000 yards with intersecting north-west to south-east and south-west to north-east runways of 1,500 yards each. These too were of concrete.

Joe Bright, the Mayor of Poole and the man voted 'Best Baker in Britain', proudly announced that he had raised £3,600 in aid for Uncle Joe. To help Stalin's epic struggle and relieve some of the appalling suffering on the Eastern Front he worked tirelessly for the Medical Aid to Russia and China Fund which he founded. Bright's Bakery was at 117 High Street, Poole.

Levelling off runways and the rolling of relayed turf led to some changes in the usual pattern of aircraft movements at the Fleet Air Arm station near Charlton Horethorne. One of these caused a serious accident at 09.00 hours on 1 October when a Fulmar of 790 Naval Air Squadron, being moved by Lieutenant Commander Hodgson, was involved in an accident on the ground with a postman from Sherborne. W. J. John was riding a Post Office combination motor-cycle when he collided with the Fulmar, hitting the propeller, which severed his right arm at the shoulder. He was taken to the Royal Naval Hospital at Coldharbour, Sherborne, in a state of severe shock, from which he recovered.

On 7 October the Admiralty commissioned The Lake camp-site at Hamworthy and the adjoining Hamworthy Common, plus Round Island two miles away towards the opposite shore of Poole Harbour, for a new shore-base to be named HMS Turtle. It was tasked with training British, Canadian, and American crews in the handling of landing craft at sea and their use in beach assaults.

BELLS RING OUT BUT NOT FOR INVASION

On the night of 13 October, a Coastal Command aircraft spotted the German auxiliary cruiser *Schiff 45 Komet* attempting to break out from Le Havre, westwards into the Atlantic. She was being escorted by the 3rd Schnellboot Flotilla and German minesweepers. The Royal Navy proceeded to intercept them with a flotilla of Hunt-class destroyers and motor torpedo boats plus another destroyer, HMS *Albrighton*. The engagement took place five miles north of Cap de la Hague where *Komet* was sunk with the loss of all her crew. She had been hit by two torpedoes fired from *MTB 236*.

From Portland a supporting force set sail. This comprised the British destroyers HMS *Brocklesby* and *Tynedale* with the New Zealand destroyer HMNZS *Fernie* and the Polish destroyer *Krakowiak*. They tangled with the German E-boats with *Brocklesby* taking a large number of casualties though she survived the action. In a separate incident the armed trawler HMT *Jasper*, making for Portland from Dover, was sunk by German Schnellboot *S81*.

Royal Blue express coach services to London finally ceased operation on Saturday 17 October, after months of steadily slimmer timetables, as a result of the gravity of the national fuel shortages. Half of the familiar dark-blue fleet was already reserved for manoeuvres and other military uses.

Just a few coaches, however, still carried civilian passengers, as the Ministry of Transport licensed five services to run seven days a week. They were allocated 370 hours of driving time. This concession was granted because it was accepted that alternative ordinary bus services and rail facilities were less than adequate in many parts of Dorset. These were the surviving Royal Blue routes:

'Service 400. Bournemouth – Southampton. Four journeys each way of 88 minutes.

Service 402. Bournemouth – Dorchester – Bridport – Exeter. Two journeys each way of 250 minutes. Re-booking will be necessary at Dorchester as through tickets cannot be issued. The licence for the run specifies two separate stages (Bournemouth – Dorchester and Dorchester – Exeter).

Service 403. Bournemouth – Blandford – Sherborne – Yeovil. One journey each way of 136 minutes.

Service 404. Honiton – Crewkerne – Yeovil – Sherborne – Shaftesbury. One journey each way of 167 minutes.

Service 405. Bournemouth – Blandford – Shaftesbury – Trowbridge. Two journeys each way of 215 minutes.'

Fuel shortages continued after the war and the coach express service to London did not resume until 15 April 1946.

During October 1942, Weymouth's famous aviator, Wing Commander George Stainforth, was killed in a night-fighter in the Middle East. He rose to fame in 1931 when he took the world air-speed record in Schneider Trophy flights. He pushed his Supermarine S-6B round the Spithead course at an average speed of 340 mph and then raised the world's absolute speed record to 379.05 mph. Other records included flying upside-down for a duration of 11 minutes 7 seconds. He was also the RAF revolver champion.

Those living north of Bournemouth must have realised that 'something big' was about to happen from the aerial activity through the week beginning Sunday 25 October. The Army Co-Operation Squadrons left RAF Hurn en mass. Mustangs of 170 (Army Co-Operation) Squadron and the Whitleys of 297 (Army Co-Operation) Squadron departed for Thruxton on the Hampshire Downs. The other Hurn Whitleys, those of 296 (Army Co-Operation) Squadron, left for nearby Andover. Hurn was being evacuated so that it could be used as the springboard for a major overseas operation.

A halt on the railway into Egypt, at El Alamein, became the turning-point of the war from the British point of view

Hurn visitor Brigadier-General Jimmy Doolittle, world speed record holder, who commanded United States Air Forces in Europe

General Dwight D. Eisenhower led Allied forces via Hurn and Gibraltar to capture French North Africa

On the Saturday, six Boeing B-17 Flying Fortress bombers of the 97th Bombardment Group of the United States Army Air Command touched down at Hurn with a large contingent of top-ranking American officers. They were led by Lieutenant-General Dwight D. Eisenhower who was Commander of Allied Forces North-West Africa.

Eisenhower flew out from Hurn with his staff officers and a British contingent on 3 November for a conference in Gibraltar to discuss Montgomery's break-out into the Western Desert from El Alamein and the advance towards Algiers. They were aboard five of the Flying Fortress. The sixth had to abort its take-off when the undercarriage hydraulics failed. It nearly crashed into other Fortresses in the line.

The top-brass included General Kenneth Anderson, the Commander of the British 1st Army; Major-General Mark Wayne Clark, the co-ordinator of the secret moves to see whether the Vichy French would defend North Africa; and Brigadier Lyman Lemnitzer (though he was been left behind in the disabled aircraft). Colonel Thomas J. Davis and Dr Freeman Mathews, a political adviser, were airborne.

Their transit to Gibraltar, off Cape Finisterre and down the coast of Portugal to Cabo de Sao Vicente, was codenamed Operation Cackle. Eisenhower's pilot was Major Paul Tibbets. He would end his and the world's war by flying B-29 *Enola Gay*, named for his mother, in the first operational use of the atomic bomb, on Hiroshima in August 1945.

Brigadier Lemnitzer and Brigadier-General Jimmy Doolittle, the aviator who set the world air-speed record in 1932, flew from Hurn to Gibraltar aboard the repaired sixth Flying Fortress on 4 November. Doolittle was Commander of United States Air Forces in North Africa. The pilots were John C. Summers and Thomas F. Lohr.

A total of 39 American C-47 Dakota transports of 31 Wing Troop Carrier Group of the 12th United States Army Air Force also assembled at Hurn. Their crews were briefed for the planned landing in North Africa. More aircraft followed.

The great news from General Bernard Montgomery, the desert Commander of Britain's 8th Army, was that Erwin Rommel's Afrika Korps was in full retreat. The battleground at El Alamein took its name from a coastal railway halt only 60 miles from Alexandria. Rommel had been poised to attack the Nile delta of Lower Egypt.

National jubilation continued. Hearing that the 8th Army has taken 30,000 prisoners, following the Battle of Alamein, Prime Minister Winston Churchill told the country to celebrate in a week by ringing church bells – the first time they were heard since the outbreak of war. Until this moment their sound would have warned of German invasion. He said he would like them to have rung that Sunday but there was insufficient time to mobilise decommissioned campanologists.

The prisoners in Egypt included nine generals. Only the rains in the previous two days had saved the enemy from utter annihilation. General Montgomery was to be knighted.

There remained a psychological restraint. Rommel's reputation inhibited what should have turned into a British stampede across the desert. The reality was even better than anyone could have predicted, for by now there was nothing that could have stopped them – on 9 November 1942 the Afrika Korps would not only be down to ten fighting tanks but lacked sufficient petrol to field even this number in combat.

That weekend – a week before the bell-ringing – a combined British and American force of 107,000 men landed across French North Africa at Casablanca, Oran, and Algiers. Operation Torch was under the overall command of Lieutenant-General Eisenhower and had 500 transport craft that were shepherded by 350 naval vessels.

Back home, rounding off Operation Cackle, 51 Dakota troop transports returned empty to RAF Hurn, where debriefings were attended by Major-General Frederick Browning, General Officer Commanding 1st British Airborne Division. A total of 180 transport aircraft passed through Hurn during the build-up for the operation. They included 61 Boeing B-17F Flying Fortress bombers. Operation Cackle, the Hurn-Gibraltar air ferry service, was successfully completed without a single casualty.

In deepest Dorset there were developments in the investigation of the Piddletrenthide homicide. Frederick Davis was charged with the murder of a fellow villager, Louis Stickland, on the night of 16 September. Then, on Friday 13 November, police exhumed the

BELLS RING OUT BUT NOT FOR INVASION

remains of the accused man's 32-year-old wife. Freda Davis died in August with an illness described as ulcerative colitis. Her coffin was removed to the County Hospital, Dorchester, where it was opened for an autopsy by Sir Bernard Spilsbury, the chief Home Office pathologist. The accused man watched at the graveside as it was lifted and soil samples were taken. Sir Bernard found no evidence of foul play.

Seven aircrew died on 25 November when Mark II Lancaster DS653 crashed at Sturminster Newton while on a long-distance proving flight from RAF Foulsham, Norfolk. It came over a hedge 'three elms high' and exploded in the air behind haulage contractor Harry Turk's yard, near the Red Lion Inn, beside the main road at Newton.

Aircraft cannon-fire could be heard incessantly on the heathland north of Poole, in the vicinity of Fleet's Corner, but the noise came not from the sky but the ground. The local munitions factory, in Soper's Lane at Creekmoor, made 20-millimetre Oerlikon machineguns. These were being fitted to the latest version of the Spitfire and other fighters. Production continued around the clock and test-firing had to be carried out every day.

The German 5th Schnellboot Flotilla, comprising *S81*, *S82*, *S115* and *S116*, attacked two British convoys in the English Channel on 3 December. One was in the area off Bournemouth and the Isle of Wight and the other in the vicinity of Start Point and Lyme Bay. In the latter skirmish a 1,050-ton War Programme escort destroyer, 1941-built HMS *Penylan*, was sunk though 115 members of her crew were rescued. A freighter was also lost.

Barnes Neville Wallis, assistant chief designer at the aviation section of Vickers-Armstrongs, flew on 4 December from their Weybridge works in Surrey to the Chesil Beach Bombing Range. He was in Wellington BJ895, code letter 'G' for George – an aeroplane he designed – and acted as the bomb aimer when the firm's Chief Test Pilot, Captain Joseph J. 'Mutt' Summers of Spitfire fame, came in low over the flat waters of The Fleet lagoon between the offshore pebble bank and the inshore coast of Langton Herring and Abbotsbury. Captain R. C. Handasyde acted as the observer.

Two steel spheres were dropped, with the hope that they might bounce along the surface of the water, but both burst upon impact. Neither carried explosives. The second attempt, on 15 December, also failed. It was decided to try again after Christmas.

Portland's emergency of the year began at 11.00 hours on Sunday 13 December 1942 but had nothing to do with the war. For the sea had started to seep through the pebbles of the Chesil Beach at Portland. By noon the first waves were splashing over the top. Initially a shallow layer of water spread across Victoria Square but it soon surged to a depth of over five feet. The postbox was almost totally covered and the mail floated out on the tide.

More than 100 homes in Chiswell were inundated as both the rail and road links between Portland and the mainland were dislocated. The stout stone wall beside the beach road was reduced to rubble at many points and the railway embankment breached for several yards. Sleepers were swept away and the rails buckled. The water also put the island's Gas Works out of action. A slimy trail of mud, clay, shingle and boulders lay across the low-lying parts of Chiswell. Many of those rendered homeless were told their ruined cottages would be demolished.

Portland branch of the Women's Voluntary Service swung into action with hot dinners, bedding and clothes – help comes fast when there is a war on – and by evening the extensive damage caused by chest-deep water to the Cove House Inn had been cleared sufficiently for it to open punctually at seven o'clock. England's motto was business as usual. In Portland defiance extended to the older enemy – the sea.

The Workshop of the Gunnery Wing of the Armoured Fighting Vehicles School at Lulworth Camp was devastated on 14 December in a surprise attack by two German fighter-bombers. The first one passed over the camp without incident but the second dropped a 1,800-kilogram high explosive bomb. It landed at the road junction at the edge of the camp. Though it embedded itself in the concrete, leaving several feet of casing and fins standing in the air, it failed to explode.

Then the second aircraft returned low across the camp and raked the Workshop with 20-mm cannon fire. The welder, Sergeant Jack Stevens, was fatally wounded in the head, and three other soldiers were injured. The building was an utter shambles. The aircraft had come from the east, across the Tank Park, and then turned south-west, disappearing over Lulworth and out to sea.

Devastation beside and behind East Street, Bridport, from a German air raid on 16 December 1942

A Dornier Do.217 bomber swept low over Poole Quay at lunchtime on 16 December and dropped a stick of five bombs. They fatally injured 14-year-old William Matthews and a member of the Home Guard, George Davis, who was working at Poole Iron Foundry in Thames Street. There were casualties from other blasts, at the Gas Works, in Barbers Piles, and at Newman's Shipyard. A worker died as a result of the latter blast. The fifth explosion sank a Royal Navy harbour patrol vessel, at its mooring, and killed the only rating aboard.

The air-raid sirens also wailed in Bridport that lunchtime as a single Dornier Do.217 approached the town. It had been detected by radar and engaged by the eight 40-mm Bofors guns of 439 Light Anti-Aircraft Battery, which opened up after the German bomber emerged from the clouds and crossed the coast at Cogden Beach. A total of 33 rounds were fired as it turned north-westwards to circle Bridport at 1,000 feet.

It then approached from the west, dipping to 600 feet, and dropped four 500-kilogram bombs along East Street. The first fell into the entrance of the Westminster Bank at 22 East Street. It failed to explode but nearly £1,000 in banknotes spread out into the street. Nearly all the missing money was recovered and returned to a doubly-relieved manager, Herbert Langdon, as the bomb was defused.

The second bomb fell to the south, into gardens, behind East Street and King Street. The third hit buildings between Nos. 92 and 102 East Street, where it killed two men and a child, and left 16 people injured. The fourth bomb exploded in the meadow north-east of East Bridge. The bomber then continued south-eastwards – machine-gunning Walditch

as it went – before gaining height and turning south at Abbotsbury to cross the Chesil Beach and head for home.

Bridport's Home Guard

Sergeant-Pilot Marcel Fussell (20) of Monmouth Road, Dorchester, was been killed when his Lancaster bomber was shot down in error, by anti-aircraft gunners over Cleveland while returning from minelaying to RAF Holme-on-Spalding, on the night of 17 December 1942. Shortly before he died he wrote about Came Wood – autobiographical, though presented in the third person – prophetically appreciating Winterborne Came 'for the last time, for tomorrow he was to leave his native life, his home, the fields and woods, where he had spent his life as a boy . . . to join the Air Force and serve his country'. At the top of the paper he had written one word: 'Farewell.'

As with Portland earlier in the month, the sea again showed its teeth at Swanage on 21 December when the Free French Navy's gunboat *Chasseur* underestimated the tide-flow and rough waters off Durlston Head. It capsized and sank.

For the nation as a whole, it seemed like a real Christmas for the first time since 1938, despite widespread shortages. First to celebrate the Battle of El Alamein, and now for their traditional purpose, the country was blessed with a rare sound. Notably, the bells of Christchurch Priory were put through their paces. It was an unusual and joyful treat, not that their silence over previous years had been unwelcome – had they tolled, it would have been to warn of German invasion.

New Year's Day at Poole belonged to Sergeant William Hanbury who was manning a waterside searchlight post. He illuminated a Dornier Do.217 bomber as it came at low level across the sea and sprayed it with his Lewis machine-gun. The pilot veered away but struck a gasometer and lost control and crashed into Poole Harbour. Another raider was more successful. Its bomb destroyed Bradford's store on Poole Quay which had just been completely rebuilt after being hit on Whit Sunday.

The year ended with an outcome in the trial for murder of Piddletrenthide baker Frederick Davis. Mr Justice MacNaughton, said there was a matter of real doubt for the jury to consider; as he put it to them that the defendant's story might be true. Frederick Davis maintained that he had been at home with Louis Stickland at the Golden Grain Bakery, examining a loaded gun, which misfired and discharged a single shot into Stickland's chest:

> 'When I found I had killed my best friend I was frightened. I was afraid of being found in the house with a dead man. On the impulse of the moment I moved the body.'

After being out for only 45 minutes the jury returned to the Assize Court at Winchester with their verdict: 'Not guilty.'

1943

Bombing bounces back across the water

THE BOMBING offensive intensified through 1943 but was now in the other direction, across Germany from the 'Happy Valley' of the industrial Ruhr to 'the Big City' – Berlin. Bomber Command dropped 45,561 tons of bombs (plus 6,367 tons of mines) in 1942. That became 157,457 tons for 1943 (plus 9,136 tons of mines).

Dorset's had an enabling role in the background science to pinpointing targets and the initial preparations for what turned into the most spectacular single raid of the Second World War. It had a lasting impact on morale and lives on as a legend out of all proportion to its strategic importance. Daring to be brave paid off towards winning the war but not personally for Sir Arthur Harris, Commander-in-Chief Bomber Command, who was seen in retrospect as too ruthless both in terms of the devastation to German cities and the cost of 55,513 deaths to British air-crew.

At the time, however, this surge in the bombing campaign received acclamation from the vast majority of the British public as legitimate retaliation for the Luftwaffe's blitz of British homes. Harris drove a powerful old car through the Black-out, from command bunker at High Wycombe, to RAF headquarters at Uxbridge, and the War Office in Whitehall. One night a policeman stepped out in front of him in the Great West Road:

'If you keep driving like that, sir, you will kill someone.'

Arthur Harris, at the constable's age, had been junior bugler in the 1st Rhodesian Regiment fighting in German West Africa in 1914. He replied:

'Young man, I kill hundreds of people every night of the week.'

Harris felt underestimated and was scathing about the effectiveness of the Air Ministry's 'huge public relation department', peopled with 'those who knew very little of the press and even less about air matters'. Secrecy and security were excuses for not telling the country that the RAF as a whole 'was sinking more submarines than the Navy'. On its own Bomber Command sank more German naval ships than the Royal Navy. One particular raid, however, did capture media, public and top-brass attention at the time, and has become a lasting legend of book and film.

It was the brainchild of aircraft designer Barnes Wallis, who worked on a freelance basis at weekends, outside the official Ministry of Aircraft Production's armament programme. That he was able to put it into operation was through Harris's approval and enthusiasm of Ralph Cochrane, Air Officer Commanding No. 5 Group Bomber

BOMBING BOUNCES BACK ACROSS THE WATER

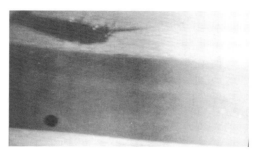

Command at Grantham, who gave the task to Guy Gibson and his Lancasters of 617 Squadron. The practical part of the story had started in Dorset in 1942 and resumed on Saturday 9 January.

In the third bouncing-bomb test, two more steel spheres were dropped by Wellington BJ895, from Vickers-Armstrongs works at Weybridge, on the Chesil Beach Bombing Range. Once again the tests were a failure. Of he six dummy bombs, five fragmented on touching The Fleet lagoon, and the other was incorrectly released and hit the land.

Wallis's bomb bouncing on The Fleet

One of the Barnes Wallis experimental devices (resembling a steel wheel filled with concrete) serving as a mooring at Langton Hive Point, Langton Herring

Overnight, Barnes Wallis carried out modifications to another of his prototypes at Warmwell Aerodrome. The aviation firm's Chief Test Pilot, Captain Joseph J. 'Mutt' Summers then took it in the Wellington, heading south-westwards for their fourth day of low-level drops over The Fleet beside the Chesil Beach Bombing Range, on the coast at Langton Herring.

This time the boffin and his team were jubilant. For the first time their dummy bomb, which had been

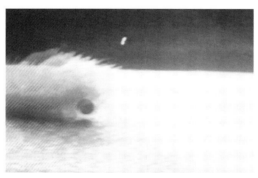

The prototype sphere ploughing through the water

strengthened, skimmed the lake-like surface of the lagoon. It spun for 50 feet and then shattered. Despite that, the principle had been proved in a eureka moment:

'It works!'

The team returned the following weekend during which refined versions of the device achieved 13 bounces on Saturday and 20 on Sunday. The latter achievement was followed by an evening spectacular in which the Wellington returned from Warmwell, turned over the sea and came along The Fleet to drop a concrete-filled bomb which not only proceeded to bounce but successfully jumped a boom simulating the wall of a dam.

On 5 February, dropped from the bomber at 300 miles per hour, a wooden version bounced 4,000 feet. Full-weight concrete-filled prototypes were tested in March – to protests that they caused distress at Abbotsbury Swannery – and the operational outcome followed in May.

As with upsetting the swans, showing wartime sensitivity, there was environmental angst that emergency ploughing of grasslands for grain production would cause the loss of public footpaths. The Rights of Way Committee of Dorchester Rural District Council expressed concern:

> 'With regard to the temporary ploughing up and diversion of rights of way consequent upon the service of directions under the Cultivation of Lands Order, the committee were extremely anxious that, during hostilities, the existence of rights of way should not be lost, and their chief anxiety was lest at the cessation of hostilities the formerly existing rights be not restored to the public.'

Dorset's county savings campaign, through the War Loan scheme, to raise enough money to buy the Royal Navy a cruiser to replace HMS *Dorsetshire* was well ahead of its original £2,750,000 target. By mid-January it had reached £3,057,703.

Lindbergh Road, a short street a stone's throw from Castle Lane in the suburb of Moordown, Bournemouth, had its name changed. This was chosen originally as a tribute to the pioneer aviator Colonel Charles Augustus Lindbergh whose *Spirit of St Louis* had just made the first solo non-stop crossing of the Atlantic in 1927. By the middle of the war, however, the memory has soured, with Lindbergh expressing pro-Nazi sentiments. Bournemouth town councillors therefore decided to re-name it Franklin Road – honouring the United States President, Franklin Delano Roosevelt.

Halifax DT684 from RAF Holmsley South on the edge of the New Forest, faltered shortly after take-off at 13.30 hours on 24 January. It made two circuits of the aerodrome and was 15 minutes into a transit flight to Talbenny, Haverfordwest, when it lost height over Wimborne and descended towards parkland beyond the town. The bomber, belonging to 58 Squadron, crashed 200 yards north-north-east of Kingston Lacy House. Its five crewmen were killed and a terrified stag jumped through a ground floor window at the elegant seat of landowner Ralph Bankes.

Bomber Command used H2S airborne radar sets, operationally, for the first time on the night of 30 January. They were deployed in a raid over Hamburg and enabled Pathfinder flares to be dropped on their target. The need for this apparatus had been apparent since of the night of 9 March 1942 when Bomber Command, in its Chief's words, 'attacked Hamborn in mistake for Essen'. Sir Arthur Harris enthusiastically backed the development of H2S – promised for the autumn of 1942 – which took its name from the chemical formula for the obnoxious gas hydrogen sulphide, because Churchill's chief scientific adviser, Professor Frederick Lindemann, hearing of it from the Telecommunication Research Establishment, said:

> 'It stinks that we haven't thought of it before!'

The invention was the product of Group 8, working from a Nissen hut in the grounds of the Establishment's eastern out-station, Leeson House, at Langton Matravers.

In an odd coincidence – given the importance of the observation in terms of contemporary weapons development – German bombs were the first described as having been caused to 'bounce'. This was through the altitude and speed at which they were dropped when fighter-bombers carried out a hit and run raid on Swanage on 3 February 1943. The censor, knowing nothing of the significance of this statement, allowed it to be printed.

In this daylight attack, Focke-Wulf FW-190s came in low across the town from the hill to the south, releasing their bombs as they cleared the High Street. One crashed through the entire length of the Congregational Church, leaving its tail-fin in the roof, before leaping out from the end wall and exploding down the slope in a disused Anglican graveyard. The nearby Methodist Church was also put out of use for the remainder of the war.

BOMBING BOUNCES BACK ACROSS THE WATER

The roof was lifted off the parish church and its windows blown out. Four people were killed. Bricklayer Reuben Churchill (70) was repairing previous bomb damage in Chapel Lane. Miss Nina Hoy (19), a visitor, was walking along the street. Mrs Winifred Swaine and Miss Florence Turner were at home.

A week later, the Officer Commanding Troops at Blandford Camp, Colonel Harold Woodhouse of the local brewing firm, died from a heart attack induced by the exertion and stress caused by a stick of German bombs. A single bomber attacked the camp where the only blast damage was to a cookhouse. Another bomber, a Dornier Do.17, reached South Buckham Farm, Beaminster, where it was shot down by Wing Commander Rupert Clarke in a Beaufighter of 125 (Newfoundland) Squadron from RAF Fairwood Common, Glamorgan.

Offshore, from 24 to 28 February, the 3rd Schnellboot Flotilla harried a Channel convoy in Lyme Bay and onwards between Portland and the Isle of Wight. Two of the escorts protecting Convoy CHA172 were sunk – the armed trawlers HMT *Harstad* and HMT *Lord Hailsham* – as well as the 4,858-ton freighter *Modavia* and a new tank landing craft.

On land, rifle-range shooting by the 2nd Special Services Brigade on Canford Heath was under the supervision of the author Evelyn Waugh as Staff Officer to Acting Admiral Louis Mountbatten, Commander of Combined Operations, with country house head-quarters at Anderson Manor, near Bere Regis. The brigade also trained with landing craft in assaults on Brownsea Island and Shell Bay and Studland beach which were being cleared of their anti-invasion scaffolding and mines.

The previous year, Waugh published *Put Out More Flags* and *Work Suspended*, but the confinement and constraints of war now proved conducive to turning from sophisticated satire to suave sensuality. The result, *Brideshead Revisited*, appeared in 1945 and Waugh turned his experiences with the Royal Marines into the *Sword of Honour* trilogy.

Such was the growing sophistication of this Second World War that Exercise Spartan was marked by the appearance of the 'first daily newspaper of its kind to be printed specially for the purpose of a military exercise in this country'. It covered the invasion of southern England by the British Expeditionary Force (with the underlying premise that southern England represented northern France). 'On to Eastland,' the headline put it:

> 'We are not on the defensive; we are passing to attack, but if we carry the Spartan determination into attack, then the battle will be won.'

This unusual newspaper was 'Not to be published'. It carried a reminder that participants were not to play in the vicinity of RAF radar stations which were waging the real war:

> 'All vehicles, especially armoured fighting vehicles, should avoid operating, or coming to rest within 400 yards of RAF wireless stations. The RAF, you know, will probably be engaged with the real enemy and we want to avoid interfering with their functional efficiency.'

Blandford Camp commandant Colonel Harold Woodhouse died of a heart attack during an air raid on 10 February 1943

(Left) Wing-mounted 20-mm Hispano cannon being re-armed on a Typhoon of 257 Squadron at RAF Warmwell

(Right) Squadron Leader Ronnie Fokes (left) and his Typhoon pilots of 257 Squadron at RAF Warmwell on 13 May 1943

(Left) Typhoon Mark 1B and pilot at RAF Warmwell

(Right) Whirlwind P7094 'Bellows' of 263 Squadron at RAF Warmwell with Flying Officer J. P. Coyne from Manitoba

On 8 March, E-boats failed to ambush a coastal convoy off Devon and escaped eastwards pursued by the Polish destroyer *Krakowaik* until she had to pull into Poole to refuel. Six-inch coast defence batteries then opened up from Brownsea Island, Hengistbury Head, and Mudeford, aided by 3.7-inch dual anti-air and anti-ship emplacements and the 40-mm Bofors anti-aircraft guns along the Bournemouth cliffs. There were German losses in Poole Bay. Two bodies and four survivors were brought to Mudeford Quay by the picket-boat *Robert T. Hillary*, a former lifeboat crewed by the Royal Navy Volunteer Reserve.

(Left) Though carrying the name of Flight-Lieutenant H. K. Blackshaw, Whirlwind 'Bellows' was loaned for the day to Flying Officer J. P. Coyne – who had just been awarded the Distinguished Flying Cross – at RAF Warmwell

(Right) Whirlwind P7094 'Bellows' at RAF Warmwell with pilots in 263 Squadron from around the Empire – (left to right) Flight-Lieutenant E. C. Owens (Adjutant), Squadron Leader G. B. Warnes (Commanding Officer), Flight-Lieutenant H. K. Blackshaw (Flight Commander), Sergeant S. D. Thyagarajan (from India), Flying Officer C. P. King DFM (West Indies), Flight-Sergeant F. L. Hicks (Australia) and Flying Officer J. P. Coyne DFC (Canada)

A Royal Artillery officer fouled his parachute on the airframe of a Dakota in a jump that went tragically wrong on 18 March. He found himself hanging from the aircraft and the pilot headed for the South Coast and the nearest area of calm sea. He chose Poole Harbour and circled at 1,000 feet over the Wareham Channel before coming in low, to within 50 feet of the harbour, at which point the soldier dropped off. Tragically it was to no avail as the gunner died on impact with the water. A Hurricane pilot was luckier when he crashed off Green Island and was picked up by the Air-Sea Rescue launch *Commodore*.

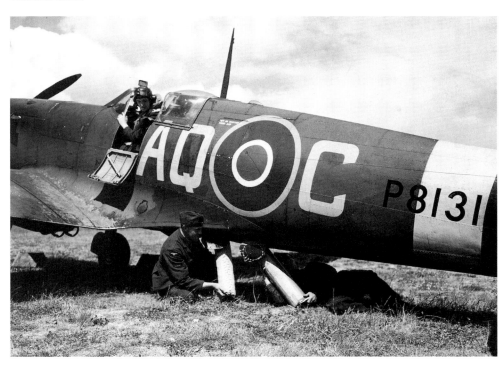

Air-Sea Rescue Spitfires operated from RAF Warmwell, with P8131 belonging to 276 Squadron

BOMBING BOUNCES BACK ACROSS THE WATER

The harbour's next drama occurred at 20.55 hours on 21 March. Flight-Lieutenant Manger was leaving RAF Hamworthy with Sunderland flying-boat T9111 of 461 (Royal Australian Air Force) Squadron. He began lifting off from the 'Trots' – as sea runways are called – when he lost power. The flying-boat careered into the mud-flats of Poole Harbour and was a total loss. Manger and his eleven crewmen were able to clamber free and stagger to the shore with only superficial injuries.

There was another mishap was on the 23rd. Having successfully returned to Poole Harbour on the last leg of a trip from Lagos, Nigeria, BOAC Catalina DA took off for a training flight. Everything was routine until her second homecoming of the day. This turned into a disaster. The flying-boat ploughed into a dense raft of flotsam and crumpled into a mass of wreckage with the loss of three crewmen.

Overseas, at the end of the month, the siege of Malta was lifted and the 1st Battalion of the Dorsetshire Regiment sailed for Egypt. They were welcomed at Fayid by General Sir Bernard Montgomery.

Burmese pilots serving with 257 Squadron at RAF Warmwell included Pilot Officer M. H. Yi from Pegu and Pilot Officer T. Clift from Shan States

> 'This morning I have seen some magnificent soldiers. These fine Regular battalions who have been shut up in Malta, and have now joined us, will be an asset to the 8th Army.'

Springtime in Bournemouth saw rabbits replacing exotic birds in aviaries at the Pleasure Gardens. Parks department staff began supplying bunnies to British Restaurants in the town though there was reluctance at putting rabbit pie on the menu. Likewise, throughout the suburbs, animal husbandry took over where the tedium of spade-work caused relapses into boredom for those who reluctantly responded to C. H. Middleton's *Dig for Victory* wireless broadcasts. Chicken and even the occasional pig now rooted around beneath rabbit hutches. From cock-crow to sunset, Bournemouth resonated with sounds of the farmyard. There was also a revival of the Victorian allotment movement. Gardeners took over open spaces, bomb sites and building plots, and there, at least, Middleton's words were heeded:

> 'These are critical times, but we shall get through them, and the harder we dig for victory the sooner will the roses be with us again.'

Tiring of the usual pranks, such as swapping over householders' gates and front-door mats, some Bournemouth-bound schoolboys played a more contemporary wheeze on their mates this All Fools Day. They spread the rumour around the bus that sweets and chocolates had been removed the food ration and would no longer require coupons. 'I bet dozens of chaps will run into the shops,' said the joker. He was proved correct.

Repainted with the white and blue roundels of the South-East Asia theatre, two BOAC Catalina flying-boats left Poole Harbour for Trincomalee, Ceylon. Catalinas FM and FL were seconded to the RAF (and survived to become peacetime flying-boats *Altair* and *Vega*). Then 461 (Royal Australian Air Force) Squadron left RAF Hamworthy and took their Sunderland flying-boats to Pembroke Dock in South Wales. They were replaced at Poole by military Catalinas of 210 Squadron.

On 21 April the United States Coastguard Service vessel *Apache*, bound for Cowes from Boston, Massachusetts, was forced into the River Avon at Christchurch for repairs after hitting a mine in the English Channel. On the night of the 27th, a German VJ submarine-chaser, *140Z*, was sunk by the Hunt-class destroyers of the Royal Navy's main coast protection flotilla, off St Alban's Head, whilst escorting Axis Convoy code 37K/MS.

May Day saw elements of the first massed United States Air Force daytime bombing raid against Germany crossing Dorset on their way to the Channel. The Royal Observer Corps log at Dorchester records:

Firemen in Newland, Sherborne, where blitzed buildings from 1940 provided an authentic setting for Exercise Demon in May 1943

(Left) Mopping up German resistance in Exercise Demon at Sherborne (genuine uniforms, apart from wellies instead of jackboots, and broad-Darzet spoken)

(Right) Realistic casualty with a detached eye (courtesy the butcher) in Sherborne's Exercise Demon on 9 May 1943

'09.30 hours. 20 Liberators spotted south-west. 10.45 hours. 47 Fortresses flying south.'

The aircraft returned individually through the afternoon. The Observer Corps, incidentally, had been awarded the 'Royal' cachet on 11 April 1941.

Bomb-damaged Newland in Sherborne, one of the streets blasted by the Luftwaffe on 30 September 1940, provided a realistic setting for Exercise Demon on 9 May. Spectators watched from rows of seats on the rise that looks down towards Castleton as troops, firemen, ARP wardens, and the Women's Voluntary Service practised their crafts – from street warfare to the arrival of WVS tea urns.

Time for tea with the arrival of the Women's Voluntary Service van (right) in Newland, Sherborne, during Exercise Demon on 9 May 1943

Halifax bomber DG390 of 295 Squadron crashed on 16 May whilst flying from RAF Hurn to nearby RAF Holmsley South. Only a mile short of its destination, at Bransgore, it dived to starboard from 1,200 feet and two of the crew were killed on impact. The third crewman, Canadian Flying Officer D. J. Smith (21), was dragged out of the wreckage but died in Boscombe Hospital. Another Halifax, towing a Horsa glider, was lost with its crew in a crash near Fordingbridge.

The RAF's presence in Dorset doubled its capacity on 17 May. An advance party took control of the aerodrome at Tarrant Rushton (henceforth RAF Tarrant Rushton) as part of Army Co-Operation Command, through No. 38 Wing, though the aerodrome was not yet operational. The Wing was responsible for training aircrew in an Army airborne-support capacity.

That day it was Bomber Command and the nation as a whole that had something to celebrate. Operational versions of the bouncing-bombs that were first tested in Dorset had been dropped overnight by Lancasters of 617 Squadron, to breach the Möhne and Eder dams in the Ruhr. Air Marshal Sir Arthur Harris recalled that he:

> '. . . rang up Washington, where Churchill and Portal were at the time, to give them the news. The telephone personnel seemed never to have heard of the White House, and there was some little difficulty. When I did get through I was intercepted and asked for an assurance that the person I was calling was reliable. I don't know whether she was persuaded that Winston Churchill came into that category, but I got through to Portal in the end and told him that two dams had gone.'

(Left) Dam-busting outcome for the bouncing bomb tested in Dorset, taken to the Möhne Dam by Lancasters of 617 Squadron

(Right) The Ruhr floods from the Mohne Dam – hit precisely in the middle – on 17 May 1943

Eight of the 19 Lancasters failed to return. The main aim had been to cause a shortage of water for industrial purposes in the Ruhr, rather than sweeping everything away in a flood, which is how we tend to remember the exploit. Not that there were many happy farmers in Kassel when 330 million tons of water spread across their fields. Several hundred Russian prisoners-of-war were among the 1,294 people who drowned.

Psychologically, and as a momentous example of what could be achieved by a defiant combination of personal initiative and precision flying, it will retain pre-eminence among the achievements of aerial warfare. Wing Commander Guy Gibson DSO, DFC was awarded the Victoria Cross.

Sunday 23 May was a very different day with 101 people being killed in Bournemouth's worst air-raid. Beales department store was reduced to a burnt-out shell. West's Picture House and the former Shaftesbury Hall in Old Christchurch Road were destroyed. The Central Hotel in the Square was in ruins. Facing, it drapers Bobby and

Beales of Bournemouth burning, with its clock having collapsed into Old Christchurch Road, after the lunchtime raid of 23 May 1943

Burnt-out Beales (left) and the flat roof of J. J. Allen's store (right), after bombing on 23 May 1943, from St Peter's Church

Blown-out frontage of Bobby's drapery store in The Square, Bournemouth, May 1943

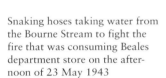

Snaking hoses taking water from the Bourne Stream to fight the fire that was consuming Beales department store on the afternoon of 23 May 1943

(Right)The biggest loss of life on 23 May 1943, including more than 24 Canadian and other Empire airmen, was in the collapsed Hotel Metropole at the Lansdowne, Bournemouth

BOMBING BOUNCES BACK ACROSS THE WATER

Co were shattered by blast damage; the omnibus standing area beside the Bus Station in Exeter Road covered in glass – from 25 Hants and Dorset buses that lost all their windows – Punshon Memorial Church, on Richmond Hill, ripped apart; and the Metropole Hotel at the Lansdowne collapsed. Shamrock and Rambler coach depot in Holdenhurst Road was devastated.

Bombs also fell into residential areas at Bethia Road, Cotlands Road, Dean Park Road, Drummond Road, Howeth Road, Lansdowne Road, Vale Road, Queen's Park South Drive, and between Pokesdown and Iford Bridge. Of the 3,481 buildings that were damaged about 40 had to be demolished.

Seventy-seven civilians were killed and the bodies of 24 Empire airmen and other military personnel recovered from the debris of the Metropole Hotel. Firemen of the National Fire Service, with a new 100-feet turntable ladder, rescued a further 35 airmen who were trapped on the upper floors of the elegant Victorian building, dating from 1893, which occupied the triangular corner between Holdenhurst Road and Christchurch Road. A a total of 196 people were treated for their injuries.

All this happened within about five minutes, at 13.00 hours, when 22 Focke-Wulf FW.190s swept in low from the sea and bombed the central shopping areas of The Square and Lansdowne. But for the fact that the attack coincided with Sunday lunchtime the casualty figures could have been much higher.

Two hours later the conductor of the BBC Orchestra, Sir Adrian Boult, took the Bournemouth Municipal Orchestra through the 'Nimrod' passage from Sir Edward Elgar's *Enigma Variations* in memory of those who had died. The bombs marred what had been intended as a celebratory concert to mark the 50th anniversary of the Bournemouth Orchestra.

Meanwhile, at 14.20 hours, Bournemouth ARP Control Centre requested rescue parties from Christchurch and Poole. A major fire was still burning around Beales, where the bombs fractured a gas main, and at one time threatened the adjoining department store of J. J. Allen and St. Peter's Church. Pumping parties dragged multiple snakes of hoses to the Bourne Stream to supplement the reservoir-fed gutter network of the emergency on-ground water supply. Others formed a chain to pass buckets of water up the slope.

The show went on with guest conductor Sir Adrian Boult (centre) taking Bournemouth Municipal Orchestra through its 50th anniversary concert two hours after the bombs fell on 23 May 1943

Not only the concert proceeded as planned. Window-less buses went back into service during the afternoon with sacks tied across the front of the vehicles to reduce draughts. Five FW.190s were reportedly shot down. One crashed beside St. Ives Hotel, at 34 Grove Road, with an unexploded bomb still attached. The pilot, Unteroffizier F. K. Schmidt, was killed. Though the bomb failed to explode, the aircraft caught fire and the hotel was gutted. Another aircraft, seen to crash in the bay, was credited to a machine-gun post of the 87th Light Anti-Aircraft Regiment of the Royal Artillery, emplaced on the former flat roof of J. E. Beale Limited. Its triple Lewis guns were manned by Lance-Bombadiers John Howard and Norman Lawrence.

RAF figures show the five destruction claims against the FW.190s as overstated. Two had been destroyed, as described, and two more were damaged. Falling masonry then killed a workman who was finishing the demolition of Beales. The principal buildings remained as bomb sites for more than a decade. West's Picture House is now the Burlington Arcade, Beales was replaced, and Bobby's repaired. Other lost landmarks were replaced by shops and offices.

Allied fighter-bombers passed over Bournemouth three days later. Ten P-51 Mustang fighter-bombers of 2 Squadron Royal Air Force, based at RAF Sawbridgeworth, Hertfordshire, had taken off from Thruxton in Hampshire on Ranger Operation Asphalt. The cross-Channel offensive action was to have been against rail movements in the Rennes-Laval area. They flew south-west in line abreast formation until reaching a wall of fog between Kimmeridge and St Alban's Head. The order to climb was given by Flight-Lieutenant G. Kenning at 17.35 hours.

Seven of the aircraft were able to clear Smedmore Hill but the other three – code letters U for Uncle, W for William, and Y for Yorker – crashed into the northern slope. Their three pilots were killed – Flying Officer N. J. Miller, Flying Officer D. Hirst, and Pilot Officer J. B. McLeod. The remaining Mustangs returned to Thruxton after having failed to locate the missing aircraft. Flying Officer M. P. Dunkerley returned later with hydraulic failure but was able to effect a safe landing. The operation was cancelled.

Westland Whirlwinds of 263 Squadron at RAF Warmwell, turned into bombers with racks fitted under each wing, crossed the Channel through May to 'work on the railway' in northern France. Bomb loads were delivered from 50 feet or less. They proved to be formidable fighter-bombers, using the aircraft's four 20-mm Hispano cannon, to press home their attacks on trains. Their named Whirlwind P7094 *Bellows* was a war weapons donation from the Bellows Fellowship of 70,000 wealthy British expatriates in South America. It was joined by others from the same sub-continent with P7116 being named *Bellows Argentina* and P7121 *Bellows Uruguay No. 1*.

Catalina flying-boats of 210 Squadron of Coastal Command moved into the seaplane base at RAF Hamworthy in May to operate long-range flights into the Atlantic in the battle against the U-boats. It was reported during the month that Major Robert Hambro, the only son and heir of Captain Angus Hambro of Merley House, Wimborne, was mortally wounded whilst serving in a reconnaissance regiment of the 8th Army. He died in Tripoli.

A total of 321 German mines and 84 barrage protection floats were laid off Dorset and the Isle of Wight in the first week of June through the combined efforts of the German 2nd, 4th, 5th and 6th Schnellboot Flotillas. The Royal Naval Mine Sweeping Service simply noted the areas concerned and proceeded to clear them as and when resources and weather conditions allowed. On 23 June a mine in the Swash Channel claimed the Dutch vessel *Leny* at the entrance to Poole Harbour. Only two crewmen were rescued.

At 19.54 hours on 25 June a Royal Navy Seafire, being flown into Christchurch Aerodrome from Donibristle, Scotland, overshot the runway and crashed into a bungalow in Caroline Avenue at Stanpit. MB315 was piloted by Sub-Lieutenant P.M. Lamb who was taken to hospital with head injuries, which were stitched-up, though he had to let his hair grow to cover the scars. He wrote in his log:

'Not my best landing. Engine tired of living. Fortunately I didn't join it.'

Seafires were a frequent sight over Christchurch as the Airspeed factory converted 160 of them, from standard Spitfires, for use by the Fleet Air Arm. During June an RCL – a tank landing craft modified at Poole to carry batteries of rocket launchers – was tested in live-fire exercises at Studland Bay and Kimmeridge. It fired more than 1,000 explosive rockets in about 30 seconds, delivering them to a small area of the beach. The aim was to annihilate enemy strong-points with firepower that was devastatingly concentrated.

No. 3 Overseas Aircraft Despatch Unit at RAF Hurn co-ordinated a massive shuttle service as No. 13 Maintenance Unit fitted out Halifax bombers as tow-craft for the Horsa troop-carrying gliders which had been made ready by No. 1 Heavy Glider Maintenance Unit. That unit then moved to Netheravon, Wiltshire, and the Halifaxes of 295 Squadron towed the gliders, built by Airspeed at Christchurch, to Portreath, Cornwall.

Meanwhile, 296 Squadron had been flying its Albemarle paratroop carriers out of Hurn since 3 June. Twenty-eight had left by 21 June. The squadron was equipped with Albemarles in February and began training with the Rebecca radio navigation system. From Cornwall, the Albemarles and Halifax-Horsa combinations flew out, in Operation Beggar, to Sale in Morocco. They were then moved eastwards to Kairouan, in Tunisia, to be handed over to 1st Air Landing Brigade Group, preparing for Operation Husky. These were the logistics for the invasion of Sicily, into the 'soft under-belly of Europe', as Churchill put it.

The 1st Battalion of the Dorsetshire Regiment sailed into the Mediterranean aboard the ex-Peninsular and Oriental liner *Strathnaver* among the armada bound for the beaches of Sicily.

BOMBING BOUNCES BACK ACROSS THE WATER

13 Corps landing in Sicily on 10 July 1943, after a night assault by 'C' Company of the 1st Battalion, the Dorsetshire Regiment

The 1st Air Landing Brigade Group, with aircraft from Hurn and Christchurch-made gliders, was tasked to begin the invasion of Sicily between 22.10 and 22.30 hours on Friday 9 July with a drop west of Siracusa to capture the Ponte Grande over the Anapo River, take out the coast batteries to the north, and also attack a seaplane base. Seaborne landings were to follow with the commandos arriving four hours later and then the main force of 13 Corps.

In the event, airborne operations were disrupted by high winds, with some gliders coming down in the sea and many paratroops falling far from the drop-zone. Few reached the Ponte Grande but they held the bridge heroically for 18 hours. Fortunately the seaborne assault proved to be a complete success.

On the 19th, 'C' Company of the 1st Dorsets, under Captain A. C. W. Martin, went over the side of the troopship *Strathnaver* at 03.00 hours to effect a scramble-landing on a rocky promontory at the right-flank of the projected bridgehead in Sicily. They took the village of Marzamemi and were able to secure the proposed landing beach to the south.

Tracer shells fired vertically from a Bren gun was the dawn signal of success to the Commanding Officer offshore. The battalion's 'A' and 'B' companies then landed to establish themselves inland.

The Royal Navy lost two submarines in the Sicilian invasion. One was HMS *Saracen*, commanded by Lieutenant M. G. R. Lumby of South Eggardon Farm, Askerswell, who was taken prisoner with his crew. Poole commando Major Geoffrey Appleyard DSO (26) – 'The Apple of Combined Operations – was killed in the landings, as deputy commander of the 2nd Special Air Service Regiment.

The sea was also lively off the Dorset coast in an action towards the Channel Islands. HMS *Melbreak*, a Hunt-class destroyer from Portsmouth, sustained serious damage, and the German 2nd Schnellboot Flotilla lost minesweeper *M135*. Thirty-eight Spitfires of 66, 131 and 504 Squadrons flew into RAF Hurn on 10 July as cross-Channel escorts for American Flying Fortress bombers. Spitfire EB687 was wrecked on arrival when it collided with a parked Whitley bomber. The fighters were led by Wing Commander C. E. Malfroy DFC who brought the Wing back for similar escort duties on 14 July.

On the morning of 13 July a Lancaster bomber of 49 Squadron, returning from the mass raid over Turin, crossed the English Channel on an almost empty fuel tank. Pilot Officer B. S. Tomlin then put JA851 down on to the 2,400 feet of grass that is Christchurch Aerodrome.

He brought his aircraft and its six crew to a perfect landing. Two-and-a-half hours later they were refuelled and airborne again, after an excellent short take-off, en route to RAF Fiskerton, Lincolnshire. Bomber Command strays were not uncommon in Hampshire and Dorset but it was the first time anyone could recall a four-engine bomber arriving at Christchurch.

'Let us open the Window,' Winston Churchill decided and it was done on the night of 24 July. Window was the codename given by the Telecommunications Research Establishment's A. P. Rowe to what became the parting shot of the Worth Matravers scientists before their radar laboratories were moved from Purbeck to Malvern. It was deployed from the air in the form of millions of thin strips of aluminium foil that created a smoke-screen effect upon enemy radar scanners at the onset of a mass bombing raid.

Window had been perfected in Dorset early in 1942 but opposition from Fighter Command and Robert Watson-Watt, radar's British pioneer, blocked its operational use. It had been feared that it might give the Germans the idea at a time when they were liable to carry out major attacks against Britain. The scientists and Bomber Command were elated with the results of Window in causing confusion and consternation to the German defences. Forty tons of Window were dropped (a total of 92 million strips) and all but twelve of the 791 bombers returned from the raid on Hamburg. Losses which statistically should have been about 6.1 per cent were reduced to 1.5 per cent. Window was credited with saving 36 aeroplanes and their crews.

Hedges and ditches were removed across flat farmland to the north-east of Sopley, beside the lane from Winkton to Ripley, for a temporary Advanced Landing Ground. This enabled additional fighter capacity to be brought into the Christchurch area for protection of the Channel convoys and the build-up of invasion shipping, plus cross-Channel ground-attack missions. The runways of RAF Winkton were laid as sheets of steel mesh directly on to the grass. There were two runways, one north-south from east of Parsonage Farm to west of Clockhouse Farm, and the other east-west from the Ripley road to within a third of a mile of the cottages at Bransgore village.

During the morning of 9 August the Free French bombers of 88 Squadron, flying Bostons alongside those of 107 Squadron and 342 Squadron, headed back across the Channel to the safety of RAF Hurn. The three squadrons had been in action over Rennes, in Brittany, where they lost two aircraft. The 21 surviving bombers were short on fuel when they landed at Hurn.

Gas-mains were set alight, water pipes fractured, and 1,455 properties damaged at about 01.10 hours on 12 August when eight high explosive bombs dropped on Bournemouth. Thirteen people were killed and 21 had to receive hospital treatment. The bombs fell at the corner of Firs Glen Road and Woods View Road; at the junction of Boundary Road with Beswick Road; at the corner of Wilton Road and Gloucester Road; in Spring Road; Charminster Avenue; and Shelbourne Road.

At about the same time there was an explosion near the railway, close to Christchurch Station, and then another high explosive bomb caused widespread damage in Ringwood Road, Walkford. Many houses were shattered and one bed-ridden lady rendered homeless. Three people were injured.

A training flight had a tragic ending at 04.25 hours on 24 August when Pilot Officer Duff brought a military Catalina of 210 Squadron back to Poole Harbour. They descended into thick fog and the flying-boat missed the clear waters of the 'Trots' in the channels of the northern harbour. Instead it ploughed into the cord-grass salt-marshes that surround Round Island on the shallow Purbeck side of the harbour. Ratings from the island's naval camp dragged eight bodies and four survivors from the debris.

Later that week, at 14.00 hours on Saturday 28 August, there was a VIP landing in Poole Harbour. The arrivals included Anthony Eden (Secretary of State for Foreign Affairs), General Sir Alan Brooke (Chief of the Imperial General Staff) and Admiral Louis Mountbatten (Chief of Combined Operations). They were aboard the BOAC Boeing Clipper *Bristol* and had returned across the Atlantic from the Quebec Conference which set the location and timetable for launching the Second Front.

The decision had been taken to go for the beaches of Normandy and forgo the need to capture a port by towing across prefabricated concrete caissons, codenamed Mulberries, to make two instant harbours. The provisional date for the invasion of Europe was 1 May 1944.

There was an echo of the Monmouth Rebellion and the Battle of Sedgemoor on 31 August when *The Daily Telegraph* reported that a Lyme Regis hotelier received a stamped addressed postcard from an anxious prospective visitor asking for 'the date of the last enemy attack on your town'. The manager sent the card back with the year – '1685'.

BOMBING BOUNCES BACK ACROSS THE WATER

Just before dawn on 8 September, support landings took place at Pizzo, on the Toe of Italy, to establish a rearguard to ease pressure on the Allied troops in the Reggio beachhead. The commandos went astray, however, and the first craft to beach contained the headquarters unit of the 1st Battalion the Dorsetshire Regiment. The landing was led – not that he realised his bravado at the time – by an NCO with a mailbag slung nonchalantly over his shoulder.

That moment passed uneventfully but later the battalion's 'B' Company came under heavy counter-attack on the nearby coast road. Though the Dorsets knocked out a Panzer Mark IV tank, with one of their 6-pounders, they had two anti-tank guns destroyed and many crews became casualties. Without any gunnery to support him, Sergeant W.J. Evans single-handedly immobilised an approaching armoured car, which was leading an enemy column. He tossed in a grenade and killed all the crew with the exception of a German officer. Sergeant Evans then shot the survivor as he tried to bale out. The other enemy vehicles reversed and withdrew.

Arrival in Pizzo of Sergeant W. J. Evans of the 1st Battalion the Dorsetshire Regiment (to win his second Military Cross) to secure the Toe of Italy, as sketched by Bryan de Grineau for the *Illustrated London News*

The company's left-flank was under infantry attack. This was held off by Lieutenant L. G. Browne's platoon in fierce hand-to-hand fighting which left 20 enemy dead.

At one point the Brigade Commander called up air support. Kittyhawk fighter-bombers duly arrived on time but they then confused the British positions for those of the enemy and proceeded to bomb and strafe them. Several vehicles were destroyed. It had been that sort of day, from which Sergeant Evans won a bar to his Military Medal, and Lieutenant Browne was awarded the Military Cross.

Arrivals at RAF Tarrant Rushton included 2851 Anti-Aircraft Squadron from RAF Friston, Sussex, and a dozen Ventura aircraft from RAF Sculthorpe, Norfolk. They were joined on 23 September by a prototype Albemarle Mark IV transport flown by Group Captain T. B. Cooper DFC Its potential was to be assessed in towing trials with a view to using the aircraft as a tug-plane for troop-carrying gliders.

One of the more bizarre weapons of war, a Great Panjandrum rocket-fired assault wheel, was tested by commandos of Combined Operations from Poole on their explosives firing ground at Clouds Hill, near Bovington Camp. The cylinder at the centre of two 10-feet high wheels contained 4,000 pounds of high explosive.

The rockets were intended to send the wheel out of an invasion landing craft and up the beach to blow a hole in the 10-feet concrete of the German Atlantic Wall defences. The rocket propulsion was tried out on the sands of Westward Ho! and Instow, Devon, on 7 and 8 September with unpredictable results. Nevil Shute Norway, the aeronautical engineer and writer, figured out the size of the charges needed to breach the Atlantic Wall and took part in the experiments.

A final trial took place at Westward Ho! in January 1944. It was filmed by motor-racing photographer Luis Klemantaski who had to run for his life as the machine reached 100 miles per hour and suddenly veered towards him. Onlookers tried to escape up the beach and became entangled in anti-invasion barbed wire. The Panjandrum, meanwhile, wobbled seaward again as rockets spiralled across the beach; one being chased by an Airedale hound, Ammanol.

With this the project was abandoned, though it had served its purpose as a feint, by demonstrating that there were active plans to attack the concrete coast between the Seine and Calais, rather than the soft sands of Normandy. Hence the unprecedented testing of a 'secret' weapon before an audience in a holiday resort; it was a deception that the public and the Germans could hear about. Few, if any, of those involved would have been privy to the ruse.

News from Germany included the following card, written in a camp at M. Stammlager, which was typical of those being received by the Society of Dorset Men:

MARRIED WHILE ON LEAVE
Oliver—Whitaker
Union at Weymouth

Home on leave from the B.L.A., Driver Leonard Drake Oliver, R.A.S.C., son of Mrs. B. Oliver, 9, High-street, Weymouth, and the late Mr. J. W. Oliver, was married by special licence at Holy Trinity Church, Weymouth. The bride, Miss Mary Margaret Whitaker, was daughter of the late Mr. and Mrs. A. Whitaker, formerly of Glusburn, near Keighley, Yorkshire. The Rev. M. Gutch officiated and Mr. Alfred Stevens was at the organ for the choral service.

The bride, given away by a friend, Mr. Joseph Jobling, was attired in a turquoise two-piece with wine accessories. Her brides-maids were Miss Jessie Oliver and Miss Ann Oliver (sister and niece of the bridegroom), attired respectively in pink and white dresses. Pink carnations, blue iris and anemones composed the bouquets. Gunner Percy Oliver, R.A., was best man.

The reception was at Tett's Restaurant. For the honeymoon at Bournemouth, the bride travelled in a dusty pink dress with brown accessories. The bridegroom is a partner in Messrs. Oliver Bros., fish merchants, Weymouth.

Wartime ambulance driver Leonard Oliver on home leave in Weymouth to marry Mary Whitaker

'Kriegsgefangenenlager. Dear Sir, Thank you very much for your letter of September. I have today received a parcel of 200 cigarettes. I believe they are from the society. Cigarettes mean such a great deal. I am a Dorset man, born and bred, and to me it is still the finest little place in the world. Thanking you once again. Yours sincerely, G. W. Harris, 6848.'

To most Britons, the invasion of Europe would be a Second Front, but there were already other overseas battlegrounds from Italy to South-East Asia. On Monday 11 October, Field-Marshal Sir Archibald Wavell, Viceroy of India and Supreme Commander Allied Forces in India and Burma, left Poole Quay by launch to board a BOAC flying-boat bound for Bombay.

Whirlwind P7094 'Bellows' at RAF Warmwell with pilots in 263 Squadron from around the Empire – (left to right) Flight-Lieutenant E. C. Owens (Adjutant), Squadron Leader G. B. Warnes (Commanding Officer), Flight-Lieutenant H. K. Blackshaw (Flight Commander), Sergeant S. D. Thyagarajan (from India), Flying Officer C. P. King DFM (West Indies), Flight-Sergeant F. L. Hicks (Australia) and Flying Officer J. P. Coyne DFC (Canada).

The same day, No. 38 Wing of the Royal Air Force, comprising the support units for British airborne forces, changed its name to HQ 38 Group. The week also started with movements on the ground from RAF Hurn to RAF Tarrant Rushton. 'A' Flight of 295 Squadron followed with Halifax tow-craft for troop-carrying gliders and re-formed as the nucleus of the new 298 Squadron. They were joined by the Sterlings of 196 Squadron. By the end of the week, 298 Squadron was taking to sky for Exercise Thresher. Three gliders were towed by their Halifax tug-planes and released over Salisbury Plain to land at Netheravon, Wiltshire.

On 28 October a Mitchell bomber, damaged by German flak off Cherbourg, made a successful emergency landing at RAF Tarrant Rushton. It was flown by Lieutenant Loeffe of 320 Squadron, from Lasham Aerodrome, Hampshire.

Another of hit-and-run raid struck Bournemouth at tea-time on 1 November. It consisted of 23 high explosive bombs which left 1,284 properties damaged. The casualty toll, however, was light, with just one person killed and 27 injured. Widespread damage was reported from Cecil Avenue, Howard Road, Campbell Road, Borthwick Road, Avon Road, Chatsworth Road, Bennett Road, Orcheston Road, Shaftesbury Road, and Shelbourne Road. Bombs beside Queen's Park Avenue did little more than crater the golf links.

Saturday 6 November was a red-letter day for Dorset's Regular Army soldiers, the 1st Battalion the Dorsetshire Regiment, as they disembarked on the Clyde at Gourock from the troopship *Durban Castle*. They were played ashore by a Highland band. The survivors of the Malta siege and assault landings in Sicily and Italy looked forward to their first home leave in seven years – they had been overseas since their transfer to the North-West Frontier Province of India in 1936.

BOMBING BOUNCES BACK ACROSS THE WATER

A week later, psychologically at least, the war turned from defence to the offensive. Fighter Command ceased to exist and became part of the Allied Expeditionary Air Force, which was the umbrella command for all British, American, and other Allied fighting aircraft and air stations in the United Kingdom. Its Commander-in-Chief was Air Chief Marshal Sir Trafford Leigh-Mallory.

There was a shock on 12 November for the Adjutant at the headquarters of the 7th (Boscombe) Battalion of Hampshire Home Guard. A shooting incident occurred shortly before 21.00 hours, as Sergeant G. A. Miller reported to his commanding officer:

> 'When rifles were being loaded, previous to proceeding to the Operational Patrol, one round was accidentally fired by a member of the patrol, Private G. H. Thomas. The round passed through the ceiling of the guardroom and lodged in the wall of the room above. I am able, fortunately, to report that no one was hurt. The bullet passed within one inch of the Adjutant who was sitting in the room above.'

By 15 November, three squadrons of Albemarles were based at RAF Hurn, with the formation there of 570 Squadron. 'We launch the spearhead,' was the motto chosen for the taxi service of the Airborne divisions. The station's existing 295 Squadron was re-equipped with Albemarles and reunited with those of 296 Squadron returning from Italy. The squadrons would co-operate in paratroop drops and in exercising towing Horsa gliders, together with a detachment from 570 Squadron, based at RAF Stoney Cross in the New Forest.

On 16 November, Major-General Charles Harvey Miller, the officer commanding administration at Southern Command, issued eviction notices to all persons living in an area of ten square miles of western Purbeck. The entire

Gas bomb being dropped by a Lysander on a Sherman tank in an exercise beside the Purbeck Hills at East Lulworth

3,003-acre parish of Tyneham was being requisitioned along with considerable areas of heath and downland in the adjoining parishes of East Lulworth, East Stoke, East Holme, and Steeple. The village of Tyneham and hamlets of Povington and Worbarrow had to be evacuated by 19 December, along with many isolated farms and cottages.

The land was to be used as a live-fire battle training area for the tanks of the United States Army as well as the Gunnery Wing of the Armoured Fighting Vehicles School which had its ranges at Lulworth Camp, next to the requisitioned area. Practising tank warfare became a top priority in August, when the Quebec Conference decided that the Overlord plan for the so-called 'Second Front' invasion of Fortress Europe should be launched against Normandy.

Eight Halifax transports from RAF Tarrant Rushton carried out Exercise Fledgling on 16 November. 298 Squadron dropped men of the 8th Battalion the Parachute Brigade on Cranborne Chase. They jumped over Thorney Down, beside the A354, two miles south of Sixpenny Handley.

Studland Bay disappeared in a cloud of smoke on 24 November for Exercise Cumulus during which landing craft were obscured by a dense smoke-screen. Thirteen Mitchell and 24 Boston bombers dropped the canisters. They operated for the day from RAF Hurn. Four Typhoons of 181 Squadron came low across the sea to test the effectiveness of the screen against attacking fighters.

December's training flights started with Halifax tug-planes pulling Horsa gliders from 298 Squadron at RAF Tarrant Rushton to meet up in aerial formation with 295 Squadron from RAF Hurn. Exercise Stickies also involved aircraft and gliders from RAF Stoney Cross. It was followed by Exercise Hasty with loaded gliders.

RAF Hurn, apparently during an exercise on 1 December 1943 (as the photograph pre-dates the D-Day stripes of airborne invasion) with Horsa gliders along the north-eastern extension to the aerodrome and Albemarle tug-planes on the grass

Eviction notice to Tyneham parishioners issued by Major-General Charles Miller of Southern Command in order to double the capacity of Lulworth tank gunnery ranges for the upcoming invasion of Europe

On 8 December, the 184th Auxiliary Anti-Aircraft Gun Battalion became the first unit of the United States Army to arrive at Blandford Camp. Its 716 enlisted men and 25 officers were tasked with providing protection around the beach landing assault area at Studland.

Lord Brabazon, the previous Minister of Aircraft Production, was the principal speaker at a ceremony in the Town Hall, Bournemouth, on 17 December to present a plaque and certificate of merit on behalf of the National Savings Campaign. The town collected £2,033,894 in the 'Wings for Victory' week, held from 8 to 15 May. The award of the plaque was made by Group Captain Hutchinson of the Royal Canadian Air Force. Councillors and collectors were told that the money had been invested in a flight of six Sunderland flying-boats; three squadrons of 15 single-engine fighters; three squadrons of twelve 4-engine bombers; plus three 2-engine bombers. That was a grand total of 90 aircraft – at an average price of £22,598 each.

Ralph Bond, the platoon commander of Tyneham Home Guard and a Purbeck magistrate, left his Elizabethan mansion along with his servants, farm labourers, and the fishermen of Worbarrow Bay on Sunday 19 December. The whole of the parish of Tyneham plus other land on either side of the Purbeck Hills was depopulated by order of the War Cabinet.

The area became a firing range for American Sherman tanks of the Second Armored Division which was the backbone of V Corps of the First United States Army. No mention of this extension of the Lulworth Ranges was permitted in the press. Neither was there any consultation with local councils.

Tenancies, however, were maintained and each occupant reassured:

'This means that when the War Department has no further use for the property and it is handed back, you have every right to return to your property. It should not be assumed by you that, because the War Department has turned you out, you lose the right of occupying the premises again.'

As a Christmas present for the 1st Battalion the Glider Pilot Regiment, it arrived back in England on the 25th, from Taranto, Italy. The flyers were re-united with their Hamilcar gliders and the four-engine Halifax towing-craft of 298 Squadron and 644 Squadron at RAF Tarrant Rushton. In theory the festivities were on hold, for Exercise James, but aircraft and paratroops were grounded by cloudy weather. Exercise Wizzard followed with Exercise Novice to round off the year for airborne forces.

Ralph Wightman, known to the press as 'the Dorset farmer' though he never actually farmed, progressed from his career as Dorset's senior agricultural adviser to being the worldwide voice of the English countryman. He talked into the microphone as if he were having a chat among friends in the village inn – the King's Arms Hotel at Puddletown – where he lived in a 16th-century stone-built thatched house.

In 1942 he was heard on the wireless, in the *Country Magazine*, with established rural pundits such as A. G. Street and S. P. B. Mais. Wightman's dulcet tones, warm humour, and practical down to earth common-sense immediately appealed to listeners. He found himself invited back by the BBC to 'star' in the programme. On Boxing Day in 1943 he was given the honour of delivering the *Sunday Postscript* which was relayed by the Forces Broadcasting Network to all theatres of war, as well as across the British Empire and North America.

Ralph Wightman went on to do 290 consecutive weekly broadcasts, describing the countryside at war and into the peace, for listeners in the United States. He was to compere the bulk of the *Country Magazine* series as well as make regular appearances in

SOUTHERN COMMAND

TRAINING AREA, EAST HOLME, Nr. LULWORTH

IN order to give our troops the fullest opportunity to perfect their training in the use of modern weapons of war, the Army must have an area of land particularly suited to their special needs and in which they can use live shells. For this reason you will realise the chosen area must be cleared of all civilians.

The most careful search has been made to find an area suitable for the Army's purpose and which, at the same time, will involve the smallest number of persons and property. The area decided on, after the most careful study and consultation between all the Government Authorities concerned, lies roughly inside of the square formed by EAST LULWORTH—EAST STOKE—EAST HOLME—KIMMERIDGE BAY. *Including your properties – all overleaf.*

It is regretted that, in the National Interest, it is necessary to move you from your homes, and everything possible will be done to help you, both by payment of compensation, and by finding other accommodation for you if you are unable to do so yourself.

The date on which the Military will take over this area is the 19th December next, and all civilians must be out of the area by that date.

A special office will be opened at Westport House, WAREHAM, on Wednesday the 17th November, and you will be able to get advice between the hours of 10 a.m. and 7 p.m., from there on your personal problems and difficulties. Any letters should be sent to that address also for the present.

The Government appreciate that this is no small sacrifice which you are asked to make, but they are sure that you will give this further help towards winning the war with a good heart.

C. H. MILLER,
Major-General i/c Administration,
Southern Command.

16th November, 1943.

S.C.P. 24. 400. 11/43 S.P. 92944

BOMBING BOUNCES BACK ACROSS THE WATER

Country Questions, *On the Land*, and *Any Questions*. For those who grew up with the wireless he was the best known Dorset man of his generation.

Thirty-seven P-47 Thunderbolt fighter-bombers of the United States Army Air Force landed at RAF Hurn on 29 December on their return from offensive operations over northern France. So too did two flak-damaged B-17 Flying Fortress bombers. The Thunderbolts had been protecting Liberator bombers that were also returning from raids.

There had been intense activity over the Cherbourg peninsula in which Hurn played its part. On 22 December there were 24 Spitfires at the station, from 131 Squadron and 165 Squadron, to escort bombers to Triqueville. Eight 'Ski-sites' were accounted for in the vicinity of Cherbourg. These were being prepared for the new terror weapon, the FZG76 (Flakzielgerat = Anti-aircraft target device) or Vergeltungswaffe I (V-1 = Retaliation weapon 1) as the Germans started to call it. The V-1 was a flying bomb which required a concrete ramp – vulnerable to air attack – if it was to be launched with any accuracy.

The Catalinas of 210 Squadron left RAF Hamworthy by the end of the year to enable its concrete slipway to be used in training exercises to load landing craft with tanks and other heavy vehicles. There was a gathering armada of these vessels dispersed along the creeks and estuaries of the South Coast. Air Marshal Sir Arthur Tedder, appointed General Eisenhower's Deputy Supreme Commander of Allied Forces Western Europe, began his military career with the Dorsetshire Regiment in the Great War. He served in France in 1915, transferred to the Flying Corps in 1916, and rose to Vice-Chief of the Air Staff in 1942.

In December a heavy tank proceeding through Longham, between Ringwood and Poole, skidded off the road and careered into the public bar of the King's Arms Inn. The side of the building would have collapsed but for the turret of the tank which ended up supporting the bedroom floor and the bed of Michael Weaver, recovering from a bout of influenza. He was the son of landlord Leslie Weaver. One soldier in the tank was slightly hurt but all the occupants of the bar, in the process of leaving at closing time, had remarkable escapes.

There was an unfortunate incident at Portland Royal Navy dockyard where some boys mocked a decent, self-respecting soldier, of the Buffs, and told him he was no better than a Home Guard. Instantly, in a fit of pique, the sentry shot dead John Groves (17) of Williams Avenue, Wyke Regis. It was silly and unintentional; manslaughter rather than murder, and the situation rather than the participants was to blame. Give a man a gun and he may defend his pride as well as his country.

Perhaps the kindest sequel to a war story was that of RAF Sergeant Ronald Foss, from Bridport, who was on a Coastal Command flight over the Bay of Biscay. The first person to know he was missing happened to be his wife, whom he married in April 1942, as she was serving in the operations room of the same air station. Ronald, in fact, was still alive, and would be picked-up from the sea a week later with enough experiences of the war to fill a book.

Ronald Foss had in him not just one book but three. *In the Drink* would be followed by *Three of us Live*, and *Famous War Stories*. He was to enjoy a long retirement, with his wife, in London, Ontario.

"I AM NOW 50 YEARS OLD I PREFER A WAR NOW TO WHEN I AM 55..." – HITLER AUG. 23. 1939

Cartoonists had a field day when Der Fuhrer celebrated his 55th birthday (reminding Hitler of his prophetic words from 1939)

1944

The American year

THE DIE WAS cast. General Sir Alan Brooke heard on New Year's Day on BBC wireless news that he had been promoted Field-Marshal. He opened a letter of thanks from the nation's best-known soldier whose star was also in the ascendant. Despite Eisenhower's reservations, Brooke had persuaded Churchill to appoint General Sir Bernard Montgomery as commander of land forces for the invasion of Europe. Montgomery emphasised to the Prime Minister, recuperating at Villa Taylor in Marrakech, that landings had to be 'on the widest possible front' and that 'British and American areas of landing must be kept separate'. The concept coalesced as the Western Task Force under Rear-Admiral Kirk of the United States Navy and the Eastern Task Force shepherded by Rear-Admiral Sir Philip Vian. Each sector, Monty argued, needed air superiority supported by deployment of the four Allied Airborne Divisions and four United States Parachute Regiments. Monty wrote to Brookie:

> 'I must thank you for promoting me to command the armies in England. It is a big job and I will do my best to prove worthy of your selection. There is a terrible lot to do and not much time to do it.'

The D-Day date, previously set for 1 May, had been postponed to 1 June when Churchill celebrated his 69th birthday in Teheran with Roosevelt and Stalin on 30 November 1943. General George Marshall, Chief of Staff of the United States Army, was to have been its midwife but he was considered 'too big for the job'. So it was delegated to General Dwight Eisenhower who had the assault landings of North Africa, Sicily and Italy under his belt and made it clear he had no wish to be prematurely returned to the Pentagon.

The war-plan was to be finalised by Eisenhower as the Supreme Commander and his deputy, Air Chief Marshal Sir Arthur Tedder, in the Supreme Headquarters Allied Expeditionary Force (SHAEF), initially in Grosvenor Square before removal to Castle Combe

The Great Panjandrum, a spoof weapon of the secret war, tested at Bovington in 1943 and in public trials at Westward Ho! in January 1944 (to deceive the Germans that the forthcoming assault would be against concrete defences around Calais)

at Bushy Park, Teddington, with an advance command post at Southwick House, Corsham, near Portsmouth. *Time* magazine executive C. D. Jackson reported home to his boss, Henry Robinson Luce, on the effect of Eisenhower's arrival from the Mediterranean, via Washington:

> 'Now there is a new hustle and bustle, and the dawning of a sense that what is being put on paper really means something in terms of lives and logistics.'

Operation Overlord was destined to attack the beaches of Normandy but for public and German consumption there was a parallel deception plan – Operation Fortitude – in which the Second Front was to be launched from 'Caesar's Coast' across the narrow passage of the Strait of Dover directly at Fortress Europe towards the Pas de Calais. Plans for a real Third Front on the French Riviera (Operation Anvil, re-christened Operation Dragoon) were still being progressed though Montgomery protested that he needed its landing craft. There was the further bluff of an assault in the Aegean – a latter-day Gallipoli favoured as Churchill's pet project in 'the underbelly' – which ranked as another diversion. Churchill still hankered for his 'oft-rejected'

Allied Supreme Commander General Dwight D. Eisenhower and General Sir Bernard Montgomery planning the invasion of Europe, at the Carlton Hotel, Bournemouth, in February 1944

Operation Jupiter, to re-run the 1940 landings in northern Norway. There was also an Operation Caliph to attack Bordeaux as a follow-up to the Normandy landings. No wonder the Germans were confused, not least because just about all their spies had been turned into British agents, by MI5 through Maxwell Knight's 'Double Cross' scam.

Round the clock production in the three yards of Poole shipbuilders J. Bolson and Son Limited at Hamworthy brought about the completion of one assault landing craft every day. The LCAs were tethered in Holes Bay. The yards, formerly the Skylark boat business which built yachts and other pleasure craft, also produced Air-Sea Rescue speed-boats and Royal Navy minesweepers, as well as carrying out repairs on tank landing ships. Work practises were revolutionised. One squad was given responsibility for the complete production of a single vessel. This helped Bolson's into their premier position as the main assault landing craft manufacturers in Britain.

(Left) British rocket-firing landing craft *RCL 'B' 640* under construction at Bolson and Son's shipyard in Poole

(Right) LCAs (Landing Craft Assault), built by Bolson's at Poole, moored in the Holes Bay backwater of Poole Harbour

RAF Tarrant Rushton was handed over to 38 Group, Airborne Forces. Long-distance troop carrying was put to the test in Exercise Spook on 14 January with 13 Halifaxes of 298 Squadron flying across England's maximum width to deliver 115 paratroops over a dropping-zone at Winterton, on the North Sea coast. Starting on 20 January, for Exercise Manitoba with Canadian participants, the four-engine Halifax tug-planes at Tarrant Rushton began a series of take-offs with Hamilcar gliders. Some carried a 7.5 ton Tetrarch Mark VII light tank which only just fitted into the glider. The gliders were released at 1,000 feet above a dropping-zone. One Hamilcar and its Tetrarch overshot the landing area and split a Nissen hut apart as the tank shot forward out of the glider. Both vehicle and driver survived. A total of 670 troop-carrying Horsa gliders were constructed at the Airspeed factory beside Christchurch Aerodrome.

Air Chief Marshal Sir Trafford Leigh Mallory visited Tarrant Rushton on 12 February. He was given demonstrations and shown a display of German equipment in order to learn from the enemy's innovative ideas and methods. Elements of 208 Squadron split to form the new 644 Squadron at the airfield on 1 March. A detachment of 181 American paratroops from the 101st Airborne Division took part in Exercise Sailor on 3 March. As a mark of its growing use and importance, 2733 Anti-Aircraft Squadron of the RAF Regiment transferred to Tarrant Rushton from North Weald, Essex.

On 24 March, Air Marshal Sir Douglas Evill and Air Commodore Francis Masson Bladin watched as four Halifaxes, each towing a Hamilcar, lined-up for synchronised take-off and were all successfully airborne within 100 seconds. At times it must have seemed as if faltering Halifaxes and stray gliders were falling out of the sky all over Dorset and the New Forest. If anything, despite half a dozen of each being lost, it was surprising that the attrition rate was not much greater.

(Left) Hurn Aerodrome massively extended, along the entire northern side, for D-Day related activity

(Right) 'Georgia Peach' with oomph-girl Ann Sheridan gracing Lieutenant Curry Powell's Thunderbolt of 510 Fighter Squadron at Christchurch which became Station 416 of the 9th United States Army Air Force in March 1944

Several breeds of light tank and armoured car were converted for amphibious operations. Duplex-Drive (DD) versions of the British Valentine, turned it into a floating tank with a skirt, and American Stuarts had their exhausts turned into funnels, so they could wade ashore. These were tested in February on Weymouth sands. The objective was to reach the shore in six minutes on a day when the sea was obligingly flat.

Several teams of boffins and engineers tested a variety of Scam Projects in Dorset. Practical devices included rocket-fired grapnel hooks fired up cliffs for commando assaults. More problematic were the Lily floating airfield, tested in Studland Bay with a Swordfish biplane, and the Swiss Roll floating bridge which was laid across Weymouth Harbour, for a Bedford lorry. The Great Panjandrum, a loose-cannon of a Catherine-wheel that was stuffed with explosives, seems to have been a deliberate spoof, to imply that the invasion would be against the up-Channel Atlantic Wall rather than the down-Channel sands of Normandy.

(Left) Thunderbolt 2Z-N 'Touch of Texas' of 501 Squadron of the 405th Fighter Bomber Group operating from Christchurch

(Right) Lieutenant Charles Mohrle and 'Touch of Texas' on the ground at Christchurch (with 2Z-P behind)

(Left) The distinctive twin-boom lines of the Lockheed Lightning fighter-bomber came to Dorset in the spring of 1944 as Warmwell became Station 454 of the USAAF

(Right) Two-pounder Pom-poms firing Star-shells, silhouetting dragon's teeth anti-invasion defences at Abbotsbury, as they light up Lyme Bay

The Build-Up Control Organisation (BUCO) for the British assaults was matched by the Major Port structure that the Americans brought to Weymouth and Portland. Massively increasing its capacity, the runways at RAF Hurn were extended by half their original lengths, across a square mile of heathland, in work completed in February 1944.

Dorset's veteran assault troops, the 1st Battalion the Dorsetshire Regiment, were watched by King George VI as they attacked a strongpoint in a training exercise at Halstead, Essex, on 23 February. Eisenhower and Montgomery discussed detailed plans at the prestigious Carlton Hotel on Bournemouth's East Cliff. It hosted the American Forces Bureau of Investigations and some crews of self-propelled guns but still aspired to moments of five-star style.

Devon was initially given over to Force O of the United States Army and Dorset to British Force G. The order was given that no enemy aircraft was to be allowed to return with photographs of build-up preparations west of Selsey Bill, whereas pretend plans for the phoney assault from Sussex necessitated the reverse. The RAF had to be dissuaded from shooting down reconnaissance flights that observed dummy airfields, landing craft and tanks that were part of the great deception. As the Churchillian maxim has it, 'in war truth must have an escort of lies'.

Montgomery, returned to his old school – Saint Paul's at Hammersmith – as his headquarters, and set about compiling the Cossack Plan. These D-Day secrets were only to be shared with those who received Bigot security clearance. Monty visited units of 21st Army Group in Dorset on 18 January and received a hero's welcome when he drove through Bridport. A lady pushed forward through the crowd in East Street and reprimanded a policeman who tried to restrain her:

'Constable, you cannot stop me from thanking the man who has saved his country!'

The United States 7th Field Artillery Battalion was stationed on Wardon Hill, above Evershot, and at Maiden Newton. Wesley Henson and his mates caught the train at Holywell for the Great Western Hotel in Dorchester where they were introduced to dances such as the Bumpsie Daisy, Hands Knees and Okie Pokie. Less energetic combination pairs (each comprising GI and regular) played darts for pint prizes.

Christchurch Aerodrome became Station 416 of the United States Army Air Force as nearly 1,000 officers and men of the 405th Fighter Bomber Group began arriving by train from Liverpool on 7 March. They sailed from New York on 27 February on the liner *Mauretania* which cruised at 25 knots, without escorts, and changed her course every seven minutes 'to prevent U-boats getting a head on us'. Master Sergeant Horn observed:

'You don't know how good North America looks until you see 'er a-slippin' over the horizon.'

Their aircraft, which arrived the following week, were P-47 Thunderbolt fighter-bombers of 509, 510 and 511 Squadrons of the USAAF. Their first day trip to France, a suitably uneventful low-risk sweep, took place on 11 April.

Tragedy marred the transfer of the former Battle of Britain aerodrome at Warmwell to the 474th Fighter Group of the USAAF. One of four RAF Typhoons of 263 Squadron, taking part in the welcoming display on 12 March, spun out of control at 15.00 hours after having stalled in a vertical roll. It crashed at West Knighton, killing Flying Officer Graham Smith, and setting fire to the heather.

American graffiti from 1944, with a few RAF contributions, on a beech tree in Knighton Heath Wood beside Warmwell Aerodrome

GI haircuts on the shingle at Freshwater, Burton Bradstock, in April 1944.

Local lads showing off a beech-found gun belt to their American friends under the sycamore tree on the triangle of village green at Burton Bradstock

(Far left) Assault Landing Craft firing rockets with grapnels, trailing rope ladders, for the scaling of vertical cliffs in an exercise at Burton Bradstock

(Left) Retired Petty Officer Podger of the Royal Navy pointing the way to the NAAFI in Burton Bradstock to Roy St Jean from Springfield, Massachusetts

Village boy Barry Knell manning the pumps at A. E. Cheney's Red House Garage, Burton Bradstock, as another lad cleans the windscreen of an American 'Headquarters' Jeep

Propaganda point for American consumption as Revd. Arthur Dittmer points out the date on one of his table-tombs in St Mary's churchyard, Burton Bradstock (the significant year being 1775, before which Britain and America share a common history)

(Left) Burton Bradstock blacksmith Benjamin Burton presenting a lucky horseshoe to the commanding officer of a United States unit (with a plaster on his forehead to a wound probably resulting from recent intensive training)

(Middle) Benjamin Burton in the Smithy at Burton Bradstock, showing according to the contemporary caption 'that the Britisher is not as stand-offish as he is said to be'

(Right) Cliffside pillbox at Burton Bradstock with NBC studio musician Corporal Bert Markowitz from New York City serenading T/5 G. R. Miller from Louisville, Kentucky

Revd and Mrs Arthur Dittmer introducing Lieutenant S. M. Weitzner of Ridgewood, New York, and Major E. M. Beebe of Burlington, New York, to the English ritual of tea on the Rectory lawn

RAF Warmwell was designated American Station 454 on being handed over to three squadrons of P-38J Lightnings for cross-Channel operations to prepare for D-Day. Its distinctive twin-boom shape and fearsome reputation led the Luftwaffe to dub the Lightning 'the forked-tail devil'

RAF Hurn was transferred to No. 11 Group, Air Defence of Great Britain (as Fighter Command was renamed) on 14 March and became a forward base for rocket-firing Typhoons of 438 (Royal Canadian Air Force) and 440 (RCAF) Squadrons plus 439 (RCAF) Squadron of Hurricane fighter escorts. They comprised 143 Wing of 83 Group of the 2nd British Tactical Air Force. Typhoon dive-bombers were the most formidable attack aircraft available for both air to ground and air to sea offensive actions.

A colossal bang occurred near Sherborne at midday on Monday 20 March 1944. It came from a point 500 yards east-south-east of Sherborne Castle, about 50 yards on the Haydon side of the public footpath between Home Farm and The Camp on the south side of Sherborne Park.

'It was a tremendous explosion, the loudest anyone had ever heard,' said Tod Frost (16) who was threshing a corn rick for Arthur Jennings of Horsecastles Farm on the private road in front of Sherborne Castle He had a Land Army girl hurled on top of him, in the straw, close to being impaled on his pitchfork:

'It was a predicament I would have enjoyed under different circumstances. Bits of lorry and bodies were strewn across half a mile.'

One truck had totally disintegrated and others were mangled. Troops and ambulances from the nearby camp came to clear up:

'Open lorries passed along the road directly beneath us. We could see the rows of mutilated bodies covered with ground-sheets. It was an appalling sight.'

It had been, a spokesman for United States Forces confirmed, the largest single loss of American servicemen since their arrival in England. The number of casualties was given as 29 (now listed on the commemorative plaque in Half Moon Street, Sherborne), 35 to 40, and up to 140. All the accounts agree that there were only bodies to be counted and no injured to be tended. Betty Warner (23), living in Coombe on the other side of the town, wrote that 'the whole of Sherborne heard the explosion' and recorded in her diary a death-toll of 37, including her new-found friends Joseph B. Henning and Lucien P. Pessoz:

'Another American, Frank, came to tell us Joe and Lucien had been killed with 35 others.'

The accident happened when a lorry slipped back on to a mine during clearing-up after an exercise with anti-tank and anti-personnel mines by the 294th Combat Engineer Company of the United States Army. The wheels came to rest on an 8-pound anti-tank mine – the bellows of which needed a pressure of 250 pounds to trigger its detonator – and that explosion caused simultaneous detonation of all the mines in the truck.

(Left) Burton Bradstock's village canteen with Gunner Weightman of the Royal Artillery handing home-made cakes to his American counter-parts

(Middle) Deliberate disinformation in that this photograph from April 1944 of GIs drinking with the locals at the Dove Inn, Southover, Burton Bradstock, features a poster of H. & G. Symonds' Reading Brewery

(Right) Staff Sergeant Daniel Ewton, a Military Policeman from Chicago, who did his best to control Weymouth's GIs

What happened next was that a myth was spun. Sherborne Park, it was said, had been infiltrated by German agents who brought a truckload of mines into an Army physical training course. The culprits were named as Kurt Henlein and Ernst Buchner, who would be executed by the military, at Salisbury, in May 1944.

Censorship and news management was the norm. Such manipulation was vital to avoid giving indications to the enemy of the size and disposition of the American Army that was assembling on the coast facing the Cherbourg peninsula. Secrecy and security became a cloak for incompetence.

Revelations that came to light in 1997 under the American Freedom of Information Act show that the 'enemy agents' cover-story was invented to conceal the fact that a combat exercise course had been laid out within the confines of the 228th Field Hospital

(Left) Revd Arthur Dittmer (left) and American officers being treated to a display of country dancing by Burton Bradstock schoolchildren

(Right) General Montgomery in his Royal Tank Corps beret for a visit to Bovington Camp on 19 April 1944.

General Sir Bernard Montgomery, appointed overall land-force commander of Allied armies in Western Europe for the forthcoming invasion

Humber armoured car going into Weymouth Bay from a landing craft in an amphibious landing exercise

Daimler scout car 'Razzle' heading towards Belvidere and Victoria Terrace on the Esplanade at Weymouth (with anti-invasion barriers visible on the beach)

Humber scout car, carrying the Wyvern emblem of the 43rd (Wessex) Division, splashing into Weymouth Bay

Humber armoured car heading for Weymouth sands

A Humber scout car plunging into four feet of water in the Weymouth amphibious exercise

Stuart tank driving through more than six feet of water with not much more than its gun and cockpit being visible off Weymouth

Flag to signify the Stuart tank has achieved the required six minutes of immersion in the Weymouth exercise

Valentine floating tank in its 'land' mode

Valentine tank with its skirt lifted, ready for the water

Studland memorial to six Dragoon Guards who went down with their 'floating' Valentine tanks in Poole Bay on 4 April 1944

Unit of the United States Army. That meant that the site of the massive explosion came under the auspices and protection of the International Red Cross by the terms of the Geneva Convention and should not have been used by armed personnel, nor for the storing of ammunition, let alone for the laying of a live minefield.

Hurricanes of 439 (Royal Canadian Air Force) Squadron returned to their home base at RAF Hurn from Lincolnshire on 21 March but two American fighters were unable to resist joining their dog-fights over the Avon valley. As Hurricane LD972 levelled off from a manoeuvre it was hit by the metal airframe of a Thunderbolt which sliced off the tip of its wood and canvas starboard wing. Norval E. Pollock pulled the Hurricane out of an initial spin but then lost control and spiralled to his death in meadows near Sopley.

The seven-man crew of Halifax JP137 and two civilians were killed at 00.35 hours on 22 March when the bomber crashed into open ground below Meadow Court flats, beside Wimborne Road, in the Bournemouth suburb of Moordown. It had just taken off from RAF Hurn three minutes earlier, fully loaded with fuel, ammunition and medical supplies, for an RAF base in North Africa.

Swimming tanks, as a concept, could work, the 79th Armoured Division proved by taking modified Duplex Drive tanks through an oil-fired 'flame barrage' on to Studland beach on 27 March. Practising for invasion then brought tragedy on 4 April 1944. Amphibious tanks were now being tested in more realistic – and challenging – conditions, with approaches to the sands of Normandy being closely matched by the geography of Studland Bay. Several Duplex-Drive Valentine tanks rolled off a landing craft beside the Milkmaid Bank on the west side of Poole Bay and began to sink. Six members of the 4th/7th Royal Dragoon Guards were drowned. They were named as C. R. Gould, V. Hartley, A. V. Kirby A. J. Park, E. G. Petty and V. N. Townson.

Mosquito night-fighters of 125 (Newfoundland) Squadron were on the sidelines for Exercise Eric across the New Forest on 7 April. They flanked 25 Lancaster and Stirling bombers which took advantage of the coastal blind-spot in German radar caused by the Isle of Wight to drop strips of metalled paper – codename Window – which created spoof images. The object was to practice the dropping of Window in a pattern that would suggest to a radar operator the steady approach of a convoy at about 7 knots. This was to be created by a long series of orbits that gradually overlapped and edged towards the enemy coast over a period of five hours.

More than 100 aircraft took part in the actual deception, in the early hours of 6 June, including the Lancasters of 617 Squadron of Dambusters fame. The feint was intended to make the enemy think that the D-Day landings were taking place in the area of Boulogne (Operation Glimmer) and Cap d'Antifer (Operation Taxable) though the Germans went one better than this and thought the invasion was taking place further east in the Pas de Calais.

Devon's Americans continued to spill over into the Dorset countryside and on 16 April the battle-plan was amended to fit the reality on the ground. The embarkation zone based on Weymouth and Portland was given over to United States Force O for Omaha and British Force G for Gold was relocated eastwards to Southampton. There were more than 80,000 American soldiers and sailors in Dorset of whom more than half were tasked to take part in the invasion.

Under the revised battle-plan, the 'Fighting Firsts' or 'Big Red One' as America's 1st Infantry Division is known – from its badge – moved its Divisional Headquarters to Langton House in parkland at Langton Long Blandford. The Commanding General, Major-General Clarence R. Huebner had at his command 34,142 men and 3,306 vehicles.

Burton Bradstock and its GIs, from nearby Freshwater Holiday Camp, featured in a remarkable photo-shoot by an unknown American photographer in April 1944. The theme was the instant bond of friendship between residents and visitors. Tea on the Rectory lawn was with Revd and Mrs Arthur Dittmer. Old table-tombs in St Mary's churchyard were particularly poignant because they pre-dated 1775 and therefore represented a common heritage. Blacksmith Benjamin Burton showed officers how to shoe a horse. GIs received a haircut on the Chesil Beach whilst NBC studio musician Corporal Bert Markowitz from Queens played his violin from a disused pillbox belonging to an earlier phase of the war. Retired Petty Officer Podger pointed the way to the NAAFI. London evacuee Betty 'Freckles' Mackay and Dorset boy Chris Kerley were handed cups of cocoa. Local lad Barry Knell manned A. E. Cheney's pumps at the Red House Garage, opposite thatched Guildford Cottage. The ubiquitous Jeep carried 'Headquarters' stencilling which confirmed the importance of the occasion. The presence in the Dove Inn of a framed poster featuring a Reading brewery – H. and G. Simonds Limited – implies the insertion of a piece of deliberate misinformation to suggest a location much further east when deception was still the order of the day.

To British military cynics, proved on the ground wherever they camped, Americans had brought their own taxi-service. They were wedded to their Jeeps and trucks. It was crucial for the success of the Normandy landings that transport and supplies could be unloaded during the second phase of the invasion, after beach-heads had been secured but before the strongly-defended ports were captured and restored to use.

The great secret of the back-up logistics was the making of two artificial Mulberry Harbours. Mulberry A for the Americans was destined for the United States sector and Mulberry B for the British was to be towed to Arromanches. The concept came from an engineer, Allan Beckett, who designed the telescopic floating spans, with British companies Oscar Faber and Maunsell, for the War Office Port Engineering Branch formed under Major Bruce White. It was estimated that they could handle 12,000 tons of stores a day.

The codenames for constituent parts were brilliantly British in being totally inscrutable (unlike German terms which could be worked out like crossword clues). Phoenix concrete caissons, to be towed across and sunk, would form harbour walls. They were 200 feet long, in six sizes varying from 2,000 tons to 6,000 tons, with a maximum draught of 20 feet.

Gooseberries were breakwaters, to be formed by blockships (Corncobs) 'who will steam to the far shore and will be sunk early in the operation'. Bombardon units – 'floating steel structures 200 feet long and drawing 19 feet' – weighed 1,000 tons and were to be be towed across and moored, with Kite anchors, 'to form an outer floating breakwater'. Whales – the only nautical name – were floating roadways to connect to the shore and form pier-heads. Building the Phoenix caissons consumed vast quantities of sand from pits at Stephen's Castle, near Verwood, and finished sections were concealed in the Beaulieu River and Portland Harbour where one caisson remains close inshore, off Portland Castle, at Castletown.

The other great idea was Pluto (acronym for Pipe-Line Under the Ocean). This was a flexible undersea pipe unrolled from a floating Tweedledum spool coiled 60 feet in diameter with cone-shaped ends. These had been developed by the British Petroleum Warfare Department and pulled by HMS *Conundrum* and a tug out of Poole Harbour in a test passage to the Isle of Wight. Initially, however, before it could become operational, a team of Dallas oilmen from the American Gasoline Distribution Group were to make do with Tombola. Its system of buoyed pipes, between tankers and the shore, was theoretically capable of delivering 8,000 tons of fuel a day.

The starting point for Pluto was at Sandown, Isle of Wight, from where two pipes were taken to terminals near Port-en-Bassin. One was for the Americans and the other for the British. They took a couple of months to come on line and were followed by a third Pluto connection later from Dungeness to Boulogne.

Dorset's great invasion rehearsal day was Exercise Smash across Studland Heath on Tuesday 18 April 1944. The 1st Battalion, of the Dorsetshire Regiment, wallowed about offshore waiting to return to its native heath. Watching them, having been awoken in the royal train at Swanage Station at 04.00 hours, was King George VI. Police toured the town and villages to warn people to open their windows – to minimise blast damage – before the air and ground of the Isle of Purbeck began to vibrate to the concussive thud of Studland's war. VIPs and military commanders viewed the landings in Studland Bay from a massive concrete observation bunker, Fort Henry, on Redend Point. Major-General Percy Hobart's AVREs [Armoured Vehicles Royal Engineers] of the 79th Armoured Division included Churchill tanks which unrolled Chespale Carpet – coils of chestnut fencing – for Shermans to follow across the dunes.

The recessed slit in three feet of concrete from which King George watched Exercise Smash in Studland Bay on 18 April 1944

Fort Henry, the VIP blockhouse constructed by Canadian Engineers as the Observation Post for monitoring live-fire rehearsals of the D-Day landings from Redend Point, Studland

British tank coming ashore from Landing Craft 2307 in Exercise Smash (with Haven Hotel, Sandbanks, visible in background)

United States Landing Ship US526 having disgorged machines, men and material on Studland beach, mid-morning on 18 April 1944

Failure for Churchill tank 'Iroquois' trying to climb a sand dune at Studland

Enter one of 'Hobart's Funnies' – the AVREs (Armoured Vehicles Royal Engineers) of Major-General Percy Hobart's 79th Division – to lay a carpet from a giant bobbin

A road of fabric and chestnut paling laid by the AVRE across the Studland sandhill

'Iroquois' climbing Hobart's underlay

Mission accomplished as 'Iroquois' goes over the top of the dune

Unlike normal manoeuvres, Exercise Smash was distinguished by widespread use of live ammunition, from small-arms fire and artillery to bombs and rockets. Users of the binoculars at Fort Henry included His Majesty King George, Prime Minister Winston Churchill, General Dwight D. Eisenhower, General Sir Bernard Montgomery, General Omar Bradley (commanding the First United States Army), Lieutenant-General Miles Dempsey (commanding the Second British Army) and Field-Marshal Sir Alan Brooke (Chief of the Imperial General Staff). The day ended with the King and the generals dining in Swanage at the Hotel Grosvenor.

That weekend, on 22 April, Eisenhower and Air Chief Marshal Sir Trafford Leigh-Mallory, Commander-in-Chief of the Allied Expeditionary Air Force, with Air Vice Marshal Leslie Hollinghurst, visited RAF Tarrant Rushton to address the 700-strong air and ground crews of 198 Squadron, 644 Squadron and 'C' Squadron of the Glider Pilot Regiment.

The wartime reminiscing that has become this book has enabled me to re-write the story of one of the most famous disasters of the Second World War and claim it for Dorset. My initiation into the intrigues of the great Portland cover-up took place in the drawing room of Holbrook House Hotel, near Wincanton, in 1985 when I was working on the proofs of the first of what became a series of books on Dorset at war. A softly spoken 45-year-old from some arm of military intelligence, staying there while on a visit to the Royal Navy Air Station at Yeovilton, asked me what I knew about Exercise Tiger. This was the rehearsal for the D-Day landings at Slapton Sands, Devon, on the far side of Tor Bay, on 28 April 1944 in which an audacious attack by German motor-torpedo boats sank two United States tank landing ships and killed more than 600 American soldiers and sailors. Correct, he said:

> 'Except that the location is wrong. The attack on the Americans took place slap bang in the middle of your coast, off Portland Bill, but that fact had to be kept secret. So they moved it westwards and even gave the enemy credit for a brave assault right under the guns of Allied cruisers. The memorial has been put there rather than in Dorset.'

So I began to change my account accordingly. A decade later, a copy of the book found its way to Barry, in South Wales, with the result that I received a telephone call from an ex-Gunner. Lance-corporal Tecwyn Morgan, 31-years-old and serving with a coast defence battery, was billeted in a tent beside the Chesil Beach between Ferrybridge and Castletown dockyard. It was the third time he had tried to tell his story. Scott Wilkinson, a reporter, had visited him on behalf of *The Mail on Sunday*. Mr Morgan then reminisced with a Captain Murphy, also serving on Portland at the time, whom he thought was a newspaper proprietor. Nothing, however, appeared in print, so he now wanted someone else to know:

> 'We saw an LST [Landing Ship Tanks] unloading bodies but were sworn to secrecy, not to mention it to anyone, and it has played on my mind for decades. The ships of Delta Force were inside Portland Harbour, and they didn't want them to see the carnage, so the LST was towed into Balaclava Bay and the bodies were taken off there, around the corner from the harbour. They were driven round the top of the island and stored in Castletown dockyard. They were never buried – they were packed in the tunnels, which were collapsed by explosions in 1994, before the dockyard closed. What they write [about Slapton Sands] isn't true as we could virtually see it [the attack] from the coast battery.'

Enter my next informant. Leading telegraphist Nigel Cresswell, alive and well and living in Wimborne, was the 20-year-old Senior Wireless Operator aboard *MTB 701* of the Royal Navy's six-strong 63rd Motor Torpedo Boat Flotilla. For the previous three nights they had been on patrol in enemy-occupied waters off the Channel Islands and France. On the morning of Thursday 27 April 1944 they returned to base in Portland Harbour.

Nigel Cresswell was visited by a Wren Mechanic, named June Caswell:

> 'Her surname is almost the same as mine. She had a long face and I asked what was wrong. June replied that her American boyfriend had told her that he was going on an exercise with landing craft in Lyme Bay. I asked her where she had been told that and she replied in a Weymouth pub.'

The loose talk seemed unlikely in retrospect, given the vessels at Slapton Sands had sailed from Brixham or Plymouth, but my published report broke ranks with the accepted accounts, in raising the possibility that they had rounded Portland Bill from the Solent. Mr Cresswell commented:

> 'If the GI was coming from Dorset, no way could he have got there [Slapton Sands] from Weymouth [under wartime conditions]. However, if he was sailing from the Solent, as you suggest, then he could easily have got the train or his own Jeep to a port on the Solent.'

THE AMERICAN YEAR

Later in the afternoon of 27 April, the 63rd MTB Flotilla was put on stand-by in Portland Harbour:

> 'I was called to the Skipper's cabin and informed that the Senior Officer of the 63rd had offered the flotilla to escort some LSTs who were to be on an exercise in Lyme Bay. The dockyard buzz was that the sole escort was to be a veteran V&W destroyer from the Royal Navy.'

This was almost correct. In fact the destroyer was from the old S-class, being the 905-ton HMS *Scimitar* – armed with three 4-inch guns – dating from the Emergency War Programme of 1918. She was assigned to shadow the LSTs which were designated as Convoy T-4. So too was HMS *Azalea*, a Flower-class corvette of 925 tons, with one 4-inch gun and smaller calibre anti-aircraft and machine-guns.

Then things began to unravel. *Scimitar* collided that morning with a LCI [Landing Craft Infantry] and was detained in Plymouth Naval Base for repairs to her bow. Despite this, and no replacement being available, no one told the 63rd Flotilla to take her place. The result was a tempting and vulnerable target through which German E-boats ran amok. One of the attacking vessels, Schnellboot *S130* of the Kriegs-marine, survived the war and was in 2009 being restored in Dartmouth for its present owner, Kevin Wheatcroft of Donington Grand Prix Museum. The Allied ships were less fortunate, with these being the unpublished bullet-points from the official list of losses:

* 441 dead from the United States Army
* 197 dead from the United States Navy
* and 'a handful' [unspecified] of Royal Artillery dead, on board the vessels to man Bofors anti-aircraft guns
* an unspecified number of injured men
* the loss of *LST 507*, sunk by torpedoes.
* the loss of *LST 531*, sunk by torpedoes
* severe damage to *LST 289*, hit by a torpedo (which limped westwards to safety at Dartmouth)
* gunfire damage to *LST 511* (which escaped eastwards into Weymouth Bay)

Tecwyn Morgan told me that the one-sided battle had been watched by Royal Artillerymen at Blacknor Fort, high on Portland's western cliffs. The men had the E-boats in their sights, within range, but were ordered not to fire, by an American officer, because of the number of Allied personnel fighting for their lives in the water.

Nigel Cresswell was awoken at about 03.00 hours on 28 April when alarm bells rang across Portland Harbour. The crews of two MTBs of the 63rd Flotilla were ordered to put to sea:

> 'MTB 701's engines were warmed up and myself and Telegraphist Ken Leigh switched on both our W/T [Wireless Telegraph] sets. There was a fair amount of W/T traffic on the longer distance receiving set but it was all in code; a code that Coastal Forces boats were not issued with. The high frequency W/T set, an American TCS set, provided no traffic at all even though we tried all the crystals provided for pre-set tuning.'

By 04.30, *MTB 701* was stood down, but only for a couple of hours as the boat's log reveals:

> '[701] slipped from jetty at 06.45, passed the harbour gate at 07.00, proceeded at 21 knots on various courses into Lyme Bay.'

What followed was never to be forgotten. *MTB 701*'s wartime Navigator wrote to Nigel Cresswell in retirement, stating that they had nosed their way through floating

(Left) LCIs (Landing Craft Infantry) coming ashore on Slapton Sands in Exercise Tiger

(Right) LSTs (Landing Ship Tanks) of the type involved in the 'Slapton Sands Disaster' coming ashore there on 28 April 1944

Costly victory – more than 600 Americans had been massacred by E-boats off Portland before Exercise Tiger concluded with the capture of Slapton Sands on 30 April 1944

The Schnellboot was the principal E-boat (standing for 'Eil Boot' meaning 'Fast Boat')

Supposed (left) and actual (right) positions of the 'Slapton Sands Disaster' plotted on the Admiralty Chart

bodies and brought four or five on board for identification. Mr Cresswell then set down his own vivid memories of that fateful Friday:

> 'On a bright sunny late spring morning, I saw us approach what looked like an outdoor swimming pool but there were hundreds of bodies in the water and they were all dead. I was not quite 21, and had seen the odd dead body, but nothing to what we saw before us. It had a profound effect on us young men and I will never forget it, ever. I remember examining two or three bodies that had been brought on board. Their Army denim uniforms had buttons crimped so that the buttons could not be removed; I remember that two of the dog-tags had 'Rome City, New York'. Their life jackets were different from ours; with two circular rings sewn together with a small cylinder of gas at one end. When depressed the life-jacket would inflate. We were ordered by another MTB to return the bodies to the water.'

Another member of the crew, Able Seaman Torpedoman Wood, confirmed that they had been told to puncture the life-jackets. Here and there they saw a British Army khaki battledress with the square red badge of the Royal Artillery.

That evening all six boats of the 63rd Flotilla were back 'on the other side' as they resumed cross-Channel patrols. Returning to Portland on the morning of the 29th, Nigel Cresswell wandered through the dockyard in the hope of seeing his current girlfriend, Wren Torpedo Mechanic Doreen Smedley:

> 'Looking into the Torpedo Workshop from a distance of a few yards I saw lots of shrouded bodies. I was quickly ushered away.'

What concerned the Allied High Command was that 20 United States officers with the security classification BIGOT were missing and had to be accounted for. They not only knew when and where the invasion of Europe was to take place but the build-up details for both its American sectors (codenames Utah and Omaha) plus elements of the subsequent battle-plan.

Eisenhower, as Supreme Commander, had given strict instructions that no BIGOT personnel should go on any journey or operation before D-Day which carried a risk of being captured by the Germans. This explains why Slapton Sands has been substituted for Portland in the records, then and now, because an inshore misadventure off Devon under the guard of 30 large warships hardly came into that category. On the other hand it was foolhardy for them to be far out in the English Channel with only one lightweight escort vessel.

As it happened, no one had been fished out of the water and taken back to France for interrogation, with the dog-tags of the 20 'in the know' having been collected by military intelligence. The D-Day secret was secure.

As the definitive evidence for the cover-up I can now give the precise locations of both Tank Landing Ships with references courtesy the Admiralty Chart:

LST 507 lies at Latitude 50 degrees 26 minutes 08.00 seconds (north) – Longitude 2 degrees 44 minutes 01 seconds (west).

LST 531 lies at Latitude 50 degrees 26 minutes 08.00 seconds (north) – Longitude 2 degrees 43 minutes 39 seconds (west).

That puts them under between 19 and 33 metres of water, 10 miles west-south-west of Portland Bill and 12 miles south of Burton Bradstock – which is 45 miles from Slapton Sands. Dorset's case proven.

Post-disaster eye-witness Nigel Cresswell of *MTB 701*

Commonest shoulder flash in south Dorset was the 'Big Red One' of the 'Fighting Firsts' – the 1st Infantry Division of the United States Army, heading for Omaha Beach on D-Day

The United States 2nd Infantry Division – 'Second to None' – were to be the reinforcements in Normandy from D-Day plus One

The emblem of the 14th Major Port of the Transportation Corps of the US Army was ubiquotous around Weymouth and Portland and commonplace from Bridport to Poole

Evaluation of Exercise Smash also showed failings at Studland. In particular there were operational problems with the LCGs [Landing Craft Guns]. Difficulties were encountered in drawing down accurate fire on to the coastal hinterland, such as crossroads, which could not be observed from the sea or the beach-head. There was a repeat experiment at the start of May. It was decided to synchronise the position of an LCG on the grid of a local map, by using a Royal Artillery Survey Regiment on the shore, and to check the precision of the resultant gun-laying. Locations were picked as far inshore as Wareham.

(Left) American half-tracked towing vehicles and their trailers, as far as the eye can see, between Dorchester and Weymouth in May 1944

(Right) Ordnance depot with American Engineers laying a temporary road of wood and wire at the foot of an escarpment near Weymouth

(Left) Smiles from an American motorcyclist and an under-age driver (climbing on to the Jeep) at Weymouth in May 1944

(Right) Masses of American armor in a 'Tank Park' near Dorchester, awaiting transit via Portland to the Battle of Normandy

Frank Hamer of Poole recalled that though the technique worked it still lacked the required accuracy:

'The arrangement for D-Day was therefore changed so that the Survey Regiment could land and erect beacons along the landing beach, surveyed into the local map grid. The co-ordinates for each of these beacons would then be sent to the ships by Beach Signals and the ships would fix themselves by re-section. A small party of surveyors – one officer and 13 other ranks – were allocated to each self-propelled Artillery Regiment and split into three teams in separate ships in the hope that at least one group would manage to reach the shore. In the event all the teams did so but they found that smoke from fires and shelling had reduced visibility to almost nil. A bearing was eventually obtained from a sun-shot and later a lighthouse – for which there were co-ordinates – was sighted. Beacons were erected and surveyed in, with the details being sent to ships, via Beach Signals.'

For many in Britain, events on the other side of Asia were 'the forgotten war', but Dorset's strong connections with British India were cemented by the presence there of one of the county regiment's five battalions. Dorset was also pivotal in providing the air link between Britain and the Raj with RAF Hamworthy having been handed over in January 1944 to Sunderland flying-boats of 44 Group, Transport Command. They were tasked to operate from Poole Harbour to Karachi – via Gibraltar, Tunis and Cairo – to carry aircrew and other personnel needed in India and Burma.

The turning point in the far-off war, between Nagaland and Manipur, saw the Japanese advance into India being halted by hand-to-hand combat across the remains of a shattered jungle hill-station at Kohima on 13 May 1944. The 2nd Dorsets lost 75 men in three weeks of fierce fighting that ended with the recapture of a tennis court. For the Japanese it was a major strategic disaster but for the West Country infantrymen it was a visit to hell. Many of their dead had to be left where they fell since battle commenced on 27 April. War correspondent Richard Sharp of the BBC was there when the padre held an aftermath service:

Kohima hill station in India, recaptured from the Japanese by the 2nd Battalion the Dorsetshire Regiment on 13 May 1944, after losing 75 men in a three-week battle

'We are still on the six hills in the centre of Kohima. We've mopped up nearly all the Japs on them, and we've taken the famous tennis court. A half-smashed bunker on one of the hills was giving us a good deal of trouble; but we took it at one [13.00 hours] today, and I've seen the hill myself. It's covered with dead Japs. I've counted up to 40 of them and then stopped. Our men have been sprinkling them with quicklime – a necessary precaution in this weather.

'The men who took it came from a battalion of a West Country regiment [2nd Battalion, the Dorsetshire Regiment]. They've been plugging away at that tennis court for 16 days and they'd become personal enemies of the Japs there, who used to taunt them at dusk, calling across the tennis court "Have you stood-to yet?" Today they're on top and they walked on their toes, laughing, among the bulges in the earth of dug-out roofs; their muscles limber, ready to swivel this way or that in an instant.

'There was a company commander [Captain Clive Chettle], a robust man with a square, black jaw covered with stubble. The skin between his battle-dress trousers and his tunic was bloody, and he swayed as he stood with his legs straddled. But his brain was working at full speed, and he laughed and shouted to his men as they went eagerly from fox-hole to fox-hole with hand grenades and pole charges – that's 25 pounds of explosive at the end of a six-foot bamboo.'

Horsa Mark B glider, supplied in kit form by Airspeed at Christchurch, laid out for inspection at RAF Tarrant Rushton on 25 May 1944

Twin-engine Albemarle tug-plane (left) towing a troop-carrying Horsa glider into the air from RAF Tarrant Rushton

Tetrarch tank being loaded into the belly of a Hamilcar glider

Tetrarch tank being unloaded at Netheravon for the benefit of King George and Queen Elizabeth

Representative aircraft and men of the British 6th Airborne Division being reviewed at Netheravon by King George and Queen Elizabeth

Hamilcar 770 and airborne forces preparing for D-Day at Tarrant Rushton

Four-engine Halifax tug-plane with Hamilcar glider (left) preparing for take-off from RAF Tarrant Rushton

Halifax tug-plane and Horsa glider lift off from Tarrant Rushton

'Going over the edge' with a Halifax (left) and Hamilcar glider above The Cliff escarpment between Tarrant Rushton and Tarrant Monkton

Coming back, after release at 8,000 feet – required height for manoeuvring – a Hamilcar returns to Tarrant Rushton

Invasion stripes on a Halifax-Hamilcar combination above Crichel Estate woodland (with Badbury Rings visible in original print) in May 1944

Halifax-Hamilcar combination, with invasion stripes, above Blandford Camp and heading north-west in May 1944

That day, back home in the New Forest, General Eisenhower visited their compatriots of the 1st Battalion – part of 231st Infantry Brigade – at Cadlands Camp, near Fawley. After being trained by British Commandos in Scotland, the elite United States 2nd Ranger Battalion moved south, via Somerset, to practice climbing techniques on the chalk cliffs of Swanage Bay at Whitecliff Farm and Ballard Point. They were commanded by Lieutenant-Colonel James Earl Rudder.

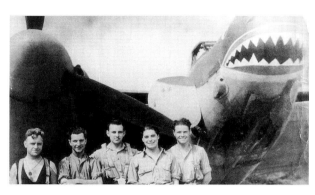

While on routine defensive patrol at midnight, a Beaufighter Mark VI night-fighter of 68 Squadron from RAF Fairwood Common in the Gower peninsula, made visual contact with an enemy reconnaissance aircraft high over the English Channel. It was approaching the big American fleet gathered off Portland. The interception, at 25,000 feet, was initiated by radar control, from Hope Cove in the hills above Salcombe, Devon. The brief encounter was brought to a conclusion at 00.43 hours on Monday 15 May.

Beaufighter pilot Flying Officer Gilbert Wild and his observer, Flying Officer Frederick Baker, detailed the kill of the Junkers Ju.188 in their combat report:

Pilot, navigator and ground crew pose beside the shark's teeth nose of their Mosquito of 604 Squadron at RAF Hurn in May 1944

'Bandit had been gently waving during the chase. On closing in to 300 feet, bandit was identified as a Ju.188 by the oval-shaped nose, long pointed wings and tapering tail-plane with single fin. From 25 yards range a two second burst of cannon fire was given and strikes were seen on the fuselage and port engine. We then got into the enemy aircraft's slipstream and dropped to port and below.

'On coming out with a slow starboard turn, we noticed that the bandit was turning slowly to port and falling. We closed in to 150 yards and gave a long burst, from dead astern, of about four seconds. Strikes were then seen on fuselage and starboard engine, which burst into a bright orange flame, spreading along the fuselage. Bandit then fell away vertically below fighter's port wing with flames growing larger and brighter.

'We then did a hard port turn and dived after bandit but by the time we got round the enemy aircraft fell into hazy cloud about 10,000 feet below, well ablaze. It was then 00.43 and position some 35 miles south-south-west of Portland. As soon as bandit went down we gave 'Murder' over the RT [radio telephone] and understood that a fix was taken by Hope Cove at Z 0560. No window [radar-confusing foil] was seen, enemy aircraft was interrogated [asked to Identify Friend or Foe] three times on AI [Airborne Interception] set and gave no response. No return fire experienced. No exhaust flames were seen.'

Having taken off at 22.22, the Beaufighter returned to Fairwood Common at 01.30 hours. Its four cannon, mounted in the fuselage, had used a total of 787 rounds of 20-millimetre ammunition, principally heavy explosive incendiaries. There had been stoppages. The six smaller calibre wing-mounted Brownings were not used. The kill was confirmed on 17 May when wreckage was found by the Royal Navy.

On 16 May, Sir Bernard Ramsay, the Allied Naval Commander, reluctantly agreed to a request from the Prime Minister that he should witness the D-Day landings:

'Briefly the plan is that you are to embark on HMS *Belfast* in Weymouth Bay in the late afternoon of D-Minus 1, the ship being called in on her passage from the Clyde for the purpose, and rejoining her squadron at full speed. I consider that nothing smaller than a cruiser is suitable for you during the night and the approach.'

On the morning of D-Day, the Prime Minister would be transferred to a destroyer which had completed her bombardment of the Normandy coast and return with her when she headed home to re-ammunition:

Map reading – not of Dorset but Normandy – for the crew of a Sherman tank of the United States 2nd Armored Division, near Dorchester, 1 June 1944

Blackened faces of American infantrymen being debriefed after their last exercise in the Dorchester countryside

American GIs filing into a tent behind barbed wire in woodland near Dorchester for their top-secret D-Day briefing on 30 May 1944

Lieutenant Chandler from Clevedon, Ohio, giving his men a final briefing behind the wire in a wood near Dorchester on 30 May 1944

Inside a Dorchester D-Day briefing on 30 May with foreground figures (left to right) in an American Engineer unit being Private Albert V. Ottolino of Billings, Montana, Private First-class Howard D. Kraut of Brush, Colorado, and Private J. H. James of Woodville, Texas

Signal Corps men with an assault unit waiting to board United States Landing Ship 374 on specially constructed Castletown Hards, Portland, 30 May 1944

All GIs were familiarised with the German signs for the obstacles they would encounter

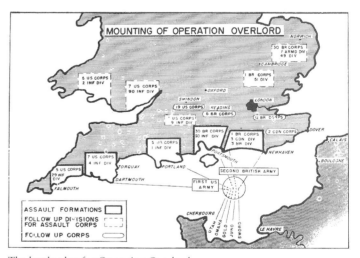

The battle-plan for Operation Overlord

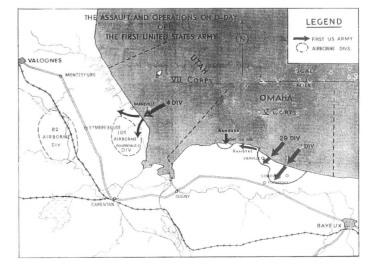

V Corps of the United States Army, from Dorset, formed Force O for Omaha

'You could have a short tour of the beaches, with due regard to the unswept mine-areas, before returning in her.'

The Chiefs of Staff were horrified and did their best to block the plan. Churchill persisted, however, and was only dissuaded by the direct intervention of King George. On the eve of the invasion the King succeeded with a letter that the Prime Minister could hardly ignore:

'I want to make one more appeal to you not to go to sea on D-Day. Please consider my position. I am a younger man than you, I am a sailor, and as King I am head of all three Services. There is nothing I would like to do better than to go to sea but I have agreed to stop at home; is it fair that you should then do exactly what I should have liked to do myself?'

(Left) Men of the 2nd Armored Division changing their training rounds for live ammunition, in a field between Dorchester and Weymouth, 1 June 1944

(Right) Destruction in Melcombe Avenue, Weymouth, from an air raid in the early hours of 28 May 1944

(Left) Unexploded bomb, deactivated and raised from 28 feet below ground beside Weymouth and District Hospital

(Right) Melcombe Avenue and the scale of damage from what was to be Weymouth's last heavy raid of the war, on 28 May 1944

Churchill's private secretary, Jock Colville, had returned to the RAF in a Mustang fighter of 168 Squadron at Odiham, and would fly over 'a sea boiling with ships of all kinds heading for the landing beaches'. Churchill had shared that determination to be 'among the first on the bridgehead' and thought 'what fun it would be to get there before Monty'.

Bournemouth received an incendiary raid on 27 May and the air-raid warning warbled across Weymouh at 01.00 hours on 28 May. One bomb hit Weymouth and District Hospital, starting a fire, and a second embedded itself – unexploded – 28 feet into soft ground beside the buildings. Colonel Knoblock and the Medical Corps of the United States Army evacuated the patients and established an Emergency Hospital in Weymouth College.

Troops were confined to their camps and the coastal areas sealed on 28 May. The D-Day maps were unveiled in the Prime Minister's map room in the underground Cabinet War Rooms. A full-scale glider exercise from Tarrant Rushton Aerodrome took place in moonlight on 30 May as final preparations for the real thing.

'Fair stood the wind for France, when we our sails advance,' Churchill mused as the weather seemed to meet the expectation in Michael Drayton's lines, revived by H. E. Bates's novel which was filmed during the war at Cutt Mill, Hinton St Mary. Though it was restricted information at the time, because of the military significance of things meteorological, Whit Monday – 29 May 1944 – turned into the hottest May day on record.

The temperature reached 92 degrees Fahrenheit (32.8 degrees Celcius) and generated fierce thunderstorms, the most violent of which flash-flooded through Holmfirth, Yorkshire, destroying houses, shops and factories. Three people died and dozens of families were left homeless.

There was a remarkable Dorset sequel to one of the invasion support missions. Halifax Mark II bomber LV792 of 158 Squadron, flying with No. 4 Group of Bomber Command took off from RAF Lissett, Yorkshire, on the night of 2-3 June to attack railway marshalling yards at Trappes, near Versailles, to disrupt German reinforcements bound for Normandy in the aftermath of the impending invasion of Europe. En route home, over Evreux at 01.17 hours, it was peppered by 'Nacht Musik' – an upward firing cannon – from a German night-fighter. The Halifax's air bomber, Flying Officer Eric Tansley, surveyed the damage around him:

'The fire in the bomb bay was hydraulic fluid burning, so the flaps fell half down, and later the undercarriage control could only be lowered by the emergency release. All radio and electrics and hydraulics were out of commission.'

Three members of the crew baled out. The rear gunner, Sergeant Dave Arundel, was jammed in his turret and could do nothing until he backed his way out with his axe. He then went forward to see the situation. He used-up two extinguishers on the fire and then

Halifax LV792 of 158 Squadron which miraculously arrived at RAF Hurn as the war's 'most damaged bomber' on 3 June 1944

Seven-man crew of bomber LV792 at RAF Lissett – one died, two baled out alive and four narrowly made it to Hurn

One of 146 Phoenix caissons of the two Mulberry Harbours being prepared for towing across to Normandy on D+3 (if weather conditions permitted)

Elite forces of the United States 2nd Ranger Battalion marching along the Esplanade, Weymouth, led by Lieutenant-Colonel James Rudder (foreground) with Lieutenant Bob Eldin running (right) towards him

GIs singing on Weymouth Quay as they wait to board USS *Henrico*

Amphibious American DUKWs KS lined up beside the Chesil Beach, awaiting their turn to go into landing ships at Castletown, Portland

An Engineer unit edging towards United States Landing Ships 374 (left) and 376 on Castletown Hards on 3 June 1944

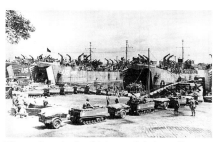

Lines of tracked vehicles and their trailers being loaded into a row of American Landing Ships from the specially constructed additional 'hard' slipway at Castletown, Portland

Frenetic American activity on Weymouth Quay with the loading of the Assault Landing Craft of Force O for Omaha, 3 June 1944

Barrage balloons, to protect the American armada, and loading operations beside the Pavilion Theatre, Weymouth Quay

Five LCAs (Landing Craft Assault) being manoeuvred into position in Weymouth Harbour for loading at noon on 3 June 1944

First Lieutenants Robert T. Eldin of Los Angles and Stanley White from New Jersey, at the controls of a Landing Craft Assault opposite Cosens's steamer office in Weymouth Harbour on 3 June 1944

African-American 'Static Troops' pass down boxes of 'C&K' rations into LCAs moored to the west of the railway station on Weymouth Quay, 3 June 1944

Bombardment battleship HMS *Rodney* in Portland Harbour

'On the double' as the cream of the American Army – the Rangers tasked to take the most difficult objectives at Pointe du Hoc and Vierville – move into LCAs beside Weymouth Quay on 4 June 1944

Rodney in profile

Assault infantrymen packed like sardines, in an LCA at Weymouth Quay, starting what became a long wait before a nightmare voyage

Already packed, those in an LCA moored at Weymouth Quay have to find room for five more GIs on 4 June 1944

'Brass City' half-track reversing on to a landing craft at Castletown Hards, Portland

Reversing on (so they could drive out forwards) with this being the ninth of twelve vehicles to be packed upon United States Landing Ship *195* beside Portland Harbour on 4 June 1944

Signal Corps attached to an assault unit waiting to join 'Queue UF' beside US Landing Ship *374* at Castletown Hards

A pointed finger as an American spots the cameraman during waiting time in Portland Harbour through 4 June 1944

beat out the remaining flames with his feet and hands. The pilot, Flying Officer Doug Bancroft of the Royal Australian Air Force was unaware that the P4 compass had been jammed by shrapnel and was stuck on the course being flown at the time of the attack. Eric Tansley resumed his account for me:

'Some time later the navigator asked the pilot what course he was flying and Doug replied, 'Oh, about north.' I looked ahead of the cockpit and saw the Moon dead ahead. Something registered with me and I said to Doug, an Australian, that we never have the Moon in the north. His mental view of the sky was that in the southern hemisphere. Then he looked around for the Pole Star, by which time we were apprehensive about how far we had flown in a south-westerly direction, and whether we would still reach England on a northerly course.'

Infantrymen aboard USS *Henrico* in Portland Harbour on 4 June 1944

Though problematic, that new line proved to be their salvation, as it kept them clear of the higher cliffs of Dorset to the west and the Isle of Wight to the east. Between these obstacles is a low plateau, at the 120 feet contour, rising up to 200 feet with in-depth hazards such as rooftops, steeples, and chimneys, which was enough of a barrier. They were continuing to lose height:

'These coastal cliffs were only just cleared and the landing was made inland, fortunately as it was by complete chance, on Hurn Aerodrome behind the town of Bournemouth. The bomb bay was still burning. As we came to rest it was the sight of an RAF ambulance that made us realise that by a miracle we had happened to land on an airfield.'

It was 02.49 hours. This combination of low cliffs and an operational base with full-length runways, only four miles inland, occurs on only a few locations along the South Coast. The Air Ministry began to prepare a press report – omitting such topographical details – that this was the 'most damaged' plane to return to England. The four returnees were rewarded with three instant Distinguished Flying Crosses and one Distinguished Flying Medal. News management then went somewhat awry with envelopes or wires being crossed. For it is Pilot Officer Bancroft of Pennant Hills, Sydney, who became the hero for the London *Daily Telegraph*. And the story of Flying Officer Tansley, from St Alban's, Hertfordshire, appeared in the *Sydney Sun*.

At 09.00 hours on Sunday 4 June the codeword for 'Go' was received by airborne forces at Tarrant Rushton. Faces were blackened and all clambered aboard, but then found they could go nowhere, as windy weather caused cancellation of the flights. Some American assault units had already put to sea from Cornwall and Devon but had to turn around and seek shelter. Bombardment ships were already en route to the invasion coast from northern ports. A message was issued to all ranks of 21st Army Group from its Commander-in-Chief, General Montgomery:

'The time has come to deal the enemy a terrific blow in Western Europe. To us is given the honour of striking a blow for freedom which will live in history.'

Captioned 'arms across the sea', British sailors give a helping hand to United States Rangers at Weymouth Quay on 4 June 1944

The weather, however, indicated otherwise. The wind forecast at 21.00 hours on 4 June, for the morning of what should have been D-Day, on Monday 5 June, was revised to west-north-west Force Five [19 to 24 miles per hour] in sea-area Portland. Termed a 'fresh breeze' this would mean mid-Channel waves six feet in height. The report on weather conditions continued bad to indifferent into the evening. Group Captain James Martin Stagg presented it to General Eisenhower at SHAEF headquarters with a series of Atlantic weather maps showing one deep depression passing to the north of Scotland and another positioned to take its place, though not immediately, as it was currently 2,500 miles to the west, off the coast of Labrador and Newfoundland. It was 'chancy' and below 'minimum requirements', Stagg said, 'but it does represent something of a lull

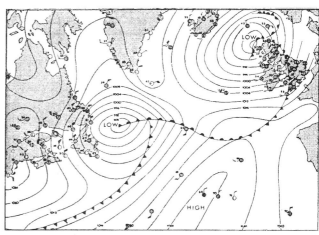

(Left) Stewards Mates Jones and Furrell Browning, from Dallas, manning a 5-inch anti-aircraft gun on USS *Henrico* in Portland Harbour on 4 June 1944

(Right) Group Captain James Martin Stagg's weather map of 21.00 hours on 4 June 1944 delayed D-Day for 24 hours (from Monday 5 June to Tuesday 6 June)

on Tuesday'. He promised 'fair conditions' with a drop in the wind and broken cloud above 3,000 feet.

There were two other major complications. Bombardment ships, already at sea, would need to put into port for refuelling if there was further delay. The invasion window was already closing, as the latest date with the required tidal conditions was 7 June. High tide was necessary for naval reasons and because it brought the matching period of low tide required for Sappers to dismantle underwater obstacles during the time when they were exposed. Deployment and delivery of an assault force of 176,000 men and 20,000 vehicles, protected by 7,000 guns and rockets, was a complex plan that had 'overflow berthing' in estuaries around England and Wales and as far away as Northern Ireland and Scotland.

The operation had to be postponed for 24 hours. Eisenhower decided that Tuesday 6 June would be D-Day:

> 'I am quite positive we must give the order . . . I don't like it, but there it is. I don't see how we can do anything else.'

To prove the point about the weather, the French battleship *Courbet* – filled with concrete and turned into a Gooseberry blockship – was forced to anchor in the lee of Durlston Head, Swanage, at 22.00 hours on 4 June. Later, as she had no power with which to weigh her 7-tonne anchor, this had to be slipped in order for *Courbet* to be towed to her final resting place across the Channel. There was much continuing discomfort in harbours and estuaries, where men were incarcerated in landing craft, packed like sardines and bobbing up and down in the swell. Ernest Hemingway was aboard the troopship USS *Dorothea L. Dix* in Portland Harbour where he had a crash initiation into Morse code on Monday, 5 June:

> 'Three dots, one dash. Those are the lights tonight. Constantly. The letter is "V" for Victory.'

Dr Reginald V. Jones, the chief of scientific intelligence at the Air Ministry, flew over the Solent and realised the invasion was 'on' as the armada that had been in Spithead two days before was no longer there. He then flew westwards to RAF Hurn:

> 'I was silently wishing them good luck when we had a head-on encounter with a whole wing of American Thunderbolts [taking off from Christchurch Aerodrome]. It was like standing in a butt whilst a covey of enormous grouse is driven past you on all sides. What was more, the Thunderbolts with their big radial engines were climbing, and so none of their pilots could see us.'

Having managed to land at Hurn they heard that the Norwegian Wing Commander had been taking part in the cross-Channel attacks on German radar stations:

'He had been shot down earlier in the day, picked up out of the sea by one of the Air-Sea Rescue launches, and had already flown another sortie.'

Twenty-eight Typhoons delivered 96 rockets, each of 60 pounds, and seven tons of bombs on German coastal radar stations. They had to take care to keep that at Fecamp intact so that it could report spoof activity aimed at convincing the enemy that the main thrust of the Allied invasion was further up-Channel, east of the Seine. Five squadrons of Typhoons and Mosquitoes were operating from RAF Hurn, together with P-61 Black Widow night-fighters of the 9th United States Army Air Force and B-26 Marauders of the American 97th Bombardment Group.

Weymouth Bay saw its largest gathering of warships since the Reserve Fleet was dispersed in 1939. The danger of air attack then prevented anything larger than a destroyer operating from Portland Harbour. Naval Operation Neptune brought five American and two British cruisers to the Dorset coast, plus the distinctive silhouette of the 34,000-ton battleship HMS *Rodney*. The terrific destructive force of her broadsides – nine 16-inch, twelve 6-inch and six 4.7-inch guns – was to bombard German batteries at Le Havre.

The last walk across Tarrant Rushton Aerodrome to Horsa gliders with their D-Day stripes on the evening of 5 June 1944

The great armada of smaller craft was to sail east up the English Channel, being joined by more vessels from Poole and the Solent, to gathering point Z for Zebra in a huge circle 40 miles south-east of the Isle of Wight from where it then turned south for the assault crossing.

Field-Marshal Sir Alan Brooke, Chief of the Imperial General Staff, confided to his diary:

'It is hard to believe that in a few hours the cross-Channel invasion starts! I am very uneasy about the whole operation. At the best it falls so very far short of the expectations of the bulk of the people, namely those who know nothing of its difficulties. At the worst it may well be the most ghastly disaster of the whole war. I wish to God it were safely over.'

It all started at 22.56 hours with take-off of the first of 36 Halifax tug planes of the British 6th Airborne Division, towing a troop-carrying Horsa glider, from RAF Tarrant Rushton. Their commander on the ground was 47-year-old Brigadier Richard 'Windy' Gale. Flown by Staff-Pilot Jim Wallwork, the 1st Platoon of 'D' company of the 2nd Battalion, the Oxfordshire and Buckinghamshire Light Infantry, were commanded by Major John Howard in Operation Coup de Main.

From 00.15 to 00.30 hours, Sergeant Victor Swatridge of Dorset Police was patrolling Victoria Park, Dorchester, where he was due to rendezvous with his beat constable. He witnessed the beginning of the airborne armada:

Horsa glider at Tarrant Rushton with graffiti message 'The Channel stopped you, but not us. Remember Coventry, Plymouth, Bristol, London. Now it's our turn. You've had your time you German . . .' ('bastards' was censored and 'swinhunds' substituted).

(Left) Tug-planes and gliders lined-up at Tarrant Rushton on 5 June 1944, along the north-south runway, with Badbury Rings being the wooded hill on the skyline to the south-east (left)

(Right) Horsa gliders from Tarrant Rushton on the ground in Normandy on 6 June 1944

'Suddenly I became aware of the heavy drone of aircraft coming from inland. As it drew nearer, the sky lit up. Thousands of coloured lights had burst forth and the whole atmosphere exploded into activity. It was an amazing transformation as hundreds of bombers, towing gliders with their masses of human and vehicle cargo, flew overhead and across the English Channel. This huge armada was a continuous procession for more than two hours. It was clearly evident that the invasion of Europe had commenced.'

Miss Barbara Baker, a 22-year-old Weymouth teacher, wrote in her diary:

'Early this morning was awakened by the throbbing of low-flying aircraft. Looked out of the window and saw the sky full of bombers towing gliders. Presume airborne troops are being dropped behind enemy lines in France. Heard later that all ships anchored in Weymouth Bay had sailed across the Channel to land troops in Normandy. The long awaited invasion has begun.'

'Pegasus' Bridge over the Caen Canal was the prime target captured by airborne forces from Tarrant Rushton (note their gliders under the trees)

Wallwork and Howard were flying towards a 'promised' gap in the German flak at Cabourg and were cast-off at 5,000 feet to land near Benouville, west of the pair of bridges over the Caen Canal (codename 'Ham') and the River Orne (codename 'Jam'). Coup de Main proceeded smoothly and four of the gliders arrived within yards of the target. They were the first Allied soldiers to arrive in France on D-Day.

Both bridges were secured intact. 'Ham and Jam. Ham and Jam,' Lance-Corporal Edward Tappenden radioed from a captured pillbox just 15 minutes after the attack on what is now known as Pegasus Bridge. It confirmed the successful conclusion of the first D-Day battle. The 'Ox and Bucks' had also liberated the first building in France, namely the Cafe du Tramway, owned by the Gondree family, on the other side of the canal in Ranville. The sadder superlative was the fate of Lieutenant Dennis Brotheridge, shot by a German guard on Pegasus Bridge, who thereby became the first man in the Battle of Normandy to die from enemy action. The Glider Pilot Regiment also lost 34 men on D-Day.

Operation Tonga, involving the other 30 Halifax-Horsa combinations from Tarrant Rushton, encountered more problems. Five of the aircraft failed to release their gliders within the landing zone and Halifax K288 went down with its port wing ablaze.

On the water, the biggest armada in history was underway, in naval Operation Neptune. A total of 6,488 vessels were under Admiralty orders. The main launching points were:

Plymouth to Torquay for Force U for Utah. Weymouth and Portland for Force O for Omaha. Poole to Portsmouth via the Solent for Force G for Gold. Poole to Portsmouth via Spithead for Force J for Juno. Chichester to Newhaven for Force S for Sword.

Major John Howard whose men captured – intact for Allied use – two key bridges over the Caen Canal and the River Orne before dawn on D-Day

Swanage-born Roland Hammersley was among those overhead, in a Lancaster bomber of 57 Squadron, en route to attack German coastal gun batteries at La Pernelle. He

(Left) Midway across – showing a fraction of the Allied sea armada with each vessel protected from air attack by a barrage balloon – at dawn on 6 June 1944

(Right) Offshore as the French coast burns on the morning of 6 June

recalled that they were alarmed by blips from their Fishpond airborne radar, and looking round for enemy fighters, before they realised it had been activated by flotillas of landing craft. What Roland did not know at the time was that his brother, Walter, was down there on the water.

H-hour for Dorset's Americans was set for 06.45 hours. In the event, 06.34 was the moment the first troops splashed ashore, but that was about all that went ahead of schedule for V Corps of the First United States Army with 34,000 troops and 3,300 vehicles due for delivery on D-Day. The initial American assault was by 'C' Company of the 2nd Ranger Battalion who were transported by eight British LCAs [Landing Craft Assault].

(Left) Invasion – the view from a landing craft bridge in the British sector

(Right) Landing craft heading into Omaha Beach with Force O's flagship – USS *Augusta* – offshore

They attacked on a broad front – ten miles wide – with two regimental combat teams, one each from the 29th Infantry Division and the 1st Infantry Division, supplemented by Ranger Battalions. The Rangers had to scale Pointe du Hoc. The 29th Division was tasked to capture Vierville-sur-Mer as its first target. The 1st Division was to secure Colleville-sur-Mer, about three miles to the east. St-Laurent, a village half a mile inland, was at the centre of the main assault, between Vierville and Colleville.

It was almost a disaster from the start. Heavy seas and numerous underwater obstacles caused considerable losses to the leading wave of Americans in landing craft and amphibious tanks. The latter went down ramps into the water about 6,000 feet from the shore. All but two sank with their crews, 'going down like stones'. Resistance was strong from the start. Murderous fire began to take its inevitable toll. It was obvious that aerial bombardment had been inadequate – impaired by poor visibility – and mostly fell some distance inland. Naval bombardment was also largely ineffective, due to the topography of the ground, and went over the top of its targets.

Worse was soon to follow. German coastal forces had been freshly augmented by the 352nd Infanterie Division. This field formation happened to be holding a stand-to exercise and was manning the defences as the Americans waded ashore. They therefore ran into an enemy division that was ready for action and were consequently pinned to the beaches. Likewise the Ranger Battalions on the western flank met with stiff resistance.

Major Stanley Bach, a liaison officer from Brigadier-General Norman D. Cota's 29th Division, who was attached to the 1st Division assault troops, scrawled these potted descriptions of the day on a couple of old envelopes which were his only available paper:

First wave of the assault, into deep water at dawn, towards a line of low hills held by determined German defenders

'11.30. Mortar, rifle, 88-mm, and machine gun fire so heavy on beach, it's either get to ridge in back of beach or get killed. Noon. Beach high tide, bodies floating. Many dead Americans on beach at high-water mark. 12.15. Heavy mortar and 88-mm fire started on beach from east to west end – series of five shells in spots. Direct hit on Sherman tank, men out like rats – those alive. 12.30. LCT [Landing Craft Tank] hit two mines, came on in – hit third, disintegrated and rear end sank. At burst of shell two Navy men went flying through the air into water and never came up. 14.40. More mortar fire and more men hit. LCVP [Landing Craft Vehicles and Personnel] unload five loads of men, they lie down on beach, mortar fire kills five of them, rest up and run to fox-holes we left a couple of hours ago. 16.50. Established CP [Command Post] and saw first time the 1st Division friends who were quiet, fighting men – gave me heart. 17.00. Prisoners began to come up road – a sorry looking bunch compared with our well-fed and equipped men. Duck. I've seen movies, assault training demonstrations and actual battle but nothing can approach the scenes on the beach from 11.30 to 14.00 hours – men being killed like flies from positions. Navy can't hit 'em, Air cover can't see 'em – so Infantry had to dig 'em out.'

The Americans could indeed have lost the beach if the German High Command had not held back its reserve units, thinking that the Normandy assaults were a feint, and that the main invasion force would land between the Seine and Calais. Though Operation Overlord fielded a total of 39 divisions the Germans wildly exaggerated its strength and believed that between 75 and 85 divisions had been assembled for the Allied Second Front. This miscalculation, encouraged by Allied deception and disinformation which had already caused them to reinforce Norway, had Hitler and the High Command holding back their forces from Normandy. They continued to prepare for non-existent further assaults for the rest of the summer.

Meanwhile, at 07.30 hours on D-Day, *LCH 317* [Landing Craft Headquarters], beached to the north-east of Les Roquettes with officers and men of the 1st Battalion the Dorsetshire Regiment to spearhead the arrival of the British 50th Infantry Division on Gold Beach. 'A' Company was led by Major A. A. E. Jones and 'B' Company by Major P. Chilton. Captain C. R. Whittington, the Unit Landing Officer, wore a rainbow-

Dorset's Americans wading ashore through withering fire on to Omaha Beach

On the beach, one wounded infantryman is comforted by a comrade who removes his bandoleer as a third soldier turns his anguish towards the cameraman

Relative consolidation on Omaha Beach with second wave reinforcements at mid-afternoon (splashing towards DUKWs and a half-track towing 57-mm anti-tank guns)

Barrage balloons above the wreckage on Omaha Beach, including a knocked-out Sherman tank beside the sand dunes, on the evening of 6 June 1944

The German 352nd Infanterie Division pinning down the United States 1st Infantry Division on Omaha Beach (stick-grenade and Russian-made 7.62-mm machine gun in the foreground)

American death at the first hurdle on Omaha Beach, beside a wooden stake, above a waterproof Teller mine

coloured battle bowler. He was soon wounded but continued to organise the clearing of corridors up the beach. Major Jones was withdrawn wounded and Major Chilton led both companies in crossing the minefields.

A kilometre to the east, 'C' Company of the 1st Dorsets (led by Major R. M. Nicholl) and 'D' Company (Major W. N. Hayes), helped the Hampshire Regiment to take Asnelles-sur-Mer and attack strongly-held Point 54. The Dorsets achieved all their objectives for the day, but at a heavy cost – 3 officers killed; 30 other ranks killed; 11 officers wounded and 84 other ranks wounded.

The minesweeper HMS *Lyme Regis*, paid for and adopted by the west Dorset town in 1941, cleared the channel into Sword Beach at the eastern extremity of the bridgehead. She buoyed it with French tricolour pennants. The swept waterway was prepared for the passage of General Montgomery and his Advance Headquarters staff of 21st Army Group.

The 'all beaches' listing of 4,572 fatalities, provided for the 65th anniversary of D-Day, showed the international dimension of the invasion:

2,500 American
1,641 British
  359 Canadian
   37 Norwegian
   19 French
   13 Australian
    2 New Zealanders
and 1 Belgian.

(Left) Pluto (Pipe Line Under the Ocean) being tested in Poole Bay before being unrolled across the English Channel to supply petroleum to a beached tanker in Normandy

(Right) Pluto working, to a tanker storage facility in Normandy, having been laid from Shanklin in the Isle of Wight

Allied air forces flew 11,000 series on D-Day, most of them for the Fortitude deception plan to convince the Germans that Normandy was a diversion, with the main invasion being directed towards the Pas de Calais. The following day, Typhoons of 38 Group from RAF Hurn logged 138 cross-Channel sorties, mainly in support of the Second British Army on the coast north of Caen. Saturday 10 June was even busier, with 154 sorties, and Pilot Officer Grey of 181 Squadron became the first airman from Hurn to stand upon liberated Europe. He found himself in difficulties and brought his Typhoon down on a newly-made airstrip. There the problem was sorted out and he was able to return home with the story.

Other returnees during the week included a group of American LCRs [Landing Craft Rockets] which limped into Poole Harbour. They were peppered with shell-holes during their onslaught on the enemy beaches.

RAF Tarrant Rushton moved on to the next stage of the war with Operation Rob Roy. Halifax tug-planes released Hamilcar gliders to deliver jeeps, field-guns, ammunition and fuel to Allied forces in Normandy. Back at base, aircrew of 298 Squadron, 644 Squadron and the Glider Pilot Regiment received a visit from the Marshal of the Royal Air Force, Viscount Trenchard, on 12 June. He addressed them in the briefing room, with congratulations and thanks for their 'perseverance and performance which has been brought to perfection after those months of repetitive training'.

Out in the Channel there were losses on both sides on 13 June. A Junkers Ju.188 bomber sank the 1,350-ton destroyer HMS *Boadicea* off Portland with a radio-controlled

Chain-smoking General Dwight D. Eisenhower and Major-General I. T. Wyche of the United States 79th Infantry Division, ashore in Normandy

The destroyer HMS *Boadicea*, sunk off Portland on 13 June 1944, while escorting a Normandy supply convoy

missile. There were only a dozen survivors from the ship's company of 188 men, who were picked up by HMS *Vanquisher*. A German reconnaissance plane spotted supply convoy S-NS 08 assembling in Poole Bay, enabling the 2nd Schnellboot Flotilla to intercept it, with the sinking of three coasters. The E-boats then used their superior speed to outpace the Norwegian destroyer *Stord* and the Royal Navy and escape to Boulogne. Despite such hit-and-run tactics, they were less able to slip away from the Royal Air Force, with several vessels being sunk by Beaufighters operating from New Forest airfields.

General Weather played havoc with the supply chain as half a million tons of food, munitions and medicines awaited shipment, as well as manpower and vehicles. The forecast gales blew through to devastating effect. Mulberry A – the instant harbour for the Americans – was crippled and never returned to full use, and *LST1000* cracked across the middle in heavy seas. The tank landing ship had to turn back, to Portland Harbour, where to the amazement of American Engineer James Spearman and the rest of his unit, major seam repairs were carried out underwater. Their cargo was a Bailey bridge-building outfit, plus pontoons, and trucks.

Mid-month gales also kept the United States 3rd Armored Division wallowing in Portland Harbour and Southampton Water. They were unable to embark for Omaha White Beach, near Isigny, until 23 June. Their Sherman tanks would eventually decide the Battle of Normandy. Meanwhile it was the infantry who were paying the price, including Lieutenant-Colonel J. W. Atherton from Bridport who was blown up by a tank round whilst fighting off a Panzer counter-attack.

B-17 Flying Fortress bombers of the United States 401st Bombardment Group over Portland Harbour on 15 June 1944, returning from a raid at Bordeaux to Bassingbourn, Cambridgeshire

Commanded by Rear Admiral Deyo, a formidable Allied task force departed from Portland at 04.30 hours on 25 June to bombard German gun emplacements defending Cherbourg. Taking advantage of the bombardment, advance units of General Collins's VII Corps broke into the port, capturing two of its major forts and reaching the arsenal.

Foxwood Avenue at Mudeford was blitzed on Thursday 29 June as three American Thunderbolts crashed on take-off from Christchurch Aerodrome in two separate mishaps. A total of 16 airmen and civilians were killed and 18 people injured. Warmwell also lost three Lightning pilots during the week, though they had reached northern France where the railway system was their prime target. 'You guys can just go over and hit anything that moves,' they had been told.

Bomb damage to a Luftwaffe airfield at Bordeaux, from 24,000 feet, 15 June 1944

Yanks at Christchurch leant a Thunderbolt to Lieutenant Harris of the Fleet Air Arm and he joined 511 Squadron of the USAAF in a cross-Channel mission to beat up the

railway system. Unfortunately, their British guest did not return, and the Americans went through hours of stress fearing they would face court martial for the unauthorised loan and loss of the aircraft. Then panic turned to relief as the wanderer returned. Having overstayed his flying time, Lieutenant Harris had landed at an Allied-held beach in Normandy and been given enough petrol to take-off for a nearby captured airfield where he was refuelled. The following day, 6 July, the Thunderbolts were back in France and trapped a train underground by scoring direct hits on both ends of a tunnel.

Clandestine flights behind enemy lines for the Special Operations Executive were being carried out from RAF Tarrant Rushton. There was also a key move in thwarting the secret war, to put a stop to the German V3 vengeance weapon. Mosquitoes of 418 (City of Edmonton) Squadron and 125 (Newfoundland) Squadron from RAF Hurn flew together in a bombing raid against the massive concrete emplacement of the German Hochdruckpumpe [High Pressure Pump] at Mimoyecques, near Calais. This long-range multiple barrel artillery piece, aimed at London, was still in development.

Weymouth GI bride Doris Mockridge married Private Ernest Webster of the United States 1st Infantry Division (who by the time of their wedding had lost a leg on Omaha Beach)

Rest break for the first troops to enter Caen

Regimental diaries tell what happened next as the infantry found themselves having to dig foxholes and fight from hedge to hedge across the small pastures of the Bocage. This is one story from many and is that of 30-year-old Gillingham soldier Lance-Sergeant Charles Gatehouse of the 5th Battalion, the Dorsetshire Regiment. He was stationed at Hastings prior to D-Day and sailed for Normandy from Southampton in the steamship *Ocean Vulgar*, on 19 June, in the second wave of reinforcements that followed the invasion. It made a rendezvous in the English Channel with the SS *Pampas*, from Tilbury, where personnel had their first experience of V1 flying-bombs. It had embarked with the battalion's vehicles from Victoria Dock, Canning Town.

The two vessels were pounded by a violent storm and were tossed about in mid-Channel for four days. Eventually the *Queen Vulgar* disembarked in Gold Sector near Ver sur Mer on 23 June. The men of the battalion joined their 43rd (Wessex) Division comrades in the concentration area north-east of Bayeux. Here they camped in an orchard to await the unloading of *Pampas* and the arrival of their transport.

Advance party and vehicles were united a couple of evenings later on 25 June. They spent the following day re-organising loads and removing waterproofing. Days later they relieved a battalion of the 3rd Canadian Infantry Division at Le Mesnil Patry. The village had been shelled to pieces and was smelling of death with the enemy artillery continuing to contribute to the destruction. The Canadians had repelled the tanks of a German counter-attack.

In the next village, Cheux, Dorset's 5th Battalion expected an imminent offensive from the 10th SS Panzer Division. They withstood two days of battle and were then rested at St Mauvieu. There was still great danger as they were within range of the big guns at Caen. Captain J. C. V. Davies, the Battalion Intelligence Officer, was killed by a shell while he stood at a check-point.

They prepared to attack Hill 112 and Chateau de Fontaine, along the ridge between the River Odon and the River

American Thunderbolt upside down on the Lymington Road, having landed short of Christchurch Aerodrome on 2 July 1944 (without harming the pilot)

Orne, but the planned attack of 5 July had to be postponed due to the failure of the Canadians to take the German aerodrome at Carpiquet. Meanwhile the 5th Battalion relieved the 3rd Monmouths at Tourville and found themselves within sight of German positions, from which five days' sustained shelling and mortar fire forced them to dig-in and keep their heads down. 'Dust means Death,' the men were told, as divisional artillery proved the point, by pounding the spot from which the slightest enemy movement had been seen. The Dorsets took turns to craw forward to the River Odon for a long overdue bath in No Man's Land. Their other heartening moment was the second Allied heavy bombing raid on Caen which enlivened an otherwise dull evening.

They were by no means pleased to be told they were to be relieved and would return to the so-called rest area at St Mauvieu on 8 July. Here the 'Dust means Death' adage would be again proved as their arrival was greeted by a fusillade of 30 shells. The following night they were tasked to march to an assembly area at Mouen where breakfast was eaten [03.00 hours, 10 July]. They then set off for Fontaine Etoupfour [03.45 hours], to rendezvous with the 9th Royal Tank Regiment for the commencement of a barrage and smoke-screen by 8th Corps artillery, to enable the Dorsets and their armour to attack the high ground around the Chateau de Fontaine, as the 129th Brigade advanced on their right to take Hill 112.

(Left) Typical Normandy with the 1st Battalion the Dorsetshire Regiment advancing through the Bocage (tanks having knocked holes in the hedges) on 11 July 1944

(Right) The 1st Dorsets firing a 3-inch mortar from a foxhole near Hottot, having met resistance on 11 July 1944

The Chateau de Fontaine became known as 'The Fortress' as the Germans mounted a frenzied defence and the 5th Battalion spent eight days laying siege to it from slit-trenches. Casualties were taken and many acts of bravery took place in a series of advances and withdrawals. The battalion then pulled back 500 yards, technically into brigade reserve [night of 18-19 July], to be rewarded with five days in which to make up for lost sleep.

They then spent another two days facing 'The Fortress' [24-26 July] before being marched to the River Seulles for a pleasant break at a spot untouched by the war, enjoying ENSA concerts – Entertainments National Service Association, known to the men as 'Every Night Something Awful' – and a visit to Bayeux. The 5th Dorsets took over from the 2nd Argylls of the 15th (Scottish) Division and were told to form a tight bridgehead over the stream running through Le Mesnil Leveau and to advance from there on the next village, Le Quesnay. They took over American-built dug-outs and were secure from enemy bombing which came in anticipation of their attack. This, however, was met with effective resistance from heavy machine-gun fire, forcing them to halt as intense enemy shelling stopped 'B' Company and knocked out all of its headquarters staff except for the Company Commander, Major K. Mead. It seems to have been in this action, on 30 July, that Charles Gatehouse was killed.

Escorted by two destroyers, the battleship HMS *Rodney* sailed out of Portland Harbour at 07.30 hours on 12 August, and zig-zagged southwards to the enemy-occupied Channel Islands. There her huge 16-inch forward gun turrets were turned towards four German gun emplacements on Alderney. These were pounded with a total of 75 rounds, hitting three of the batteries, in a bombardment which extended from 14.14 hours until 16.44. The ships then made their way safely back to Dorset, returning at 22.12 hours.

THE AMERICAN YEAR

More of Dorset's Americans left for France. The D-Day flyers from Christchurch and Warmwell moved to airstrips in Normandy and Hurn's Canadians shifted sideways as the war moved east, to Middle Wallop on the Hampshire Downs. They were briefly replaced at RAF Hurn by B-26 Marauders of the 596, 597 and 598 Squadrons which comprised the 97th Bombardment Group of the 9th United States Army Air Force. Though only at Hurn for three weeks, they saw some lively action, notably the spectacular destruction of a German ammunition train in marshalling yards at Corbeil, south of Paris, on 14 August.

Friendly fire in warfare long pre-dates the phrase currently in use. One of the saddest 'blue on blue' tragedies of the Second World War involved rocket-firing Typhoons of 266 (Rhodesia) Squadron from RAF Hurn, after they had flown out to Airstrip B3 near Caen. They were formed during the Great War and had as their motto 'Hlabezulu: the stabber of the skies'. Their orders in Normandy were to fly with Wing Commander Johnny Baldwin in search of German E-boats which were playing havoc with Allied shipping.

On the water, four Royal Navy minesweepers of the depleted 1st Minesweeper Flotilla from the Mulberry Harbour at Arromanches had been clearing an enemy minefield off Cap d'Antifer. On Sunday 27 August there was a fateful change of plan. Commander Trevor Crick and Lieutenant H. Brownhill reviewed progress and decided their operation needed an extra day. They amended the orders and minesweepers HMS *Britomart*, HMS *Hussar*, HMS *Salamander* and HMS *Jason* put to sea. They were joined by armed Royal Navy trawlers HMT *Colsay* and HMT *Lord Ashfield*.

The day proceeded routinely enough. The flotilla arrived on station to clear mines. In the air, a total of 16 Typhoons, escorted by 12 Spitfires – to watch their tails for the Luftwaffe – were heading towards them. At 13.15 hours, lookouts from the flotilla reported aircraft circling, and correctly identified them as Typhoons of the Royal Air Force.

Wing Commander Baldwin looked at his prospective targets. They seemed the right sort of shape and size but he puzzled over other details and in particular their dispersal pattern. There were disconcerting inconsistencies. So he radioed a Royal Navy liaison officer to check the situation.

'Are you quite sure they can't be yours?' Baldwin asked.

'Why, are you frightened?' came the reply. 'We do not have any ships in the area today.'

Cluster of four 60-pound 3-inch rockets being loaded and armed under the wing of a Typhoon of 247 Squadron at RAF Hurn

The Typhoons swung downwards and outwards, far into the Channel, and then turned into a low-level attacking sweep at maximum speed.

'Christ, they're attacking us!' was the cry of disbelief on HMS *Jason*, as cannon-fire raked the vessel and rockets ripped apart the superstructure. 'Hit the deck,' shouted the captain, Commander Crick, who tried to get wireless operator Peter Wright to make contact with the aircraft before they turned to deliver more of the same. Wright's brother, Ted, was also in the crew. Peter was unable to send the message before the devastating second-strike. Crick ordered his gunners to refrain from returning fire and indeed none of the vessels responded with a single shot.

For the survivors it would be the longest eleven minutes of their lives. The Typhoons left minesweepers *Britomart*, *Hussar*, and *Jason* sinking. *Salamander*, though still on the water, was a floating wreck, with her stern blown off. The two trawlers sustained damaging hits but were able to rescue many of their comrades, aided by an RAF Air-Sea Rescue launch which headed to the scene.

By nightfall it was clear that there had been a debacle of disastrous proportions. A total of 117 officers and men had been killed, or were presumed to be dead, and 149 seriously wounded. The 1st Minesweeper Flotilla had been virtually annihilated and Commander Crick (1902-97) would recall the horror for the rest of his life:

'The fury and ferocity of concerted attacks by a number of Typhoon aircraft armed with rockets and cannon is an ordeal that has to be endured to be truly appreciated.'

Ten days later the post mortem had been held and concluded. Naval command head-quarters was held to account, in not telling the Royal Air Force about its last minute change of plans, and then denying them. But of the three officers who were court martialled the senior two were acquitted and the guilty junior received only token punishment, for what in most circumstances would have been only a minor lapse. Apparently, the amended orders had not been correctly annotated, which prevented them reaching the right people on time.

Eight separate battalion attacks were launched on 28 August by the 43rd (Wessex) Division to put the first British troops across the River Seine. Among them was the 5th Battalion of the Dorsetshire Regiment. Lieutenant-General Brian Horrocks, commanding 30th Corps, described this as an 'epic operation'. The Allies now had two million men and half a million vehicles in France. In tanks their numerical advantage over the Germans was 20 to one.

Advanced examples of German armour – including Tiger and Panther tanks of Panzer Lehr and other divisions of the retreating Panzer Group West – were shipped to England for evaluation at the Armour Fighting Vehicles School at Lulworth Camp. In excess of 650 German tanks and thousands of other vehicles were destroyed during the annihilation of German forces caught in the Falaise-Mortain pocket. This bottlenecked salient of the enemy front-line was finally closed, in the area of Chambois, after limited escapes on 20 August. Often the Germans immobilised themselves in bumper to bumper traffic congestion which provided Allied pilots with their easiest pickings of the war. The wreckage was on such a colossal scale that in places it brought the Allied advance to a halt.

Captured German tank from Normandy, mounting a short 50-mm gun, being unloaded in Dorset for evaluation on the Lulworth Ranges in the summer of 1944

Total German losses had reached 1,500 tanks and 3,500 artillery pieces destroyed or captured in the Battle of Normandy, plus tens of thousands of other vehicles from armoured car to horse and cart. The Wehrmacht had also lost nearly half a million men. The dead and wounded were estimated to have exceeded 240,000 and the number of Germans taken prisoner by the Allies had reached 210,000.

The strategy was for the Americans to break-out from the west of Normandy, and pivot round to the Seine, whilst the British and Canadians pinned down German armour east of Caen. It was devised by General Sir Bernard Montgomery whose promotion – to Field-Marshal – was confirmed by the King on 1 September 1944. Meanwhile Monty nursed another bright idea.

Nearly a hundred gliders, towed by their Halifax tug-planes, lifted off from RAF Tarrant Rushton on Sunday 17 September to join the armada of 300 Allied aircraft that were to land behind enemy lines in the Netherlands. Operation Market Garden was in the air and the Dorset aircraft headed for the farthest dropping zone, around Oosterbeek, four miles west of the great bridge over the Neder Rijn – the Lower Rhine – at Arnhem.

This became the bridge too far. Dorchester hero Captain Lionel Queripel was awarded a posthumous Victoria Cross for taking out several enemy strong-points regardless of his multiple wounds. The nation's highest award for valour also went to an old boy of Sherborne School, John Grayburn, who held the bridge that was immortalised in the film, being played by the Richard Todd character. His citation lists highlights from three days of sustained attack, without food or sleep, before he was killed:

'Up yours!' as the defiant gesture from a British soldier who refused to cower for the Wehrmacht photographer following the Arnhem debacle in September 1944

'He directed the withdrawal from the bridge personally and was himself the last man to come off the embankment into comparative cover. He constantly exposed himself to the enemy's fire while moving among and encouraging his platoon and seemed completely oblivious to danger. There is no doubt that had it not been for this officer's inspiring bravery the Arnhem bridge could never have been held for this time.'

THE AMERICAN YEAR

The landings were a display of euphoric Allied over-confidence in the face of a mass of information that should have caused more than momentary reconsideration. Aerial photographs showed German tanks only a short distance from the drop-zone. The Dutch Resistance had reported 'battered Panzer divisions' arriving in Holland to refit.

Crucially, there was an Enigma-coded radio message released from Bletchley Park just two days before Operation Market Garden was launched. It gave the precise locations of these units. The intelligence statement was that the Wehrmacht's Army Group B under Field-Marshal Walter Model – veteran of the great tank battles in Ukraine – had moved its headquarters to the Tafelberg Hotel in Oosterbeek. This should have caused considerable alarm on two counts. Firstly, the hotel lay between the drop-zone and its target – the Arnhem bridge – and secondly they were no ordinary enemy troops. These were known to be the 2nd SS Panzer Corps which comprised the crack 9th and 10th SS Panzer Divisions.

Old Shirburnian John Grayburn whose posthumous Arnhem VC was for holding what became immortalised in books and film as *The Bridge Too Far*

The information was available to those planning Market Garden, but Field-Marshal Sir Bernard Montgomery 'simply waved my objections aside' according to Lieutenant-General Walter Bedell Smith, Chief of Staff at SHAEF. General Eisenhower admitted in 1966 that 'I not only approved Market Garden, I insisted on it'. He had been so optimistic on the course of the war, on 5 September 1944, that he went so far as to declare 'the defeat of the German armies is now complete'.

It was largely due to 'the matchless heroism' of 250 men of the 4th Battalion, the Dorsetshire Regiment – part of the 43rd (Wessex) Division – that 2,400 of the original 10,075 airborne troops succeeded in withdrawing from the Arnhem bridgehead on the night of 25 September. Few, however, of the Dorsets escaped, and some of those had to swim for their lives under fire as they crossed the Neder Rijn to do so.

That was the bad news from Arnhem. The good news was that the gamble had succeeded in taking two other bridges, across the Meuse and Waal rivers, and established a narrow corridor into the Netherlands. In the salient of the British advance, 'The Island' at Bemmel, three battalions of the county regiment (the 1st, 4th and 5th) found themselves fighting in adjacent fields for the same 'thumb print' on the map. This was the first time that events had brought them together. Other Dorsets were able to give covering fire to men of the 4th Battalion as they rescued survivors of the 1st Airborne Division and the Polish Parachute with a shuttle service of assault boats across the Neder Rijn. By dawn on 26 September, at 06.00 hours, the intensity of enemy fire made further rescue crossings impossible.

Pushing towards Arnhem with a fag break at Valkenswaard on 18 September 1944, for a truck belonging to the 1st Battalion the Dorsetshire Regiment (white 56 in dull red square), also carrying the Wyvern emblem of the 43rd (Wessex) Division and the five-pointed white star common to all Allied vehicles in North-West Europe

Men of the 1st Battalion the Dorsetshire Regiment formed the first infantry patrol to cross into Germany on 29 September. They were disappointed, however, to have been forestalled from claiming the honour of being the first unit of the British Army to enter the Reich. That was snatched from them by the Sherwood Rangers in Sherman tanks.

The Dorsets operated as support troops for the Guards Armoured Division in its breakout from the De Groote bridgehead. Trophies from the cross-border patrol included a German state flag and a black banner of the SS. That evening, at the invitation of their supporting field battery, the Commanding Officer of the Dorsets and his second in command fired token shells into Germany. One was painted with a message:

'A present for Adolf Schickelgruber.'

Captain Lionel Queripel from Dorchester who was awarded a posthumous Victoria Cross for his heroism at Arnhem

In Dorset, in mountainous seas off Wyke Regis on the evening of 3 October, American *LCT 2454* [Landing Craft Tanks] was washed on to the Chesil Beach. Ten of the LCT's British crew were drowned despite the desperate efforts of Fortuneswell Lifesaving Company who ran along the pebbles from Portland. Rocket lines were fired to the vessel and four sailors were pulled to safety through the waves but the rescue came at a price. Two of the six lifesavers – Captain Pennington Legh and Coastguard Treadwell – were swept away, never to be seen again, as they struggled to free tangled lines.

On 4 October, the 1st Battalion of the county regiment, holding what they called 'The Island' at Bemmel in the Hook of Holland, saw several V2 rockets rise towards London. They were being fired from positions to the east, north-east and south-east. The missiles rose vertically for 15 seconds then gently curved over by 45 degrees during the following 45 seconds. The first to land on London hit Chiswick on 8 September (being described as an exploding gas main) and another fell the same evening at Epping.

As for the subsonic V1 flying-bomb, the Mosquito night-fighters of 418 Squadron – based at Hurn, Holmsley South and then Middle Wallop – claimed a total of 80 scores. Those towards the Hampshire end of their arc of fire were largely shot down over the sea. The method of scoring encouraged this, with one flying bomb put into the sea counting as one enemy aircraft destroyed, while one claimed over land was rated as only being equal to half an aircraft. Newspaper reports of these interceptions included eye-witness accounts of fighters flying level with missiles and then flicking them with a wing-tip to flip them into the countryside. The pilots called it 'formating and flipping'.

A Poole refuse disposal stoker, working at the town's incinerator, literally had a close shave – a superficial face wound – when a cartridge clip exploded in the furnace. This highlighted a serious danger and the public was asked to be more thoughtful with the disposal of explosives. Not that dustmen lowered their guard. Deadly objects were lying around all over the country. Inevitably some of the smaller and less noticeable kinds found their way into the dustbin.

The vicar of Christchurch Priory, W. H. Gay, wrote in his monthly parish newsletter about allegations of having breached rationing restrictions:

> **'As some have questioned the legality of my appeal for clothing coupons to refit the choir with cassocks, may I state that the 143 coupons I have received will be sent to the Controller at Bournemouth who will issue the needed permission to the tailor. I notice that most of the coupons have come from spinsters, widows and bachelors.'**

Control of Hurn Aerodrome was transferred back to the RAF, from the USAAF, on 18 October but the military airfield would soon be stood down. Meanwhile there was celebratory partying, there and at Warmwell, on Sunday 22 October as Air Marshal Sir Roderic Hill announced that the unpopular title Air Defence of the United Kingdom had been dropped and that of Fighter Command revived. RAF Hurn ceased to exist at 00.00 hours on 1 November 1944. Control was passed from the Air Ministry to the Ministry of Civil Aviation.

Twenty-five Poole landing craft, manned by naval crews from the town's HMS Turtle shore-base, landed commandos on Walcheren Island. This German-held strongpoint blocked the approaches to the Belgian port of Antwerp. Nine of the craft, designated as the Support Squadron Eastern Flank, were sunk. A further nine were immobilised. It took the British commandos and Canadian ground forces three days to capture the island. The channel to Antwerp – Europe's largest port – opened to Allied supply ships on 28 November.

Dorsetmen of the 94th Field Regiment of the Royal Artillery, mainly recruited from Bournemouth and Dorset in 1939, became the first field gun force to cross the German frontier. They did so on 11 November – Armistice Day from the previous war – in support of the Anglo-American offensive in the Geilenkirchen sector.

With the war having moved into and across Europe there was a symbolic move towards demobilisation inside the United Kingdom with the Home Guard being stood down on Sunday 3 December 1944.

The back-up troops for the clearance of the Germans from the Bretagne peninsula – the vanguard of the United States 66th Infantry Division – left the Dorchester area immediately before Christmas. Eighty acres of huts at Piddlehinton Camp housed a total of 5,000 American infantrymen but became a winter wasteland as, to their dismay, the young men found that instead of celebrating the festivities they were going to war. They had arrived in Dorset on 26 November and sailed for Cherbourg from Southampton

Charlton Horethorne Royal Naval Air Station on 3 October 1944, with 72 aeroplanes visible despite the cloud, on a training ground for pilots preparing to join the new Pacific Fleet

Docks on Sunday 24 December. The two troopships were the *Cheshire* and the *Leopoldville*.

Cheshire carried the 263rd Regiment from Piddlehinton. *Leopoldville*, an 11,500-ton Belgian liner, cast-off at 09.00 hours with 2,237 members of the 262nd Regiment from Marabout Barracks, Dorchester, and the 264th Regiment from Piddlehinton Camp. Cards and the odd mouth-whistle, wetted by a pint of beer apiece, were about the only seasonal spirit. Canadian escort destroyers HMCS *Brilliant* and HMCS *Anthony* accompanied the ships and rendezvoused with another destroyer, HMCS *Holtern*, and the Free French frigate *Croix de Lorraine* of Spithead.

The ships went on to a war footing at 14.00 hours on passing Piccadilly Circus as the point codenamed 'PC' was generally known. Then, with the white cliffs of St Catherine's Point and the Isle of Wight behind them, almost out of sight, the convoy was ordered to increase speed and weave in a zig-zag course to lessen the chances of an encounter with a German submarine. One was detected, or at least suspected, after a 'ping' on *Brilliant*'s asdic screen. The combat watch, in an intensely cold wind, continued until 14.30 and was then relaxed. 'Bunk duty' was the next order aboard *Leopoldville* as the men attempted to recover from disrupted sleep amid bouts of sea-sickness.

By 17.45 the convoy charted a course to 5.5 miles north-east of the Allied-occupied port of Cherbourg, where lights proclaimed a confidence that wartime blackouts were now beyond their time. 'The place seems to be having a party!' someone remarked laconically. Indeed the party was for real, this first Christmas Eve after liberation.

Last Christmas card of the war to family in Bournemouth from Dispatch Rider Arthur Legg of 6 Base Signal Station (from Cairo to Tripoli and then up through Italy)

(Left) War badge trophies fished out of the sea by Weymouth Lifeboat crew (from members of the Luftwaffe; German deep seas fleet; coastal E-boat sailor; and U-boat submariner)

(Right) Kriegsmarine and other shoulder and cap flashes taken from uniforms on bodies washed up around Weymouth and Portland

A torpedo then smashed into the stern of the *Leopoldville* on her starboard side which was facing the open sea. The liner took two hours to sink, gradually at first but swiftly in the final ten minutes, after bulkheads had burst. HMCS *Brilliant* led a rescue effort that should have won medals but the help expected from partying Cherbourg never arrived.

A total of 802 Americans were drowned, killed, or missing and presumed dead. Survival time in the winter water was minutes rather than hours. When they woke to the reality of the disaster, on Christmas Day, military commanders at Cherbourg disowned responsibility for the debacle, and passed the buck back to those on *Brilliant*. The wreck of *Leopoldville* has been surveyed by Penny and Mike Rowley. It lies on its port side and the highest point is in less than 38 metres of water. The hull, superstructure, and bridge are remarkably intact. Poignantly, the bow points south towards Cherbourg, and the visible damage is restricted to the impact hole caused by the torpedo and a crumpled stern behind it.

The loss, claimed by *U486*, would be overshadowed by another disaster over this final wartime Christmas. To the east, at the other extremity of the front-line, Gerd von Runstedt's Panzers audaciously broke through the snowy forests of the Ardennes in the last great German counter-offensive of the war. Their story became a legend of book and screen, immortalised as the Battle of the Bulge, whereas the tragedy of the *Leopoldville* is hardly known.

Christmas saw a steady stream of Dakotas ferrying American casualties into Tarrant Rushton, en route to the 22nd General Hospital at Blandford Camp. Up to 500 arrived in a single night. Existing patients were dispersed across Dorset from Sherborne to Swanage, and then into Somerset, Wiltshire and Hampshire, from Weston-super-Mare to Odstock and down to St Leonards.

Another year closed with end being nigh but not yet in sight.

Card to the folks in Weymouth from Driver Leonard Oliver of the 11th (British) Light Field Ambulance Unit of the Royal Army Medical Corps, on the front-line near Brussels

1945

Into VE and VJ end-games

SQUADRON LEADER Ralph Stidson Don DFC (25) from Ferndown, flying a Mosquito PR-36 photo-reconnaissance aircraft of 142 Squadron, was reported 'Missing in action' on 23 January. He failed to return from a low-level mission to search out rocket sites and other targets inside enemy territory.

It was on a January night, at 02.45 hours, that Sergeant Victor Swatridge of Dorchester Police was called by telephone at 02.45 hours by the constable on the Broadmayne beat and told that a Spitfire had been stolen at 02.00 from RAF Warmwell. As there was a blizzard at the time he thought this a little unlikely but the Observer Corps post at Poundbury Camp confirmed they had heard an aeroplane overhead at about 02.30. The missing plane was said to have flown west from the aerodrome and the Observers reported the unmistakable sound of a Rolls-Royce Merlin engine. They reported it disappearing about six or seven miles to the north-east.

Moonlight followed the snow and Swatridge went with another officer into the Dorset Downs around Cheselbourne:

> 'At about 05.00, on approaching Cheselbourne Water, to our amazement we saw a lighted hurricane lamp in the drive to a cottage. Naked lights were regarded as somewhat treasonable and very much frowned upon, as Black-out regulations were strictly enforceable. Even the headlamps of cars were only allowed narrow slotted beams. I immediately investigated the reason for this breach and a woman, on answering my call at the cottage, stated that she had heard a plane overhead about two hours previously which appeared to have landed nearby. She went on to say, that she had been expecting her husband home on leave from France, and that it was the sort of stupid thing he would do – come by any means possible. She had placed the lighted lamp as a guide to him. Amazing as it seemed, we trudged on and clambered on to a high bank overlooking an unploughed cornfield where to our utter surprise we came upon tyre marks. On following them we found the missing fighter with its nose embedded in the hedge and bank at the other end of the field, on Eastfield Farm, a quarter of a mile north-east of Cheselbourne church. Climbing on to the wing we found the cockpit lights burning but the 'bird' had flown. There was no trace of blood inside and we found footmarks in the snow made by the culprit, when walking away from the scene, but they quickly became extinct owing to the drifting snow. I returned to the divisional station, after leaving a constable to guard the plane and a search party was sent out in daylight. A Canadian airman on the ground staff was arrested, having celebrated too liberally the previous night, and in a rash moment embarked on this venturesome journey.

INTO VE AND VJ END-GAMES

There was only slight damage to the aircraft; the man was concussed and later dealt with by the authorities. So the escapade resolved itself.'

Halifax aircraft from RAF Tarrant Rushton took part in operations over Norway for the Special Operations Executive through January and February. Off the Dorset coast, the 5,222-ton cargo ship *Everleigh* was torpedoed and sunk by German submarine *U1017* as she set off down the Channel for New York on 6 February.

The Experimental Bridging Establishment of the Royal Engineers, based beside the River Stour at Barrack Road, Christchurch, heard that the longest of their Bailey Bridges yet constructed was open for traffic across the River Meuse at Gennep, Netherlands. Its total span exceeded 4,000 feet.

Designed by Donald Coleman Bailey, in 1939, the first prototype prefabricated steel bridge was put across the Stour at Christchurch on 1 May 1941. It spanned 70 feet. The operation took 36 minutes from commencement to the first lorry reaching the other side. The record-breaking bridge across the Meuse took ten days to erect – being delayed by the fact that its approaches were under two feet of water – and complicated by the height and speed of the river. It enabled 21 Army Group to intensify its relentless pressure against German forces behind the breached Siegfried Line in the second phase of the Battle of the Rhineland. Floods were delaying progress of the 52nd Division.

On the other side of the world, in Burma, there was also an historic river to cross. The 2nd Battalion of the Dorsetshire Regiment watched the 'flyin' fishes play' in the Irrawaddy on 25 February. In Rudyard Kipling's words, the British Army was now 'On the road to Mandalay'. This led to the 2nd Dorsets' battle cry, parodying *The Green Eye of the Yellow God* by J. Milton Hayes:

'There's a dirty white pagoda to the east of Payadu.'

A Martinet from the Armament Practice Camp at Warmwell Aerodrome developed engine problems over Chesil Beach Bombing Range on 12 March. The pilot crash-landed at Burton Mere but found himself trapped in the wreckage. Two heroes ignored the flames which were about to engulf the aircraft and succeeded in freeing the pilot's feet. They were Miss Harriet Evelyn Bendy (68) and Levi Rogers (65) from Burton Bradstock. As they pulled the shocked airman to safety his aeroplane became an inferno.

As an indication that the war was moving away from Dorset, RAF Christchurch was transferred from No. 11 Group, Fighter Command, to 46 Group, Transport Command. It became a satellite airfield to the major transport base on the western side of the New Forest at RAF Ibsley. For the previous nine months, Christchurch Aerodrome had been used as a diversionary airfield when intended destinations were closed by fog or other bad weather. Incoming flights from across the Channel brought Allied wounded and German prisoners. Aircraft types regularly visiting Christchurch included the Boston, Liberator, Stirling and Douglas C-47 Dakota.

As the 1st Dorsets headed for the Baltic, the 2nd Dorsets made progress towards far-away Tokyo. On 20 March, having left 27 dead along the road to Mandalay, they had seized that objective and were mopping up final opposition as the Japanese withdraw. General Sir Oliver Leese, Commander-in-Chief Allied Land Forces South-East Asia, visited the men and told them they would have to make the next 400 miles to Rangoon before the monsoon broke – though this time, he promised, they would not have to walk all the way.

Hearing the news of the capture of the ancient Burmese capital, Winston Churchill remarked:

'Thank God they've at last got to a place I can pronounce!'

The British 6th Airborne Division, with its 60 Halifax tug-planes and their Hamilcar and Horsa gliders, left Tarrant Rushton Aerodrome on 21 March for its new location, RAF Woodbridge This Suffolk airfield was closer to the division's next objectives on the

The British 6th Airborne Division from Tarrant Rushton, having moved on to Woodbridge, Suffolk, for Operation Varsity – across the Rhine – on 24 March 1945

The 'Instrument of Surrender' typed-up in Field-Marshal Montgomery's Tactical Headquarters on Lüneburg Heath

```
                Instrument of Surrender
                          of
        All German armed forces in HOLLAND, in
        northwest Germany including all islands,,
                     and in DENMARK.

1.  The German Command agrees to the surrender of all German armed
    forces in HOLLAND, in northwest GERMANY including the FRISIAN
    ISLANDS and HELIGOLAND and all other islands, in SCHLESWIG-
    HOLSTEIN, and in DENMARK, to the C.-in-C. 21 Army Group.
    This to include all naval ships in these areas.
    These forces to lay down their arms and to surrender unconditionally.

2.  All hostilities on land, on sea, or in the air by German forces
    in the above areas to cease at 0800 hrs. British Double Summer Time
    on Saturday 5 May 1945.

3.  The German command to carry out at once, and without argument or
    comment, all further orders that will be issued by the Allied
    Powers on any subject.

4.  Disobedience of orders, or failure to comply with them, will be
    regarded as a breach of these surrender terms and will be dealt
    with by the Allied Powers in accordance with the accepted laws
    and usages of war.

5.  This instrument of surrender is independent of, without prejudice
    to, and will be superseded by any general instrument of surrender
    imposed by or on behalf of the Allied Powers and applicable to Germany
    and the German armed forces as a whole.

6.  This instrument of surrender is written in English and in German.

    The English version is the authentic text.

7.  The decision of the Allied Powers will be final if any doubt or
    dispute arises as to the meaning or interpretation of the surrender
    terms.
```

B. L. Montgomery
Field-Marshal

4 May 1945
1830 hrs

far side of the Rhine. These landings, codename Operation Varsity, began at 09.45 hours on 24 March and continued for three hours. The 6th Airborne Division took Hamminkein and the bridges over the River Issel. Fifty-two of the ex-Tarrant Rushton gliders landed successfully.

The Duchess of Kent visited the 22nd General Hospital of the United States Army, which worked with the 125th, 131st and 140th General Hospitals in a major medical complex across the former Anson-Craddock Lines at Blandford Camp. It received 17,000 long-term patients, many of whom needed complicated surgery. The commander was Lieutenant-Colonel Leonard D. Heaton.

Polish pilots claimed a U-boat in the Channel. It was sunk in the south-east extremity of Poole Bay, towards the Isle of Wight. The next Dorset airfield to lose its front-line role was RAF Warmwell. 152 Squadron – which had been operating there since the dark days of 1940 – flew out on 9 April and the station became a training base for the Central Gunnery School.

Trooper James Legg from Puddletown, aged 21, was killed in action in Italy on 17 April. Serving with the Queen's Bays, he drove the first tank to force its way through the enemy's main defensive line, in the Argenta Gap.

The air link between Britain and Australia was resumed on 26 April. After a flight of 53 hours, from Hurn, the first Lancastrian of British Overseas Airways Corporation's new civilian fleet landed in Sydney. Airliner G-AGLF carried the military markings of the RAF's South-East Asia theatre but was on a pathfinding flight to determine the feasibility of a peacetime service. The Lancastrian touched down en route at Lydda in Palestine, Karachi in India, Ratmalana in Ceylon, and Learmonth in Western Australia.

The pre-war flying-boat service from Southampton Water used to take nine days, but though so much faster the Lancastrian had restricted room, for bunks and seats for only six passengers. The Empire flying-boat could carry 24 passengers.

On Friday 4 May, at 20.30 hours, cipher clerks to the units of Dorsetshire Regiment in Germany received the following message:

'SECRET . all offensive ops will cease from receipt of this signal . orders will be given to all tps to cease fire 08.00 hrs tomorrow saturday 5 may . full terms of local surrender arranged today for 21 ARMY GP front follow . emphasise these provision apply solely to 21 ARMY GP fronts and are for the moment excl of DUNKIRK . ack.'

In other words, it was over. The times were stated in British Double Summer Time and resulted from the Instrument of Surrender which was signed by General-Admiral Hans Georg von Friedeburg, the emissary of Grand Admiral Karl Doenitz who was exercising command in Schleswig-Holstein in place of Hitler – who had shot himself – and General Hans Kinzel, as Chief of Staff to Field-Marshal Ernst von Busch.

Their unconditional surrender of all enemy forces in northern Germany was signed at 18.30 hours on the 4th in the Tactical Headquarters of Field-Marshal Sir Bernard Montgomery on Lüneburg Heath.

Celebrations at home had to wait until Victory in Europe Day on Tuesday 8 May, when at 15.00 hours war in Europe was officially at an end. Street parties, bonfires, and church services marked VE Day.

(Left) The Wehrmacht surrendering to Field-Marshal Sir Bernard Montgomery at 18.30 hours on 4 May 1945

(Right) General Hans Kinzel putting his signature to the document ending the war in North-West Europe

Next day, officers commanding the German garrison in the Channel Islands surrendered aboard the destroyer HMS *Bulldog*. The islands, which in normal times have their main English port at Weymouth, were passed by during the Battle of Normandy to avoid unnecessary Allied and civilian casualties. The War Office contingency plan, implemented in May, was for the Channel Islands to be occupied, garrisoned, and then demilitarised by the 522nd (Dorset) Coast Regiment of the Royal Artillery. The unit ceased to exist as such and was reformed for the purpose, as the 618th (Dorset) Garrison Regiment, Royal Artillery.

Halifax aircraft from RAF Tarrant Rushton spent 48 hours ferrying the British 1st Airborne Division to take over Oslo Gardemoen airfield in Norway. Phase III of Operation Doomsday, completed on 11 May, was followed by Phase IV, for their re-supply over the following week. Transport duties were now the Order of the Day on aerodromes across the continent.

```
FROM : EXFOR MAIN :                          DATE-TOO
                                             04 2050 B

TO : FOR ACTION : FIRST CDN ARMY : SECOND BRIT ARMY :
                  L of C : GHQ AA TPS : 79 ARMD DIV :
                  EXFOR REAR :
     FOR INFM   : SECOND TAF : EXFOR TAC : 22 LIAISON HQ :


GO 411 A  SECRET . all offensive ops will cease from receipt this signal .
orders will be given to all tps to cease fire 0800 hrs tomorrow saturday
5 may . full terms of local German surrender arranged today for 21 ARMY GP
front follow . emphasise these provisions apply solely to 21 ARMY GP front
and are for the moment excl of DUNKIRK . ack


IN CIPHER if liable                          DOP
to interception
                                             EMERGENCY

                          BGS .

Copy to:  All Branches Main HQ 21 Army Group
          War Diary (2)
```

Montgomery's order that 'all offensive ops' are to 'cease from receipt of this signal' though excluding 'for the moment' the enemy enclave left behind at Dunkirk

The first U-boat to give itself up in British home waters, under the unconditional surrender terms, was *U249* which sailed on the surface into Weymouth Bay on the morning of 10 May 1945. The vessel flew the German naval ensign at half-mast with a Union Flag above after Oberleutnant Kock sent a signal to the Royal Navy that he wished to surrender. The five officers and 43 crewmen of *U249* lined up on deck as the submarine was anchored off Weymouth. Commander Weir boarded and hoisted the white ensign.

The frigates HMS *Amethyst* and *Magpie* escorted the U-boat which initially surfaced 50 miles south-south-west of the Lizard and hoisted a black flag. *U249* carried ten unfired torpedoes and was followed that afternoon by *U825* which came into Portland Harbour. *U1023* joined them in Weymouth as the surrender of Grand Admiral Karl Doenitz's fleet gathered pace.

LCGs (Landing Craft Guns) putting out the flags beside Poole Quay for VE Day

Villagers at Freshwater in the Isle of Wight were amazed when a German U-boat surfaced offshore in the bay and requested someone to take its surrender on 16 May. Freshwater had a parish council but no mayor or anyone of similar standing that a German officer might respect. Anyway it had no port facilities apart from a beach and the inhabitants considered they were in line for a rollicking from the Royal Navy. So *U776* was asked to surrender somewhere else and it departed for Portland

(Left) Submarine surrender with *U1023* approaching Weymouth Harbour on 10 May 1945

(Right) Commander N. J. Weir RN (foreground left) receiving the surrender of *U249* – the first to do so – in Weymouth Bay on 10 May 1945

Harbour. Someone in the Isle of Wight had turned down a splendid opportunity. Think of how he might have answered that inevitable question:

'Grand-dad, what did you do in the war?'

The first Victory Parade to be held in Germany took place on 12 May when the 5th Battalion of the Dorsetshire Regiment marched past Lieutenant-General Brian Horrocks, commander of 30th Corps, in Bremerhaven.

(Left) Memorial day for the 22nd General Hospital at Blandford Camp, remembering the dead of the Second World War and their late President, Franklin Delano Roosevelt, on 30 May 1945

(Right) Colour party firing a salute to open Roosevelt Park, Blandford Camp, on 30 May 1945

Roosevelt Park inside the confines of Blandford Camp was the first overseas memorial to the late President of the United States of America. It was declared open on 10 May by Colonel J. Fourrier of the United States Army and a colour party fired ceremonial rounds. The park was dedicated:

'. . . to the everlasting memory of our fellow soldiers, at home and abroad, who gave their lives in this war, so that we who live may share in the future of a free and better world.'

It had been provided through voluntary contributions of members of the Army Medical Department. The landscaping was designed by a patient at the General Hospital, Private George H. Stuber. Colonel Fourrier handed the park over to Colonel T. Topham of the Royal Engineers who received it on behalf of the British Army. A six-feet high monument was under construction to enshrine the ideals behind the park permanently in stone.

Dorset's worst air-crash, killing all 27 men on board, took place on Friday 15 June. Liberator JT985 of 232 Squadron, Transport Command, took off from RAF Holmsley South at 07.20 hours for RAF Castel Benito, near Tripoli, on the first leg of a flight to India. The aircraft, with a crew of five, carried 22 aircraftmen as passengers, en route to RAF Palma where they were needed as ground-crew.

The take-off was uneventful, though in poor weather, and the Liberator headed south-west, over Bournemouth and Isle of Purbeck. Between 07.45 and 07.55 hours two radio messages were sent, saying that the aircraft was experiencing a loss of fuel pressure over the English Channel, and that they were therefore turning back towards their home base in the New Forest.

Sir Ernest Scott of Encombe House and his dairyman saw the aircraft coming in low from the sea and realised that it would be unable to clear the coastal escarpment. They then heard an explosion   That was at 08.15. The first to reach the scene were Sergeant Reginald Reynolds of the RAF, who was staying at Encombe, and an Army platoon from the searchlight battery near Kingston. Wreckage lay across a wide part of North Hill, from Polar Wood towards Orchard Hill Farm, and it was immediately apparent that there would be no chance of finding survivors. Human remains, baggage and other personal effects were littered across the ground. The bodies were taken to the mortuary in Poole.

The crew comprised Flight-Lieutenant Saxon Cole of the Royal Canadian Air Force (pilot); Flying Officer Donald Twaddle also of the RCAF (co-pilot); Flying Officer Joseph Todd, RCAF (navigator); George McPherson, RCAF (radio officer); and Sergeant George Wyke, RAF (flight navigator).

Dorset's only Battle of Britain aerodrome, at RAF Warmwell, effectively closed in June with the departure of the Central Gunnery School to Sutton Bridge, Lincolnshire. Official closure followed in November 1945.

Dummy deck (rectangle of concrete along runway at centre of photograph) for training aircraft carrier pilots at Henstridge Royal Naval Air Station

The roll of honour published in *The Shirburnian* school magazine, during the course of the war, accounted for 242 lives. It compared with a death toll of 218 in the Great War but Sherborne School was then much smaller. The most distinguished of the Old Boys in the current conflict was the brilliant mathematician Alan Turing who broke the German military's Enigma cipher codes. The bravest was Lieutenant J. H. Grayburn of Abbey House who was posthumously awarded the Victoria Cross for persistent gallantry devoted to the impossible task of holding the bridge at Arnhem. John's was among the first Victoria Crosses to be won for the Parachute Regiment and the only one by a Shirburnian in the Second World War.

Thursday 5 July was General Election Day. All the pundits agreed about the result. Wilson 'Jack' Broadbent, the political correspondent of the *Daily Mail*, told its million and a half readers that the Prime Minister 'can be certain of victory at the polls on Thursday, barring accidents'. He 'will have a working majority; he may have a substantial majority' as 'there is no general swing against his Government' and 'his personal stock stands as a high as it ever did'. Broadbent concluded:

'It is true, of course, even to the ordinary observer that the Labour Party campaign in this election has been ineptly handled, and completely lacking in inspiration.'

The *Manchester Guardian* concurred:

'There is no reason to be other than frank about these matters. The chances of Labour sweeping the country and obtaining a clear majority over all other parties are pretty remote.'

Mr Churchill told electors:

'We are going to win. I feel it in my bones that you are going to send me back to power with a great majority. The eyes of the world will be on us tomorrow. If we go down, then all the ninepins of Europe will go down with us. France and Belgium will go forward, not to decent Labour or Socialism, but to a vile form of Communism.'

Ballot boxes were sealed that night and their counting delayed for nearly three weeks, to enable the practicalities of retrieving and sorting votes from overseas forces, particularly those fighting the Japanese in South-East Asia.

American aircrew being brought to Bournemouth for a period of recuperation had a lucky escape at Christchurch Aerodrome on 15 July. Flying Fortress 866, carrying men of the 306th Bombardment Group from Thurleigh, Bedfordshire, overshot the western boundary of the notoriously short airfield when landing into a light wind. It plunged into

Women Firemen (as they were known) of National Fire Service Division 16-C marching through Bournemouth Gardens in a Victory Parade, 1945

scrubland. The near-side port engine was ripped out but the aircraft came to a halt without catching fire. No one was hurt.

Thursday 26 July was Declaration Day and the nation was stunned. Contrary to the pundits not only did Winston Churchill's Conservative Party fail to retain power but suffered a crushing defeat inflicted upon it in the General Election which took place on 5 July. Instead it had been a Labour land-slide. The state of the parties was Labour 393; Conservative 198; and the Liberals eclipsed with just 12 members of Parliament.

Individual results told the same story. There were no fewer than 26 Labour members enjoying majorities of over 20,000 votes, with the greatest of these enormous majorities being Emanuel Shinwell's 32,257 at Seaham, which was Ramsay MacDonald's old seat. Only true-blue Bournemouth was in the same league, for the Conservatives, having returned Sir Leonard Lyle with a surplus of 20,312 votes.

Pre-war memories were blamed for the scale of the Socialist success which also surprised correspondents from across the world in its rejection of the country's acknowl-edged saviour. To them and to him it was an unwarranted dismissal.

Even in Dorset it was a close-run thing for the Conservatives. The Parliamentary constituency of East Dorset returned Lieutenant-Colonel Mervyn Wheatley with 26,561 votes against 25,095 to his Labour opponent, Lieutenant-Commander Cyril Fletcher-Cooke, with Liberal candidate Colonel Mander having the remaining 8,975. Out of 80,816 voters on the electoral registers there was a poll of 60,629, which included 8,352 votes from men and women in the armed services (75 per cent of electors voted).

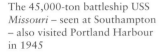

The 45,000-ton battleship USS *Missouri* – seen at Southampton – also visited Portland Harbour in 1945

Clement Attlee became Prime Minister on 27 July 1945 with Ernest Bevin as Foreign Secretary, Sir Stafford Cripps at the Board of Trade, and Dr Hugh Dalton as Chancellor of the Exchequer. Winston Churchill would return to power in October 1951 and completed his 'unfinished business' of finally removing rationing in time for the corona-tion of Queen Elizabeth II and his reward of a knighthood, in 1953.

Wednesday 15 August was Victory over Japan Day. Nowhere in Dorset were the cele-brations more heart-felt than in Stalbridge and in particular the Wrens' Quarters on the Dorset side of HMS Dipper, the Royal Naval Air Station at Henstridge which straddled the county boundary with Somerset. There a bonfire was kept burning all night, despite a soaking at 05.00 hours when the rain intensified. It was lit a few minutes after midnight when the station Tannoy roused everyone from sleep:

INTO VE AND VJ END-GAMES

INTO VE AND VJ END-GAMES

Loaded with GIs going home, the troopship *Queen Elizabeth* was given a flypast salute (top left) by a fighter formation as she sailed down Southampton Water

'Attention everybody. Attention. Japan has surrendered!'

The VJ Day party began and carried on through the night, next day, and into following night in the Red Lion and the Swan at Stalbridge and the Fountain Inn and Virginia Ash at Henstridge. This, to the end, had been an operational airfield. For Henstridge and its staff and families, VE Day had been only half the story, with young New Zealand pilots and others still under training for a war that continued to be a going concern.

What was becoming 'the forgotten war' ended with the dropping of two atomic bombs. Leaflets dropped on Hiroshima on Saturday 4 August warned:

'Your city will be obliterated unless your Government surrenders.'

That was ignored, apart from the cutting of useless firebreaks, and it was Hiroshima's misfortune to be the one of four potential targets that was basking in sunshine on the morning of Monday 6 August. The blow – with a flash 'like a thousand suns' – was delivered by a single bomb called Little Boy, which was carried by a lone United States Army Air Force Boeing B-29 Superfortress piloted by Paul Tibbets Junior and named *Enola Gay*, for his mother. Then Nagasaki was threatened with its 'rain of ruin the like of which has never been seen on Earth' which was wrought by the Fat Man dropped by another B-29 Superfortress, *Bock's Car*, on Thursday 9 August. The third atomic bomb, standing-by and apparently destined for Tokyo, did not have to be delivered. Japan began the surrender process that weekend.

Sir Ronald Lindsay, of Stepleton House near Blandford, died on 21 August. The retired diplomat was born in 1877. He rose through the ranks at the Foreign Office to become an under-secretary in 1920 and progressed to the highest postings in the service – being Ambassador to Berlin (1926-28) and Washington (1930-39). When he bowed out the war, as they say, was an extension of diplomacy by other means. His home, the classical Stepleton House and its park where Peter Beckford wrote the classic book on foxhunting, passed to Sir Ronald's nephew, Lord Crawford.

Portland's memorial to the Americans who passed through Castletown and the hards and dockyard en route to D-Day and the fierce fighting on Omaha Beach was unveiled in the rain on 22 August by the United States Ambassador to London, Gil Winant. He was welcomed by the chairman of Portland Urban District Council, A. N. Tattersall, after driving along the newly re-named Victory Road. The stone was in Victoria Gardens where the Stars and Stripes flew beside the Union Flag.

'Fine, fine, perfectly fine,' was Gil Winant's famous remark of the war, which he repeated over the trans-Atlantic telephone when President Roosevelt told him of the Japanese attack on Pearl Harbor which brought America into the conflict.

The Horishima atom bomb, photographed from lone bomber *Enola Gay* as it headed southwards and seawards from the port town of western Japan on 6 August 1945

157

United States Ambassador Gil Winant arriving in Victoria Gardens, Portland, to unveil a memorial to Dorset's Americans, 22 August 1945

By now, however, he was engulfed in personal problems and would shoot himself in 1947, after his return to the United States. He was said to have set his heart on Winston Churchill's daughter, Sarah Churchill, but she could not reciprocate his love.

Canford School's roll of war dead closed on 31 August at a total of 139 lives. This had been its first war. As the school was founded in 1923, it happened that all Old Canfordians were of an age to serve, and nearly a thousand of them held commissions.

The apparently miraculous cures brought about at Shaftesbury Military Hospital, Guy's Marsh, with M&B tablets, were upstaged by the use of penicillin. This reversed impossible infections which previously would have killed even the strongest soldiers. It took years to bring the drug into commercial production. In 1942 the entire world supply was needed to treat a single case of meningitis.

Remarkable surgery was also taking place. Strabismus was being corrected by an easing of the muscles around the eyeball. Major John Charnley carried out a pioneering hip-replacement operation at Shaftesbury which was as much a feat of carpentry as an exercise of the surgeon's craft.

The British Army returned to Blandford Camp – which saw out the war as a major American General Hospital – with the arrival of the 1st and 2nd Searchlight Regiments, Royal Artillery, in the huts of the Craddock and Benbow Lines. These units trained conscripts called-up to serve their national service with the Royal Artillery.

The first BOAC flying-boat to bring repatriated prisoners-of-war home to Britain from Japan touched down in Poole Harbour on 18 September, amid sensational press interest in the men's stories of degrading and inhuman treatment. They were given a civic welcome at a reception on Poole Quay. Many thousands were on their way home by air and sea.

An ex-military C-54 Skymaster of Pan American Airways landed at Hurn Aerodrome from La Guardia Airport, New York, on 18 September after a proving flight that took 17 hours. The airliner, carrying nine crew and ten staff as observers, stopped off en route at Gander in Newfoundland and Rineanna in Eire. This was the first time a four-engine land-plane – as distinct from a flying-boat – crossed the Atlantic on a civilian flight. Former Halifax bombers, in conversions known as Haltons, are operated from Hurn on the BOAC route to Lagos via the other West African colonies.

The Fascist hireling and traitor William Joyce smiled in the dock at the Old Bailey on 19 September as the black-capped judge told him:

'You will be hanged by the neck until you are dead.'

He gave the Nazi salute to people at the back of the court. The voice of Radio Berlin, for its wartime broadcasts to England, he had been captured near the Danish frontier, by British troops in the last week of May. He was identified and brought to London where he was charged with treason, on the grounds that although Irish-born he had put himself under His Majesty's protection by obtaining a United Kingdom passport. 'Lord Haw-Haw' was remembered in Dorset for his pre-war cottage sojourn at Farnham, as the guest of Captain George Pitt-Rivers.

Colonel Raby, the Director of the Signals Research and Development Establishment at Christchurch Aerodrome and Steamer Point, Highcliffe, test-fired a German V2 rocket which he had reconstructed from captured parts. It was flown northwards, along the coast from Cuxhaven, near Bremerhaven, into the North Sea off Denmark. Undertaken on 3 October, this was a secret test, codename Operation Backfire, and on the 4th another rocket was fired. Raby's establishment was working on a programme for British guided weapons.

A third V2 was fired by the British team on 15 October 1945; and this time the world's press was invited and billed it – wrongly – as 'the first Allied test-firing of a V2 rocket'.

The 22nd General Hospital of the United States Army finally pulled out of Blandford Camp in October. The last of its staff sailed back across the Atlantic, from Southampton, aboard the liner *Queen Mary*. Major Richard Harris of the Dorsetshire Regiment, among those killed at Arnhem, was commemorated by his parents and family with a memorial in St Peter's churchyard at Bournemouth.

Argentina, a Sandringham-2 flying-boat, lifted off from Poole Harbour for Buenos Aires, fitted out for 45 passengers. She and *Uruguay*, another Sandringham-2, had been sold to Dodero, the Argentine airline, which also purchased three Sandringham-3 flying-boats. Intended for longer flights, *Brazil*, *Inglaterra* and *Paraguay* had more spacious accommodation for their 21 passengers. Each was delivered across the Atlantic by a British Overseas Airways Corporation crew with Argentinians aboard as observers. Average flight-time was 36 hours.

V2 missile, rebuilt by Colonel Raby from the Signals Research and Development Establishment at Christchurch, prepared for firing from Cuxhaven, 3 October 1945

New Year's Eve saw the last rites for the Home Guard which was finally and formally disbanded by the War Office. Its last County Commander, General Henry Jackson, paid a glowing tribute to his men:

'The spirit of comradeship and service which was brought to life by service to the Dorset Home Guard must never be allowed to die.'

(Left) Poole BOAC flying-boat *Hanbury* (still in RAF markings) taking off for India – westwards beside Brownsea Island – in the autumn of 1945

(Right) Symbolic end of Empire for BOAC flying-boat *Hailsham* having returned a little too close to Brownsea Island when landing in Poole Harbour, 4 March 1946

The pitiful casualties of this war, beyond the help of surgery and drugs, were the psychologically distressed ex-prisoners of the Japanese brought home from the Far East to recover at Shaftesbury Military Hospital, Guy's Marsh. Many were also emaciated but the mental damage would take longer to correct. They suffered horrific memories when they were awake and lapsed into agonising nightmares in sleep.

Such dehumanised wrecks became even more pathetic as they regained their physical strength without a comparative recovery from mental anguish. They were men returned from Hell whose ordeal was worse in its way than more clear-cut cases on life's edge with tuberculosis. Its wards would once have been one-way nursing towards death but there expectations and hope had been transformed with the introduction of the wonder-drug Streptomycin.

Poole's Public Health Officer, George Chesney, sent a confidential letter to all doctors within the likely hinterland of Poole Airport. The BOAC flying-boat base in Poole Harbour remained the major national terminal for the repatriation of troops, prisoners of war and expatriates from India and Far East.

To add to the physical and mental traumas of what had been a long war, or worst an inhumane and brutal half-starved incarceration in forced labour camps, the returnees were often regarded as potential pariahs. Ships also arrived in Poole from the Far East. 'Imported smallpox' was the subject of George Chesney's letter from the Municipal Buildings:

A mine like this escaped detection and exploded on Swanage beach, on 13 May 1955, killing five boys from Forres Preparatory School

'During the past three weeks four ships from the East have arrived at British ports with cases of smallpox on board. From these ships, up to the present 19 contacts have arrived in Poole and been placed under surveillance.'

Two cases of haemorrhagic smallpox, one involving a fully-vaccinated medical orderly, proved fatal. Another case concerned a Royal Army Medical Corps officer who spread the contagion to his wife and daughter. An article was prepared for *The Lancet* warning of the hazards implicit in international travel:

'It is now possible to reach the country by air from the Far East in as little as two days, or from South America or via the United States in less than a week. Medical inspection at seaports or airports offers no protection against entry by these means of persons who are unknown contacts incubating smallpox, and it is possible for them to develop a clinical attack at any time within about ten days of their arrival. The extent of the spread of infections in such instances depends almost entirely on the prompt recognition of the illness and particularly of the mild attacks in well-vaccinated persons.'

Chesney also warned that 'modified smallpox' should be considered in evaluating apparent cases of chickenpox in persons recently returned from the East, and that any case of 'indefinite illness' in such people or their families should also be kept under observation. As well as bringing the threat of smallpox, passengers also arrived within the incubation period of typhus fever, cholera and plague. 'These diseases should be born in mind,' the Medical Officer warned.

In December the 14th Major Port of the Transportation Corps of the United States Army presented a bronze plaque to Portland Royal Naval dockyard commemorating the logistics of the invasion of Europe:

'1944-1945. The major part of the American assault force which landed on the shores of France 6 June 1944, was launched from the Weymouth and Portland Harbors. From 6 June 1944 to 7 May 1945, 418,535 troops and 144,093 vehicles embarked from the harbors. Many of these troops left Weymouth Pier. The remainder of the troops and all vehicles passed through Weymouth en route to Portland points of embarkation.'

Plaque to record the pivotal part played by Portland Harbo[u]r in the invasion of Europe

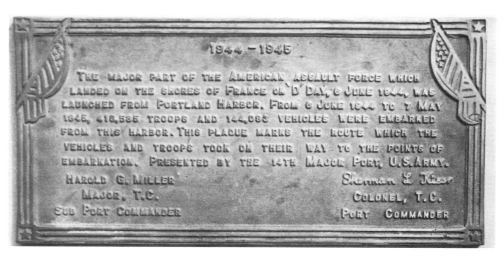

(Left) Three thousand anti-invasion mines had to be found in Ringstead Bay alone

(Right) When found, wartime devices were deactivated or blown up, here by Lieutenants Rex King and Ralph Ruby of the Royal Engineers